MW00982177

MEMORY AND DESIRE

Memory and Desire

Representations of passion
in the novella

Peter Mudford

Duckworth

First published in 1996 by
Gerald Duckworth & Co. Ltd.
The Old Piano Factory
48 Hoxton Square, London N1 6PB
Tel: 0171 729 5986
Fax: 0171 729 0015

A catalogue record for this book is available
from the British Library

ISBN 0 7156 2714 7

Typeset by Ray Davies
Printed in Great Britain by
Antony Rowe Ltd, Chippenham, Wiltshire

Contents

For Alison

Acknowledgments

I would like to record my thanks to my Colleagues and Students in the English Department at Birkbeck College in the University of London. Dr Sandra Clark read a draft of the whole book, and made invaluable suggestions. Dr David Atkinson has been of immense help in preparing the bibliography and index. I would also like to record my thanks to the Research Fund of the Literature and Languages Resource Centre at Birkbeck College for financial assistance. Finally, I would also like to express my gratitude to the late Colin Haycraft of Duckworth who offered to publish this book shortly before he died.

The French texts I have translated myself, except where otherwise acknowledged, and in the notes I have referred the reader to an easily available edition in French. Extracts from the following are reproduced by permission of Penguin Books: Lermontov, *A Hero of Our Time* (tr. Paul Foote, 1956); Tolstoy, *Anna Karenin* (tr. Rosemary Edmonds, 1954); Turgenev, *First Love* (tr. Isaiah Berlin, 1978); Mann, *Death in Venice* (tr. H.T. Lowe-Porter, 1962); Lawrence, *The Fox* (1960). Extracts from Tolstoy, *The Kreutzer Sonata* (tr. Aylmer Maude, 1924), are reproduced by permission of Oxford University Press.

Memory and desire, stirring
Dull roots with spring rain.
T.S. Eliot, *The Waste Land*

Introduction

Memory, Desire and Passion

Imagination and Memory are but one thing which for divers
considerations hath divers names.   Hobbes *Leviathan*, Book II

Desire and love are the same thing; save that by desire we always
signify the absence of the object; by love, most commonly the
presence of the same.   *Leviathan*, Book VI

The heart grown used to desiring feels nothing more to desire but
has as yet no memories.   Stendhal, *Love*

This book has its origins in an observation, and a number of
questions arising from it. European literature of the last three
centuries contains a small group of short novels or novellas which
take sexual obsession as their theme. In them, passionate love is
seen as a violent and isolating experience which ends in death.
This death may be actual, or metaphorical. Lives are profoundly
changed – in some cases burnt out, with nothing left to desire; in
others brought to a point of renewal, through the healing power
of memory. Writers who have been drawn to this theme, and to
the form of the novella as a means of representing it, include the
most celebrated in European literature.

I began to be interested by the relationship between the form
of the novella, and these tales of passionate love. Why was the
novella an appropriate form?[1] How were these forms of obsession
represented in fiction? To what extent did these novellas reflect
differing attitudes to passion within different European countries, as well as the changing historical and social contexts in
which they were written? The earliest of them, *The Princess of
Clèves*, was written by a woman, as was *Cousin Phillis*. In what
ways did this affect the representation of passion, or the perception of the relation between men and women, or the changing role
of women in society? And how was language being used to

suggest the nature of these obsessions, when much within them was inevitably half-hidden or obscure? As Freud recognised, 'being human was to be haunted by memory and desire, and entangled in a web of forgetting and remembering'.[2]

The internal structures of these stories turned out to be as interesting as the objective questions they raised. They all originated in autobiographical experience which was subsequently modified or transformed by art. In this process, memory was vital: sometimes as a means of distancing the writer from the original experience to bring objectivity and detachment to the narrative; always as a device within fiction to represent passion with the lucidity which memory allows. The formal organisation of the story was also itself worked to reinforce the action of memory: Madame de Lafayette used the historical past in *The Princess of Clèves* to confer veracity by means of distancing. More commonly the novella took the form of a reconstruction, purportedly put together out of memoirs, journals, rediscovered papers, letters and chance encounters, and published out of a desire to tell a true story (with numerous protestations that nothing had been changed). These narrative devices provided a frame for telling the story, and further lured the reader into believing what had occurred through the presence, for example, of an eye-witness, friend or listener.

Although these tales of the obsessions inspired by sexual passion arose from different cultural contexts and personal circumstances, there were many similarities in their representation of passion which related both to the form of the novella, and in a more thematic sense to the handling of desire.

Desire, the feeling which is common to both passion and creativity, has a metaphorical significance in these novellas, distinguishing them as a group from other forms of fiction. The artist, like the lover, starts from an unknown which he or she feels the need to articulate. In the course of this exploration, the desire becomes a burning obsession until the work is completed. The instances of the artist who becomes shut off from all other experiences by the need to complete the work (and understand the desire) are too numerous to need mention. The finishing of the work is again like the ending of a passion which destroys in the artist – sometimes temporarily, sometimes permanently – the desire and power to create. In this respect these narratives with their brevity, intensity and concentrated focus reflect the process of creativity, its sudden incandescence, its wrestling with form, and its eventual death.

What these novellas are concerned with overlaps with desire but is not contained by it: for relationships of passion involve the re-enactment of a *myth*, which involves self-dramatisation, and a rhetoric of love going beyond the articulation of desire. Denis de Rougemont in his fascinating book, *Love in the Western World* (to which I am greatly indebted) has described it like this: 'Passion is by no means the fuller life which it seems to be in the dreams of adolescence, but is on the contrary a kind of naked and denuding intensity; verily a bitter destitution, the *impoverishment* of a mind being emptied of all diversity, an obsession of the imagination by a single image. In the face of the assertion of its power, the world dissolves; "the others" cease to be present; and there are no longer either neighbours or duties, or binding ties, or earth, or sky; one is alone with all that one loves.'[3] And from this denuding intensity there arises, perhaps paradoxically, the desire and pursuit of the whole.

Myths are stories of which the truth is recurrent, either because they contain meanings to which the imagination responds, or because they structure the imagination. Their recurrence does not mean however that they belong completely to conscious life. However often the myth of Oedipus is retold or re-enacted, its truth belongs only partly to the light of day. The Oedipal struggle between child and parents is always conducted in the guise of something else or with a partial awareness of its repetition. (Anything else would make life literally impossible.) In the same way '*a myth is needed to express the dark and unmentionable fact that passion is linked with death* and involves the destruction of anyone yielding himself up to it with all his strength'.[4] The final chapter of this book will be concerned with the altering power and significance of this myth in the twentieth century. But in the rest of this introduction I shall say more about the recurrent constituents of the myth in these novellas of passion through their use of memory and their representation of desire and passion, leaving the following chapter for an account of the novella as form.

In a variety of ways all these narratives are concerned with memory. Those who have suffered an experience of extreme emotion are compelled to recall it, either by writing it down, or by relating it to a listener who often becomes involved in the eventual publication of the tale. But the interest of memory goes much deeper than this. In their reconstruction through memory these novellas had often the 'fierce vexation of a dream' to which the reader submits, only to share with the dreamer at the end the need to reconsider the nature of the obsession and its transforming effect on individual lives. Memory, as well as being a structural device, has become a revivification, and an attempt at coming to terms with what has occurred. As René Girard has put it, 'the inspiration springs from memory, and memory springs from the conclusion'.[5]

Like desire itself, memory is an awakening, a way of 'stirrring dull roots with spring rain'. To the sufferer, going over the past is a means of attempting to come to terms with it, of ordering what has happened in the conflicting currents of the present, and in some cases attempting to derive some moral or lesson from it. Self-narration is used by us all in dealing with grief, anxiety, or stress, just as in more formal situations it becomes an essential technique in psycho-therapy.

But the very fact that what is being told is a recreation transforms the feeling. It becomes a narration of what has occurred, with all the omissions, curtailments and dovetailing involved in giving shape to the disorder of actual experience. Memory inevitably involves a self-deceit, a shuffling of motives which are seldom transparent. The recreation in a literary form involves an additional change, by the addition of 'aesthetic emotion': that particular pleasure which is involved in any creative activity. Actual pain (passion is suffering) becomes part of an aesthetic understanding in which, as in all creativity, there is release, even at times joy (which has nothing to do with the subject, but only with the form) of what has been accomplished.

Going over the past is also an antidote to the weariness of the present, to what has been left desiccated by the violence of experience; and in the sense that it is a remove away from the present becomes also a renewal, which the form of the work completes.

The figure we meet at the start of *Adolphe*, lonely and wandering, with his head in his hands, shows little sign of this renewal; but the publisher of his papers acts as a surrogate for him. He is carrying forward what a single life did not encompass, and in doing so participating in an act of renewal. That the sufferer has become capable of writing down the experience, of fashioning it into a narrative, involves a victory, a transcendence of experience. In Girard's words, 'great novels always spring from an obsession that has been transcended'.[6]

In these first-person narratives, however, something more immediate is also present. Passion leads to self-dramatisation, because it is powerfully narcissistic. It needs language to express itself, to justify itself, and to defend itself from others' disapproval. The language of passion is one means by which it seals itself off from the world, creating a self-enclosure, which criticism and advice cannot touch. It comes to birth in that 'powerful impetus of the mind which also brings language into existence'; and 'it tends to self-description either to justify or intensify its being, or else simply in order to keep going'.[7] In other words, in a novella of passion, we are not confronted simply with a language which recreates the desire; but with the indispensability of language in the creation of the original relationship. What the sufferer does is to create in his or her mind a language which stands for the experience, even though that language may be remote from the way it would be articulated by anyone else, including the object of the obsession. Here we have something substantially different from a 'simple' expression of feeling; it is rather the birth of a language to strengthen and develop the obsession which grows by what it feeds on. I shall illustrate this at work in one novella, not discussed later, Goethe's *The Sorrows of Young Werther* (1774).

When the young Werther arrives in a country town near Wahlheim on 4 May 1771, he is nourished by his feelings for Nature, and by his belief in God. The sublime impression of the locality makes everything around him seem like a paradise. His love of Homer coincides with his love of the simple rural life; but he is already consumed by longing and desire which lack an object.

The story of Werther's growing obsession with Charlotte is told in his letters to his friend Wilhelm – letters to which we never read the replies[8] – which dramatise the passion which has no other outlet. These are letters about Werther on the stage of his own life, where, as he says, 'sun, moon and stars may pursue their course: I know not whether it is day or night; the whole world about me has ceased to be.'⁹ The increasing violence of his passion focusses his thought upon her, destroys his power to reason, and is self-consuming. The language in which he expresses himself to Wilhelm becomes the motor that drives his passion forward to the point at which his self-dramatisation has no resolution except in the murder of Charlotte's husband, Albert, or, as in fact happens, his own suicide. As Proust was later to write, 'love ... creates, so to speak, a fresh, a third, a supplementary person, distinct from the person whom the world knows by the same name, a person most of whose constituent elements are derived from ourselves, the lover'.¹⁰

Werther's letters record an intensifying passion in which neither Wilhelm nor the Editor who eventually publishes them, together with some corroborative evidence of his own, can intervene. The record when complete and published commemorates a figure who could not sustain his identity without Charlotte. But these recreative letters are already an act of memory, a means of ordering an experience which has no order in it. As he confesses, he is nothing without her.

When he learns of Charlotte's marriage to Albert (which means, Charlotte being as she is, that their relationship can have no future), he is driven towards suicide by his overwhelming desire for a union which cannot be. He is like a man who compels himself to burn more intensely out of an ever-increasing despair, to which only death can bring release; but this despair is fuelled by his ability to express it to himself. The language of self-dramatisation is the dagger with which he repeatedly stabs himself, and which leads him to see himself as a sacrificial victim. On Christmas Eve, Werther sends his servant to ask Albert for his pistols. He knows how often Charlotte's hands have touched them; and it is at her hands that he is determined to die. 'They have passed through your hands – you have wiped the dust from them. I kiss them a thousand times – you have touched them. Heavenly Spirits favour my design – and you, Charlotte, offer me the weapon. You, from whose hands I wished to receive my death.'¹¹ No action could more directly express the extremity of his mental condition; or the degree to which an articulation of his own predicament has led him to see his own self-sacrifice as propitiatory. On the stroke of midnight on Christmas Eve he pulls the trigger, dressed in his boots, blue coat and yellow waistcoat. Death does not come for another twelve hours.

The whole scene is Werther's staging of the end of his life, in which he has been both actor and producer. As designer he sees his own death in terms of social and literary fashions; and he sets it on Christmas Day. Everything about his end is a calculated dramatisation of his passion, which has been self-inspired. Charlotte, the object of his desire, has little objective reality, except as a wife and mother (though in the first version of the novella, the reader is left in little doubt that she returns Werther's love, or that Albert knows this, and is angered by it). Goethe shows little interest in the relationship as such. What interests him is that surplus of emotion which is not contained by desire; in doing so he also reflects his own and his time's man-centred world.

At the outset Werther longs to express on paper the breath of that universal love which sustains us, so that what he writes 'may become the mirror of my soul, as my soul is the mirror of the infinite God'.[12] He does just this, but in a way which goads him towards death, once Charlotte has taken the place of God. As Denis de Rougemont has put it, 'the will to expression, the will to self-description, as if in order to obtain a more intense self-enjoyment, is typical of all passion'.[13] And this in turn leads to self-destruction. In the self-enclosure of its epistolary form, *Werther* illustrates the power of language in leading to this end, which makes it the more ironic that it allegedly brought about so many imitative suicides. It is not so much about the impossibility of living as about the way in which language can make it impossible to do so.

To the Editor it remains to collect accurate information 'from persons well acquainted with his history', especially in relation to Werther's last days; but also to induce in the reader the reflection which only memory can bring, 'especially since it is so difficult to discover the true and innermost motives of men who are not of the common run'.[14] Werther's inability to free himself from the power of his obsession destroys him; but a heavy price is paid by those who survive him. The Editor concludes the narrative with these words: 'The old man and his sons followed the body to the grave. Albert could not. Charlotte's life was in danger. His body was carried by workmen. No clergyman attended.'[15] The laconic and factual nature of the language here recalls too the gap between it and the rhetoric which spurred Werther towards death.

*

If in Werther's case language dramatises desire, substituting an aesthetic emotion for the original feeling, what then of desire itself? René Girard's *Desire, Deceit and the Novel* (1966) has much to say that is pertinent. Desire is always spontaneous, but it is also imitative. As La Rochefoucauld put it, few people would fall in love, had they never heard of love. 'In the birth of desire, the third person is always present.'[16] Werther illustrates this too. The presence of Albert, and the insuperable obstruction which he offers to the relationship between Werther and Charlotte, creates the despair which intensifies Werther's ardour. Intensity of passion stands in inverse relation to the availability of the object. Conversely, the availability of the beloved can 'create a desire for her to be unfaithful so that she can be courted again'.[17] As Proust observed, 'there can be no peace of mind in love, since the advantage one has secured is never anything but a fresh starting-point for further desires'.[18]

Desire is a feeling, like hunger, with which we permanently live; unlike hunger it is never satisfied. It is impossible to imagine being alive without desire, though as W.H. Auden once observed, to be sound is to want only what one has! The unsoundness of desire results from a search doomed to failure, and which is carried on through the creation of dynamic structures, changing in shape, and overlapping one with another. In his book Girard has shown how these structures are frequently triangular, created out of rivalry and rejection, so that what was an undifferentiated feeling becomes highly defined and obsessive. Desire involves a longing to be other or Another, and the attempt to become so is structured out of a relationship with a rival, which may involve love or hate, or shift from one to another.

In some cases desire is structured by something external, as in the case of Don Quixote who lives, until shortly before his death (when he renounces all books of chivalry) in imitation of Amadis of Gaul, one of 'the most perfect knight errants'. All Don Quixote's adventures flow from this initial desire to imitate; and new adventures have always to be sought in order to desire again.

Desire feeds on obstruction. Only at the very end will Don Quixote realise the obsessive and deluded nature of his desire: 'I am the enemy of Amadis of Gaul, and of all the infinite brood of his progeny. Now all profane histories of knight errantry are odious to me. Now, by God's mercy, I have learnt from my own bitter experience, and I abominate them.'[19] (As Buñuel was wittily to observe in his film, *That Obscure Object of Desire*, a man might pursue two women without ever realising that they were not the same person. Only when a thing or person is no longer an object of desire does it appear to us in its true guise.) Desire structures a quest, and simultaneously blinds us to its nature, so that we become possessed by it as Don Quixote is by books of chivalry, or Sancho Panza by the desire to become governor of an island.

Don Quixote and Sancho Panza differ from most men in that their desires are structured by external things. More commonly, desire is structured internally by rivalry. Werther comes to Wahlheim to escape from Leonore, whose sister attracted him. He confides to Wilhelm in his first letter: 'Was it my fault that while the capricious charms of her sister afforded me agreeable entertainment, a passion for me developed in her poor heart? And yet – am I wholly blameless? Did I not encourage her emotions?'[20] Werther flees from the passion he has inspired, only to become the victim of a much more serious 'triangular' relationship with Albert and Charlotte. When Charlotte tells him that she is as good as engaged, Werther comments: 'Now there was nothing new to me in this (the girls had told me of it on the way); yet it struck me as new since I had not thought of it in connection with her whom in so short a time I had grown to like so much.'[21] In other words, his desire for Charlotte is structured by her belonging to someone else. His obsession is progressively intensified by his feelings of rivalry with Albert, and his increasing awareness that Charlotte can never be his. Albert, although increasingly irritated by Werther's presence (especially in the first version) does not suffer from the violence of Werther's feelings.

When Werther tells him the story of a servant girl who has killed herself out a hopeless passion, this merely confirms Albert's view that only a fool dies of love. Werther's desire for Charlotte is shaped by the presence of Albert; but the reverse is not the case, for a simple reason. Albert becomes Charlotte's husband; and in his contentment suffers no desire to be other than he is. Werther, however, who feels that he is nothing without her, can never complete or satisfy his desire; he can never be content with being himself; and at same time his desire to 'transcend' himself is doomed to be frustrated. As a result he becomes increasingly bewildered and unbalanced by a desire which nothing can satisfy. Like a man possessed by an evil spirit that devours him with an inner fury, Werther can only free himself from himself in death.

But a deceit exists at the centre of Werther's obsession: the cunning snare of his 'evil spirit'. He believes that he is nothing without Charlotte, whereas his obsession with Charlotte in fact arises out of a sense of nothingness which he cannot face, and from which he attempts to avert his gaze by fixing it upon another. At times his metaphors seem to reflect a partial recognition of this. When he hears of Charlotte's marriage, he comments: 'I feel like the ghost that has returned to the burnt-out castle which it had built in more splendid times.'[22] What he does not perceive is that the castle had never really existed; and that the ghost figures forth the phantom life he has 'chosen' to lead. He sees Charlotte's dark eyes as an abyss which lies before him. The image is out of his own soul: a void which he believes could be filled if he could once – only once – hold her to him. The power of the obsession, and its destructive force arise from the value he discovers in himself as a result of his passion. La Rochefoucauld expressed it like this: 'The pleasure of love lies in loving, and the passion one feels brings more happiness than the passion one inspires.'[23] Proust attributed the same discovery to Swann, enhancing it with one of his witty extended comparisons: 'And this delight in being a lover, in living by love alone, of the reality of which he was inclined to be doubtful ... enhanced its value in his eyes – as one sees people who are doubtful whether the sight of the sea and the sound of its waves are really enjoyable, become convinced that they are, as also of the rare quality and absolute detachment of their own taste, when they have agreed to pay several pounds a day for a room in a hotel, from which that sight and that sound may be enjoyed.'[24]

Werther's obsession with Charlotte originates in his lack of natural relations with society as well as in his psyche. His delight

in the simple rural pleasures of Wahlheim ('home of one's choice')
– a place where he can read Homer while shelling peas – is
inspired by his distaste for the aloofness and exclusivity of aristocratic life; but it does not give him a social role. His desire is
the product of isolation: 'Many a time I wish I were a common
labourer, so that when I awake in the morning I might at least
have one clear prospect, one pursuit, one hope for the day which
has dawned.'[25] For a time he goes away from Charlotte, and takes
a job in a neighbouring court, where he derives some relief from
his private obsessions; but soon distinctions of rank, and the
energy which needs to be expended on getting one step ahead, as
well as personal animosities, begin to become intolerable; and he
leaves this competitive environment. Lacking an occupation
again, he makes a symbolic return to his birth-place: an attempt
to find in his origins a way of self-definition which continues to
evade him. In this, a shadowy return to the womb is suggested,
which in indicating Werther's need for his parents also implies
their continuing influence on him: a theme which is developed in
novellas discussed later in this book.

Werther's desire for Charlotte releases in him a hopeless and
insoluble passion. He personifies desire in one extreme form,
which originating in a sense of being nothing without 'the other'
leads to self-destruction when he is permanently dispossessed of
her.

But a sense of nothingness can feed as well on its own frustrated attempts to find another who will satisfy an inner
emptiness. Desire, instead of being structured by the appropriation of a particular individual, becomes involved in an
increasingly relentless search for the individal who will fulfil this
role. (Nobody, alas, is perfect.) With each unsuccessful attempt,
the propensity to boredom or accidie arising out of repeated
dissatisfaction intensifies, leading to randomness and inertia. As
Stendhal remarks, comparing Don Juan and Werther, 'the curse
of inconstancy is boredom; the curse of passionate love is despair
and death'.[26]

Werther represents Stendhal's second type; Pechorin, the hero
of Lermontov's short novel, *A Hero of Our Time* (1840), his first.
Lermontov was deeply influenced by Byron. 'My love has brought
no one happiness, for I've never sacrificed a thing for those I've
loved. I've loved for myself, for my own pleasure, I've only tried

to satisfy a strange inner need. I've fed on their feelings, love, joy and sufferings, and always wanted more. I'm like a starving man who falls asleep exhausted and sees rich and sparkling wines before him. He rapturously falls on these phantom gifts of the imagination and feels better, but the moment he wakes up, his dream disappears and he's left more hungry and desperate than before.'[27] This 'strange inner need' is nothing other than that desire which needs to be satisfied, but never finds satisfaction in the objects which it fastens upon. Werther sees himself as a wanderer, but can never wander for long. Pechorin lives as a wanderer because he never cares deeply enough for anything. He grows bored, and has to move on.

'Princess Mary', which forms one of the five parts of *A Hero of Our Time*, may be seen as a novella within the novel. (The work as a whole has many similarities with the novella form, being put together and published by an acquaintance who sees in Pechorin and his Journal the story of a man's soul.) As an example of the structuring of desire at the opposite extreme to Werther's but involving the same problem of nothingness, it repays some brief further attention.

Like Werther, Pechorin takes pleasure in Nature, and in the Caucasian town of Pyatigorsk, to which he goes as an officer in the Tsar's army, he is able to indulge it. 'It's a delight to live in a place like this. Every fibre of my body tingles with joy. The air is pure and fresh, as the kiss of a child, the sun is bright, the sky is blue – what more can one want? What need have we of passions, desires and regrets?'[28] Pechorin knows that we may not need them; but that we have them, and have to do something with them. The foil for Pechorin's as yet indirected desire is the callow Grushnitsky: 'I want him to pick me as his confidant, – then I'll have fun.'[29]

As a private, without the advantages of wit, class, or attractiveness, Grushnitsky seeks the help of Pechorin in wooing the Princess Mary, who is staying in the town with her mother. And this provides Pechorin with the opportunity to torment Grushnitsky by becoming his rival: 'I was born,' he says, 'with a passion for contradiction.'[30] And contradiction in this case means denying the rival while having no genuine interest in the object of his desire: a fact which is highlighted by the presence in the town of another woman, Vera, now critically ill, who reawakens the passion Pechorin once felt for her when he realises he must lose her for ever. Desire only interests Pechorin when the goal is unattainable; it otherwise remains a game of transient pleasure. The more he succeeds in conquering Princess Mary for himself, the more he is bored by the game which he knows by heart. He enjoys the pain he inflicts on women. 'There are times,' he reflects, 'when I can understand the Vampire.' The sadism reflects a fear of the nothingness of the self for which he also attempts a more conventional compensation: 'And yet I still pass for a decent fellow, and try my best to be thought so.'[31]

When rumour spreads in the town that Pechorin is going to marry Princess Mary, Grushnitsky plans to humiliate his rival by challenging him to a duel and loading the pistols with blanks. In this, as in the account of the duel fought on a narrow ledge from which Grushnitsky will fall to his death, Lermontov reflects the hollowness and void, which Pechorin spends his life trying to fill or avoid. 'One just goes on living out of curiosity, waiting for something new.'[32] At each encounter life turns out to be like the blank which explodes and does nothing.

Pechorin's writing of his Journal in which these events are recorded, is another means of trying to assuage the boredom of feelings which he finds unrewarding. He has been born to no purpose; and has only been carried away by the allurements of empty passions. Death is the one certainty. 'And perhaps tomorrow I'll die, and then there'll be no one who could ever really understand me. Some will think me worse, others better than in fact I am. Neither will be right.'[33] The shifting nature of his desire reflects his wish to find an object which will content him: a quest in which he will fail. 'I've an insatiable craving inside me that consumes everything and makes me regard the sufferings and joys of others only in their relationship to me ....'[34] In each 'adventure' the presence of a rival gives focus to this craving and sets a challenge which is met, only to become another example of failure. He has what the French call a 'rage de vivre', but when he sits in judgement on the self who lives intensely he finds it lacking. 'Our true never-ending love might be described mathematically by a line stretching from a point into space.'[35] Like desire itself, it can never be realised. For Lermontov, as for Byron, this cannot be separated from a view of the world in which the woman only exists as an object of desire.

In Werther and Pechorin, desire is focussed through the presence of a rival. In Werther's case the unattainablility of Charlotte leads to suicide; in Pechorin's the attainability of all goals leads to boredom and indifference. He dies on his way back from a journey to Persia: a journey which had no purpose, and from which he comes back to no particular end. If death may be described like that!

For both Werther and Pechorin, jealousy is also as important as the initial desire in intensifying the passion. This too was noticed by Proust. 'Thus his jealousy did even more than the happy passionate desire which he had originally felt for Odette had done to alter Swann's character, completely changing, in the eyes of the world, even the outward signs by which that character had been intelligible.'[36]

*

When St Paul advised, 'Better to marry than burn', his metaphor for desire expressed its endlessness. To burn is to keep desire unsatisfied; and in Christendom at least, the satisfaction of desire was sanctified by marriage. But married love, with its virtues of contentment and companionship, is also at odds with its unruly partner, passion. While marriage or partnership is the usual outcome of structured desire, passion which is unruly does not necessarily lead to the same end, nor should it do so. In unsatisfied desire, there always exists a mixture of anticipation and fear, which have an uncertain place in domestic compatibility.

Denis de Rougemont has put forward a fascinating argument that passion has its origin in the courtly love of the twelfth century: a love that was secretive, unsatisfied and adulterous. He points to the absence of any tradition of love as passion in the classical world (which seems odd when we think of Dido in the *Aeneid*, or Catullus); and to its presence in literature from the twelfth century to our own time as a quasi-mystical and solipsistic force. I do not wish to argue for or against de Rougement's account of passionate love as 'a by-product' of Manichaeism. But his distinction between passionate love and Christian love is one which touches the rest of this book in many ways. As de Rougemont goes on to say: 'Between joy and its external cause there is invariably some gap and some obstruction – society, sin, virtue, the body, the separate self. Hence arises the ardour of passion. And hence it is that the wish for complete union is indissolubly linked with a wish for death that brings release.'[37] In these novellas, the tensions which arise from the conflict between inner and outer worlds (including but not confined to those identified by de Rougemont) create a shifting imbalance which forms a central part of the story's particular interest.

The word 'passion' means suffering; and in relation to Christianity refers to the Agony in the Garden, and the suffering of Christ on the Cross: in both cases the suffering involves a desire for the cup to be passed from Him. In its human form passion reflects, as Leo Ferrero has put it, 'the change of address of a force awakened by Christianity and oriented toward God'.[38] This change of address deprives the feeling of its metaphysical end, and creates an obsession incapable of being sustained indefinitely. The transference of this feeling into art confers an eternity upon it which life cannot bestow, as Shakespeare recognised in his sonnets where he claimed a special value for its fashioning into literature:

> Not marble, nor the gilded monuments
> Of Princes shall outlive this powerful rime,
> But you shall shine more bright in these contents
> Than unswept stone, besmeer'd with sluttish time.
>
> Sonnet 55

At the same time, the rhetoric of passion can involve an exorbitance and exclusiveness which attempts to banish the outside world, as, for example, in John Donne's 'The Sunne Rising':

> She is all states, and all princes, I,
> Nothing else is.

Two and a half centuries later, Wagner's Tristan, as a result of his love for Isolde, will make an even greater claim: 'I myself am the world.' Seen from any other point of view, this extreme narcissism does not involve love for another person, but a desire for self-transcendency which can only come in death, or an ecstasy, which whether mystical or sexual, is momentary. As

John Donne knows, his lovers in 'The Ecstasy' must come back to
the bodies which made an ecstasy possible. And what then? As
René Girard has wittily asked, must Tristan become Don Juan?

While desire can exist without passion, passion intensifies
desire until an eternal union becomes passion's goal. For this
reason passion can involve the destruction of anyone yielding
themselves up to it: a destruction which is willed, and the will to
which is intensified by the obstacles placed in its way. Desire
may be focussed by the existence of a rival, as Tristan's is by King
Mark; and intensified by the fact that the obstacle presented by
King Mark is made the more insuperable by the loyalty which
Tristan owes him. But what begins, and could continue, as a
triangular struggle, becomes in Wagner's rendering of it quite
different. By the love-duet of Act Two, rivalry has been forgotten;
it is day which is feared, night and darkness which are welcomed.
Day and light imprison the lovers in the material world; only in
night, and death, can the union be achieved which would make
Tristan Isolde and Isolde Tristan. This is the secular equivalent
of what the mystics described as a 'hierogamos'.

Passion of such a kind does not belong to the material world:
it seeks to vanquish and overcome that world. The importance of
the event (or the experience) transcends the individuals involved
in it. Ironically, although the lovers invoke each other with the
use of names (Tristan and Isolde, Romeo and Juliet, Antony and
Cleopatra) they lose their autonomy, as a somnambulist does,
and become potentially dangerous to themselves and others.
(Romeo seals 'with a righteous kisse A dateless bargaine to
ingrossing death'; Cleopatra in her desire for self-transcendence
and reunion with Antony has 'immortal longings' and then com-
mits suicide; Isolde's 'highest bliss' is to sink unconscious into
death, a *liebestod*.) Sexual obsession like this imagines a union
outside life, an eternal harmony which transcends mortality. The
creative imagination drawn towards chaos also seeks a resolution which is harmonious; and in doing so overcomes the disorder
of experience.

De Rougemont illustrates this through the example of Racine's
Phèdre. At the time he wrote it, Racine had conceived, it is
thought, a passion for the actress Champmeslé, when he was also
beginning to be drawn towards Christianity. By returning to a
myth which involved incestuous love, Racine was able to deny a

passion in himself which he chose to regard as 'beyond appeal'. As Racine says in the 'Preface', the frailties of love are treated as real weaknesses. Passions are brought before the eye only in order to show how much disorder they cause. The disorder becomes increasingly apparent to Phèdre herself, for whom death alone can restore to the day the light which her eyes have sullied.

> Et la mort à mes yeux dérobant la clarté,
> Rend au jour, qu'ils souillaient, toute sa pureté
> Act 5, Sc. vii

Death brings about a renewal, a restoration of the order and purity in Nature which has been violated: in the Aristotelian sense, a catharsis.

In all these novellas desire and passion overlap in different ways. In some the death of passion occurs before physical death, but the remaining life is cauterised, deprived of feeling; in others the death of passion leads to renewal; and both are related thematically and structurally to the use of memory. With that special or extreme form of passion which involves death as a means of attempting to overcome the contingency of things, I shall be concerned in the final chapter.

*

The brevity of the novella makes it an appropriate form for a narrative in which intensity, not duration, matters. (The actual length of time over which the events of the narrative occur is less relevant than the selection of events or scenes which in juxtaposition create that intensity.) In many novellas we have the figure of the hero (the one who suffers passion), and that of the listener, narrator, or editor of journals, who becomes responsible for bringing them to the notice of the public. These 'double' figures have a vital relation to one another, and to the significance of the narrative.

The hero is directly involved in the events of the narrative; but the setting down of them is an act of memory, an attempt to come to terms with an obsession, and in varying ways rediscover freedom from desire. 'The absence of desire in the present makes it possible to recapture past desires ....'[39] But passion, even recollected passion, involves a form of self-deceit, because the language of passion is always a rhetoric about the self trying to transcend the self, dramatising itself in extreme forms of feeling and behaviour. (The recurrent transposition of these novellas into plays, operas and films is evidence of their inherently dramatic nature.) The hero in writing it down (or narrating it) is trying to understand what he has lived through; and in replaying it he inevitably repeats the old self-deceits.

But he is also transcribing an actual emotion into an aesthetic emotion, and is giving form to an experience which while being lived had all the roughness and disorder of life as it is lived. In this ordering there enters the release of creativity, of the recognition of a truth (however partial) which stands against the passion undergone. Recalled or aesthetic emotion is in this respect always different to lived emotion. The subjectivity of the original emotion is transformed into a different kind of subjectivity through recollection, and through the attempt to come to terms with the obsession by making it objective. The intense subjectivity of the passion, which itself sees only in a kind of tunnel vision, is redefined in the story-telling.

The listener or publisher makes persistent claims to setting the narrative down without altering a word; but he inevitably acts an an intermediary between the hero and the reader: sometimes as a moral commentator on the tragic ends to which unruly passions can lead, and at others as a passive observer of events whose outcome he was powerless to influence. But his presence distances the obsession at a further remove, inviting the reader to consider it with the objectivity which can never be achieved by the central characters involved in it. This distancing is a further reflection of that 'calm of mind, all passion spent' which the hero or heroine is attempting to achieve through recollection; and beyond calm, restoration.

Behind these figures of the narrative stands that of the author who, through these projections, wrestles with the problem of the relation between language and desire. Tzvetan Todorov, writing about Constant's *Adolphe*, has argued for the profound relation between word and desire. 'Words imply the absence of things, in the same way that desire implies the absence of its object ... Words are to things what desire is to the object of desire ....'[40] The writer, confronted with the blank sheet of paper, is face to face with desire: the desire of writing which is comparable to erotic desire, and struggles with absence. These novellas constitute a particular image of the creative process, struggling to find a language which expresses its desire. The end of this process is an immense relief (the image of Eugene O'Neill weeping on the completion of *Long Day's Journey into Night* comes to mind) or a deep depression and sense of emptiness, as happened to Virginia Woolf. The end of desire is death, as the completion of a work is a death, leading to hopes of renewal. The writer in all these novellas shadows through the act of writing the suffering of his or her central characters' experience, and in turning desire into an aesthetic emotion finds a temporary relief from it.

For writer, and character, the starting point is an absence, a blankness which needs to be filled; and which the cost of filling will be a form of self-destruction. This is for a simple reason: it involves an encounter with 'the other' – the self or selves which we have not formerly recognised in ourselves. As in Flaubert's famous remark, 'Madame Bovary, c'est moi!'[41] The inscription of desire demands this grappling with shadows, making them embody in words what we thought we were not, as the Princess of Clèves is forced to recognise her similarity to the women for whom love has been their undoing. There is in this struggle a kind of triumph, a new lucidity which comes from confronting an obsession, and in the end overcoming it through words, seeing it for what it is. For the hero or heroine this comes about through memory, which is another way of saying that for the writer it comes about through the drawing out of the dark a myth of the self; and enlarging what exists in the conscious mind.

In writing of each of them, I have tried to show how the particular nature of the desire is related to the life and circumstances of the author, which in turn reflects the changing nature of European life. The different ways in which passion is represented are inseparable from the changing cultural context.

1

Form and the Novella

For everything I relate, I have seen; and although I may have been deceived in what I saw, I shall certainly not deceive you in the telling of it.   Stendhal, *Scarlet and Black*

The novella, as its name suggests, is a European form. The meaning of the name and the use of the form differ according to country and context. The novellas concerned with sexual obsession which are the subject of this book constitute a small subsection within a form which contains many different kinds of story-telling, and which in its economy and intensity has attracted writers as different as Kleist, James and Lawrence. Its vitality today is apparent in the work of writers as diverse as William Trevor and Gabriel Garcia Marquez.

This book is not intended as a history of the form, but the history of the form is relevant to the works on which this book focusses. As Stendhal noted in *De l'Amour*, forms of love are not independent of national character, or even forms of government; and these novellas reflect their different cultural contexts and conventions. Relations between parents and children, questions of money and social status, conventions about family, marriage and religious belief, in the broadest sense moral and ethical standards constrict (or liberate) the development of erotic feeling. Although the novella cannot explore society discursively as the novel does, its prismatic focus reflects the society outside the walls which lovers attempt to build round themselves; and criticises or approves the values by which they live.

Tales of extreme feeling are not of course confined to the novella. The first and perhaps greatest of them all occurs in Book 4 of Vergil's *Aeneid* in the story of Dido and Aeneas (a novella in verse), which ends with Dido's self-immolation on her funeral pyre. Later, Troilus and Criseyde, Heloise and Abelard, Antony and Cleopatra, Phèdre and Hippolyte, Tristan and Isolde become the subjects of diverse poetic and dramatic works. The novella in its restrictedness and concentration of focus represents such passions in their psychopathology, which tragedy, or the representation of the world as tragic, is able to transcend. In its brevity the novella is a lyric form; and several of the examples in this book have become known to an even wider public through their use as the libretti for lyric operas: for example, *Werther*, *Manon*, *La Traviata*, *Carmen*[1] and *Death in Venice*. Brevity and intensity have always played some part in the definition of the form; but their interest lies in the effects they achieve, and the uses to which they are put.

The history of the word 'novella' reflects the diversity of its use. The English word, borrowed from the Italian, does not correspond exactly to its usage in Italian; nor does the Italian correspond exactly to the German *novelle*, or the French *nouvelle*.

The word first arises in relation to Boccaccio's *Decamerone*. This is composed of a hundred and one tales told in ten days by ten Florentines taking refuge from the plague which ravaged Florence in 1348. They had found safety and shelter in a country house, where they passed the time telling tales which related to contemporary life. These were not narratives of the classical or heroic world, but of a world familiar from their own experience, in which the presence of the story-teller could be assumed. Boccaccio's *novelle* have been described as 'gossip raised to the dignity of literature'. Novellas of later periods frequently enclose the main story within a framework; and often they arise out of an encounter, a story which is recounted and subsequently written down (with nothing changed) or a manuscript which is discovered. All these devices serve to reinforce the narrative as a 'true story', an encounter with an unexpected and unique sequence of events in particular human lives, which the story-teller feels compelled to pass on, like someone possessed of a secret which cannot be kept. The narrative device of the 'glittering eye' of the Ancient Mariner who holds his audience in thrall ('they cannot choose but hear') has its parallels in the art of the novella.

Cervantes in his *Novelas Ejemplares* developed the form to exemplify some moral viewpoint; and this tendency towards a moralising element, alien to the novella in its original form, was once again taken up in the romantic novella. This was one legacy of the novel and the short story in the eighteenth century, when story-telling and moral commentary became inseparable. In the romantic period the novella writer's interest shifted from events to the inner significance of events, and the effect of transformed feelings on the lives and behaviour of those involved. Goethe's *Werther* exemplifies this shift in that extreme form where the transformed feelings become an obsession, and the obsession itself the subject of the narration.

In nineteenth-century Germany the novella becomes the predominant fictional form, provoking debate and commentary which continues to the present day. Some of this debate helps to provide the perspective in which the novella of passion can fruitfully be seen.[2]

Goethe was among the first to discuss the form of the *novelle*. He saw it as involving an unprecedented (*unerhörte*) happening which had actually occurred. The *novelle* tells a story about the world as we know it; it is embedded in that world; but the central event has about it something unprecedented and new. Ludwig Tieck – Goethe's contemporary and himself a prolific writer of stories, plays and essays who was also responsible for the publication of Kleist's work after his death – defined the unprecedented event more precisely, and in a way which determined form. For Tieck, the *novelle* involved what he described as a *Wendepunkt* (turning-point). This turning-point was something which could easily happen, was not in any way fantastic, but at the same time challenged accepted definitions of reality and involved something that was wonderful and unique. The supernatural, which was to play an important part in the German *novelle* of the later part of the century, particularly those of Hoffman, reflected this definition. But it applies equally well to stories concerning those radical transformations of personality which can come about under the influence of powerful emotions, and which for those experiencing them alter their way of seeing the world. A.W. Schlegel, another of Goethe's contemporaries, and famous as a critic and translator, put it like this: 'the novelle recounts remarkable events that have, as it were, occurred behind the back of bourgeois conventions and regulations.'[3] What is 'unprecedented' (to return to Goethe's word) challenges the norm, and demands that the reader interpret the central event on which the narrative focusses, and consider its relation to those 'bourgeois' conventions which it repudiates. In this respect it is both irrational and subversive.

But a transformation of feeling can also become a fixity of emotion, an imprisonment of a sort. All other life shrinks into insignificance; and so these extreme passions separate those who experience them from the everyday world. Being immured can involve a blindness and indifference to what those outside are thinking and feeling; and an indifference, in common with other obsessions, to the effect of behaviour on others. Whether on those who experience such emotions, or on their social milieu, the effect is likely to be disruptive and destructive. In such a narrative the intrinsic interest of the 'minor' characters becomes less. They act as grieved observers and friends who offer advice and help, but are helpless before the force of emotions they do not share. From the reader's point of view they offer another dimension of analysis and comment, a means of looking at the central relationships from a more detached perspective.

Much in the social or cultural environment is left unstated; but what happens to the central characters resonates with that background. In their fixity of emotion they may be unaware of this; but what they experience reflects in addition to their personal desires the social environment in which they live: its restricting conventions, and forms of permissiveness which are regarded as tolerable. As Taine once remarked, man like all living things changes with the air which nourishes him. In literature, language and convention prescribe the air we breathe. The limits of our language mean the limits of our world;[4] and language itself reflects the ruling concerns of an age.

These narratives are not offered to the reader directly. They are filtered through a variety of frames. It may be – as in Turgenev's *First Love*, and many novellas of the late nineteenth century in Germany – a matter of the narrator's remembering long distant events: events which transformed his life, but which are also transformed by memory. More frequently it takes the form of discovered papers, which the narrator decides to publish in edited or unedited form. Sometimes the narrator has begun by being the listener who then retells the tale to the reader. The effect is to distance the central events and the subjective emotions with which they are concerned from the reader, and provide the possibility of a commentary upon them. The reader becomes involved in the narrator's attitude towards these events as much as in the events themselves; and in doing so is being invited as another kind of listener to form a view of them. By absorbing the shock the narrator serves to relieve the events of their melodramatic surplus, and to question their relationship to the norms they offend. The narrator's interest in the unique event or situation heightens the concentration on it, and heightens and sharpens ours.

The perspective is thus very different from a story which has no mediating filter, designed to make readers, like the narrator, decide for themselves the significance of what is being narrated. In the twentieth century Brecht used this technique in the theatre, where it was given the name of *verfremdungseffekt*. There are of course many novellas in which the narrator does not have this kind of role; but he will be seen to recur in the works considered here.

Because the events in the novella are 'unprecedented' or 'unique', and involve intense concentration on one event or sequence of events, they also pose some kind of problem. The novella cannot – by virtue of its length – provide, as did the nineteenth-century novel, a 'spacious documentation' of the social world, though its central event can and often does offer a challenge to conventions, prejudices and norms of behaviour.

As the spatial dimensions of the novel are contracted to give a sharper intensity of focus, so too is the time span. The events of the novella occur within a short space of time; but a space of time which permanently changes the lives of those involved. It involves experiences which stand for, and in that sense 'symbolise' what happens to, and within, those lives; a space of time in which fateful confrontations occur, and which cannot be resolved except by being lived through.

Such confrontations may be the result of chance or fate whether malevolent or benign, as in the case of Kleist. But equally they may come about through some inner and psychological compulsion, peculiar to the individual or individuals concerned: a concurrence with unforeseeable ends. Although these events originate in a well-defined and familiar social context, they have no place in it; and as they develop they increasingly isolate those involved because their experiences are by the standards of normality and convention extreme or even pathological. As Schlegel put it, the central event is 'marginal to the broad generality of ordered social experience',[5] or to put it the other way round, the restraints of social order are challenged by experiences which cannot contain them.

I have not so far introduced the criterion of length (and some writers on the novella have chosen to ignore it completely) because it can only serve a limited purpose and is inevitably crude. A fictional narrative of thirty pages, we might say, is a short story; a narrative of two hundred and fifty pages a novel. The novella exists somewhere in between. For the sake of neatness, we might say that a novella is not likely to be much less than seventy-five pages long, or much more than a hundred and fifty. But the vagueness of the boundaries and the sterility of the argument about length make it essential to see if there are other criteria which might be applied; in particular, certain kinds of narrative for which the novella is the appropriate form.

Novels often treat of a whole life or lives. They include an account of all that happens between birth and death, or a substantial part of it. These novellas are not concerned with the whole of life, with the evolution of the individual, but with the transforming effect on particular lives of extreme states of feeling. We do not see the whole life, we see that part of it where a crucial and unredeemable event has occurred: an event which defines the quality of a particular life. In the nature of passions once awakened, an inevitability occurs from which there is release only when they are burned through. (Montaigne wisely observed in his essays that all passions which suffer themselves to be relished and digested are but moderate.) The form of the novella is appropriate for this fierce brevity; but its interest is deepened when seen through the 'belated moment of lucidity' which memory in its freedom from desire can bring. Not the least of the aesthetic pleasures of the novella of passion exists in the complexity and interest of the feelings, seen as though through very clear water. The achievement is one of style (the novella writer has no time or space to afflict his consciousness, or that of his reader, with parentheses!); but also one of narrative viewpoint.

The majority of writers in this book did not write in English. The novella of passion seems to be more the product of the French, German and Russian temperaments than of the English.

Emily Brontë's *Wuthering Heights* is the most obvious example of a work which might have been included here if it had been concerned with Cathy and Heathcliff alone. Many reasons might be advanced for this difference between European and English fiction. These novellas are concerned with extremes of emotion and of behaviour which the English imagination less frequently contemplates; and which in nineteenth-century England were more deeply repressed. The one novella of passion by an English writer which I have included here – Mrs Gaskell's *Cousin Phillis* – highlights a contrast with European writing in its lack of extremism; and in its insistence on a power of recuperation from the effects of passion that is less evident in European tales. (As will become apparent in Chapter 11, I have included D.H. Lawrence's *The Fox* to illustrate a somewhat different perspective.)

The form of the novella has been widely used; but until recently not a great deal was written about it, except in relation to the German *novelle*.[6] Over the past twenty years attempts have been made to develop a theory of the novella, of which the best is J. Leibowitz's *Narrative Purpose in the Novella* (1974). In this book Dr Leibowitz defines a number of characteristics of the novella which help to distinguish it from the short story and the novel, though it has to be admitted that 'intensity' and 'expansion' (the novella as a narrative of suggestion) to which she devotes much useful attention are categories exemplified in many short stories. She quotes Henry James's dictum that the novella aims 'to do the complicated thing with a strong brevity and lucidity', producing by means of its control 'a richly summarised and foreshortened effect'.[7] These phrases have not been bettered, either in relation to the resonance of the content, or to the aesthetic attractiveness of the form. James was aware, both as theorist and practitioner, of the cultural suggestiveness of the novella, and the values at which it hinted without probing so far that they became generalisations, and the degree to which the foreshortening could emphasise the power of particular experiences. As Dr Leibowitz rightly says, it is not the subject, but the treatment of the subject which determines form. The novella analyses intensively a limited area.[8] It often makes use of repetitions, of parallel situations and motifs, and manipulation of time to provide intensity of focus, while from the focal point the implications of the theme spread outwards into its cultural envi-

ronment and its social background. As with James's sense of
foreshortening the focus in the foreground is intensified, while all
which lies behind and around it is present in blurred or shadowy
forms. The effect is like that of a narrow depth of field in
photography.

In much that has been written about the novella it is assumed
that the form is antecedent and prescriptive. Here a distinction
between the novella and the short story seems useful. Short
stories have commonly been written with a particular publication in mind, and in the case of newspapers to fill columns, as
happened with the early short stories of Chekov and Kipling. The
novella arises more frequently from the treatment which the
author finds appropriate for the content. James in particular was
deeply conscious of the various lengths with which the same
material could be treated. He began with material which he
thought sufficient for a short story, but which grew in his imagination to an extensive fiction. The art of the novella depends on
not allowing this to happen; on achieving compression without
sacrificing resonance and suggestiveness, and awareness of social environment. The length in the end becomes like the pitch of
the ball in cricket, a means of attempting to bring about a
particular effect, of tension, control and release. The interesting
question is what is being foreshortened, to what effect, and with
what implications.

The novella as a form is particularly suited to these tales of
passion, to actions complete in themselves, explosive in content,
dramatic in development where calm of mind is only achieved
when passion is spent. Sexual passion originates in individual
impulses; but the manner in which it is worked out, the dislocat-
ing effects of its development, will depend on the society in which
it has to exist. At one extreme the novella implies much about the
conventions and restrictions of a culture; and at the other
focusses sharply on the uncontrollable forces at work in individual lives. Together they present a way of attempting to
understand in a little more detail the workings of the deepest and
most violent of human feelings, of which the outcome is always
inscrutable. In this inscrutability lies also the form's deep hold
on the imagination.

Only in imagination can we contemplate what we know we
cannot control, and find in that controlled chaos a way of recog-

nising the abysses over which we uncertainly pass. Black holes,
like all great scientific discoveries, are images drawn from our
innermost being, as well as explanations of the world in which
we live.

*

I want to conclude this chapter by referring to one work, Tolstoy's
Anna Karenina, which includes in the narrative of Anna's and
Vronsky's love much that lies close to the themes of the novellas
in this book, but where the spacious form of the novel allows the
cultural context to be revealed in detail, and where the relationship between the lovers is seen in contrast to relationships of a
very different sort. Tolstoy's novel, by dwelling upon the wider
social scene in its diversity and difference, helps to provide an
insight into what is inevitably omitted in the novella, except by
implication, but which forms part of the fascination of the form.
The pressures which exist on the boundaries make an important
contribution to its lyric intensity.

Henry James's criticism of the Russian novels as loose baggy
monsters may also be read as a description of their strength. The
so-called bagginess makes room for broadness of vision: as in the
plots and sub-plots of a Shakespeare play, narratives comple-
ment each other. Different levels of reality – practical, emotional,
metaphysical – provide the source for perspectives which accumulate and extend meaning, pushing out the boundaries of what
the form of the novel can encompass. Tolstoy's method is like that
of a painter whose canvas is always enlarging without becoming
inappropriate for its frame. His narrative method is always
exploding outwards, and at the same time tightly controlled, as,
for example, in the railway accidents which occur at the beginning and end of *Anna Karenina*.

In the novella of passion, as in *Anna Karenina*, the story
concerns a relationship so intense that those involved become
oblivious of all else, indifferent to society's conventions and codes,
but unable to live without being affected and altered by their
pressures. Anna and Vronsky wish to hide somewhere, alone
with their love; and while they live outside Russia they almost
succeed in doing so, as Marguerite and Armand (in *The Lady of
the Camellias*) also succeed for a time when they move from Paris

to the country. But in both cases their happiness is conditional, dependent on the outside world leaving them alone, and the inner world of their love being capable of sustaining them completely. Time brings about changes which break down such self-enclosures and isolation.

In *Anna Karenina*, Anna's disintegration is hastened after her return to Russia by a number of pressures. Her separation from her son, Seriozha, pains her deeply as a mother. Karenin's indecision about the divorce is exacerbated by Vronsky's desire to give his children his name. And both influence Anna's sense of herself as a fallen woman who cannot be received in society. Her attempt to ignore society's conventions by appearing at the opera results in her public humiliation. Tolstoy's genius is nowhere more penetratingly apparent than in his portrayal of Anna's mind succumbing to the pressures which she finds intolerable, and without solution, except in death.

Such a theme could have been pursued in the lives of the three main characters only; but Tolstoy's preoccupation with family and national life widens the perspective. What is involved is not just the intensities and perplexity of individual feeling, but the relationship of these to a family past; and a future belonging to the next generation. Karenin suffers from the vulnerability of a man brought up as an orphan and deprived of the secure identity which families bestow. When Anna leaves him for Vronsky, he is not simply wounded in his pride. 'He knew that people would be merciless for the very reason that his heart was lacerated. He felt that his fellow-men would destroy him, as dogs kill some poor cur maimed and howling with pain. ... His despair was intensified by the consciousness that he was utterly alone in his misery.'[9] In the extremity of his isolation he becomes an easy prey to Lydia Ivanovna's religious zeal; and her determination that those whom God has joined together, no man shall put asunder. Anna dies without knowing the finality of Karenin's decision about the divorce; but the reader's knowledge gives further poignance to Anna's anguish and despair.

Karenin has never possessed a family except in his relation to Anna; Anna loses her family in the person of her son. She can manage to tolerate this while she has no doubt of Vronsky's love, and while both of them are protected from their exile, ironically by being in exile on Vronsky's estate. Once they return to Moscow, Vronsky's prolonged absences from the house, brought about by his own need to occupy himself, arouse Anna's jealousy and lead to her conviction that he is seeing other women. The resulting quarrels quickly make their situation (and their new relationship) unbearable. To escape from Moscow seems increasingly the one way to put an end to the misery which threatens to destroy – but has not yet done so – their underlying love. Anna's disintegration occurs before they can escape, not least because as a woman she is in the power of both Vronsky and Karenin. Tolstoy does not absolve her from responsibility for her actions; but sees her as unable to control their consequences. What is intolerable for her in her sense of losing Vronsky's love afflicts him too after her suicide. His grief finds release only when he goes in search of death in a foreign war. As in other novellas, the love which embraces and encloses leaves only a residual life when its moment has passed.

What gives *Anna Karenina* its immensity of scope and imagination is Tolstoy's setting of Anna's disintegration against Levin's growth: they are not parallel or treated in exactly parallel ways, but they are complementary. Levin's intense attraction for Kitty, stopped in its tracks by her rejection of his proposal ('No, that cannot be ... Forgive me')[10] is deepened by his overcoming her humiliation of him. When they are finally married, their union seems as happy as it is appropriate. But the novel is not half way through. And Tolstoy is as much interested in their ensuing problems as in their courtship. Levin is possessive of his freedom and independence, seeing no need for Kitty's presence or help, even in dealing with his brother's sickness. Kitty's anger and jealousy is aroused by feeling excluded and unwanted in so much that concerns her husband's life. She intensely resents it when he goes to visit Anna, assuming that she must have made him fall in love with her. Tolstoy never portrays their marriage as being ideal, or without its quarrels and misunderstandings; but he does see both of them as coming to a settlement with the world they share, and taking pleasure in their common family life. Beyond this Levin's growth is of another sort.

His views on agriculture, some reactionary and others progressive, reflect those of Tolstoy as landowner. His philosophic outlook as it is expressed in the closing chapters of the book also has much in common with that of the later Tolstoy. It becomes increasingly important for him to find his answer to the questions: 'What am I? ... Why am I here?'[11] His reading in Plato, Spinoza, Kant, Schelling, Hegel and Schopenhauer gives him only temporary satisfaction. When he turns back to life, the whole artificial edifice of words tumbles down like a house of cards. As for Tolstoy, the insoluble problem of the meaning of life brings him so close to suicide that he has to distance himself from the instruments of self-destruction. When he is not thinking about the meaning of existence, he is occupied by the needs of his family, by running the estate, and by his new hobby of bee-keeping. 'So he lived, not knowing and not seeing any chance of knowing what he was and for what purpose he had been placed in the world. He was tormented by this ignorance to the extent of fearing suicide, yet at the same time he was resolutely cutting his own individual and definite path through life.'[12] A door is opened for Levin through this impasse by one of his peasants. He helps Levin to see that the solution lies in not living for one's own needs, but for God whom no one can know or define. 'All of us as rational beings can't do anything else but live for our bellies. And all of a sudden this same Fiodor declares that it is wrong to live for one's belly; we must live for truth, for God, and a hint is enough to make me understand what he means ... this knowledge is outside the sphere of reason: it has no causes and can have no effects.

'If goodness has a cause, it is no longer goodness; if it has consequences – a reward – it is not goodness either. So goodness is outside the chain of of cause and effect.'[13]

He resolves the problem of the Church's teaching by reducing it to a belief in 'serving truth rather than one's personal needs'. In this way he finds it possible to live the life of the spirit, 'the only life that is worth living',[14] and to keep intact his spiritual powers, even though everyday life will inevitably shroud them from time to time. What he has come to know is beyond reason and words, and so cannot explain why his knowledge of good and evil is apparently denied to people of other religions. 'I have no right to try to decide the question of other religions and their relations to the Deity; that must remain unfathomable for me.'[15] He also knows that his new found faith has not changed him. He will still continue to commit the same human mistakes, to lose his temper and quarrel with his wife. In spite of this his whole life, 'independently of anything that can happen to me, every minute of it is no longer meaningless as it was before, but has a positive meaning of goodness with which I have the power to invest it'.[16]

Levin's resolution of the problem of life's meaning stands against the suffering in Vronsky's and Anna's love. In the scope of its reference, and its critique of lives which are not based on anything more substantial than personal emotions, it encompasses much that the novella can only imply. The Anna who has caused Vronsky ineradicable remorse by killing herself in revenge for what she feels to be the cooling of his love for her has left him a wreck. He goes to the war indifferent to his fate. 'As a man I have the merit that my life is of no value to me. And I've physical energy enough to hack my way into the fray and slay or fall – I know that. I am glad there is something for which I can lay down the life which is not simply useless but loathsome to me. Anyone's welcome to it.'[17] Vronsky's attitude ressembles that of other lovers in the novella; like them he has to go on living. But Tolstoy's view of human passions is set in the larger perspective of Levin's faith. These lives have been endured in different kinds of reality; and even in the work of art Tolstoy makes no attempt to reconcile them. Vronsky goes with his tooth-ache to a decisive engagement, thinking only of Anna as triumphant in having carried out her threat to inflict on him futile but inescapable remorse. Levin continues his life with a new feeling which has also come to him through suffering.

But this greater detachment in Levin – possessed of a secret 'for me alone, of vital importance to me, and not to be put into words'[18] – indispensable as it is to the greatness of Tolstoy's novel, is what the novella can only touch on in the figure of the listener, the editor, or narrator. The excitement of the novella arises from what must be told, and often from a neurotic desire to exorcise. As John Bayley has said of the *nouvelle*, the writer is 'fashioning something with a secret and delightful appeal to his imagination'. The economy and precision with which this is done constitutes part of the form's interest. But it is also the delicacy with which other kinds of experience and levels of reality touch upon the central narrative which involves the reader more deeply. In *Anna Karenina*, Levin's preoccupations expose what the novella only glancingly touches upon, but is implicit in its appeal to the imagination: the question of the significance of these passions which are exclusive of all else, and self-consuming. How the novella represents them in changing social and cultural contexts will be the theme of the following chapters.

I have tried to illustrate the naturalness and effectiveness of this lyric form for this particular theme; and to show how its treatment within the form differs in the work of various European writers according to the pressures of their times and the psychodynamic forces within them. It is not a history of the novella, nor a description of what the form can encompass, but an investigation of a recurrent theme encompassed within the form, and the changes wrought in that theme by changing contexts as well as individual impulses.

We live in a time when reading – and consequently literature – seem increasingly to belong to a passing culture. The book itself is often discussed as though its days are numbered. Like the long-playing record, it will give way to more 'advanced' forms of technology, of computerised databases, and compilations of fact, thought to be more valuable than the discursive and open-ended investigations of human behaviour, relationships, attitudes, beliefs and morals with which imaginative literature is concerned. At such a time more and more works are likely to fall out of the picture of common discourse, to be replaced by theoretical discussions of ideological import, which signal the learning, cleverness and expertise of those who stagger about with portmanteaux of long words, rejoicing in a priesthood of mystification. As someone who has been fortunate enough to be a teacher of literature for most of his working life, I have remained convinced that literature, like music and painting, yields up its treasure to those who mine it for itself; that a book is, in Hermann Hesse's phrase, 'a window through which light falls on the reader', and that the imagination of the artist is more interesting that the intellect of the critic.

No doubt this reflects a preference for the view that language itself is a window on reality, and is not simply a self-referential game. The desire to write about literature expresses the belief that certain created things should not be forgotten, that they express aspirations, attitudes, ideas and feelings which enhance and enlarge our experience of being alive, sometimes by reminding us of its darkness, sometimes of its joy, and always of its contingency. The reading of a work of literature is an exploration of what we are not, a confirmation (far from consoling) of what we are, and an investigation of the circumstances of our being. It asks more questions than it ever provides answers; and in its investigation leaves none of the problems of morals in a personal sense, or ethics in their relation to society, resolved. But it does raise them. And it raises them with a clarity and an energy which enhance both in us.

Madame de Lafayette:
The Princess of Clèves

The Princess should have said nothing to her husband and yielded
to M. de Nemours.   Stendhal, *Love*

The necessity of dying, which she saw was very near, made her
used to detachment, and the length of her illness made it a habit.
                    Madame de Lafayette, *The Princess of Clèves*

The circumstances of Madame de Lafayette's life, like those of
her characters in *The Princess of Clèves*, were both fortunate and
unfortunate. Born in 1634, she was to know and enjoy Parisian
life in the age of Louis XIV. Racine, Molière, Pascal and Boileau
were her contemporaries; the Duc de La Rochefoucauld, Bossuet
and Madame de Sévigné her intimates. Her drawing-room in the
Rue de Vaugirard, where she entertained her friends, was given
the name of the *cabale du sublime*:[1] a title which indicated its
intellectual brilliance and its lack of warmth. As Madame de
Sévigné once remarked, 'I am loved there as much as one can be
in that house.'[2]
   Though not a member of the Royal Household, Madame de
Lafayette had formed a friendship in her youth with Princess
Henrietta, the daughter of Charles I of England, destined to
marry Louis XIV's brother, the Duc d'Orléans, who was a ped-
erast. She was to kneel beside the King at Henrietta's death-bed,
poisoned, as she believed, by her husband's lover. Through her
friendship with Henrietta, Madame de Lafayette was later accepted at court, and was taken round Versailles by Louis himself
to see the building in progress. The *amours*, intrigues, scandals
and ambitions of those in the court were part of her everyday life,
and she relished them. Because of her social status, she could

survey a scene which interested her, but also preserve her independence of it. As was said, she lived in a mist.

Her close friendship with the Duc de La Rochefoucauld, old and gouty as he had become, deeply influenced her life and art. His own *Maximes* had been published in 1665; and he was not *persona grata* at the court. Whether or not she was his mistress, his intimacy with her deeply influenced the final form of *The Princess of Clèves* (some even claiming that he wrote it). In her circle the progress of her *nouvelle* was frequently discussed, her friends assisting her research on the reign of Henri II which formed its background. Set in the years 1558-9, Madame de Lafayette's novella might well have become yet another historical romance of the kind fashionable at the time. But she had a sharper and more selective eye, discarding the details of daily life to concentrate on a narrative of sexual passion. In doing this, she gave the novella a theme suited to its form: a narrative in which 'violence of inclination' and a 'terrible strictness' were set in conflict with each other; and desire was shown to include both jealousy and hate. Economy of form reflected the fierce brevity of passion, and the death of desire, through withdrawal from the world, and the healing of grief.

Madame de Lafayette was married at the age of twenty-two. Her husband, the Comte de Lafayette, was a countryman and took her to live on his estate in the Auvergne. Madame de Lafayette did not like country life, nor did she find the company of her husband engaging. After bearing him children, she gained his consent to live in Paris, where he visited her from time to time on amicable terms, but without intimacy or involvement in the life she chose to lead. Surrounded by an aristocratic and intellectual circle, she developed her own tastes and discovered the environment in which her creative talent developed. As a married woman unbothered by the duties of domestic life (she was thought for many years to have become a widow), and not involved in the politics of the court, she had the advantages which derived from being a woman of brilliant intellect and perceptiveness, without the disadvantages of being confined by her position or her relationships. The free play of mind in her writing was the product of a talent, successful also in life, in getting what she wanted.

The Princess of Clèves was published anonymously in 1678.

The writer claimed to prefer not to be named so that opinions
about the man should not colour judgements about the work,
hoping that the story itself would be well received by its public.
As with George Eliot's early fiction, the female identity of the
author was well concealed to prevent criticism of the work as
being written by a woman. (Its authorship has never been proved
beyond doubt; but the attribution made after Madame de Lafayette's death has not been convincingly challenged.) It owed
something to the fashion, established by Segrais and Mlle de
Villedieu twenty years previously, for historical fictions set in
France, with characters who were *vraisemblables*. The originality of Madame de Lafayette's work lay in its understanding of
emotion and feeling; and its analysis of their development in the
relations between the three characters whom she imagined, the
Princess of Clèves, her husband, and the Duc de Nemours, in
their historical setting of the reign of Henri II. Madame de
Lafayette's novella had more in common with the dramas of
Corneille and Racine than with the work of her predecessors in
fiction. Her plot can be quite easily divided into five acts, and her
central scenes are conceived as dramatic encounters. Racine's
Phèdre had been performed the previous year; and its central
theme of a passion which is forbidden provides an obvious comparison.[3] Madame de Lafayette saw the problem more simply in
terms of the claims of virtue and loyalty, leading to less sensa-
tional consequences but scarcely less tragic ends. Virtue,
strongly inculcated in the young Princess by her mother, becomes
a standard by which she judges her own behaviour and preserves
her sense of identity. But it cannot prevent the birth of passion
or abate its violence in her relationship with the Duc de
Nemours, more especially, since, as for Phèdre, it is intensified
by the need for secrecy in a court where the destructive effects of
scandal and gossip are everywhere to be seen. In both play and
novella, the audience becomes a sharer in a secret which once
admitted can only lead to catastrophe, while the keeping of the
secret further intensifies the emotion. Subterfuge and concealment are the means of survival in the court, but the deadly
enemies of integrity of life, which is 'fame's best friend'.

By the use of historical setting, Madame de Lafayette was able
to achieve an apparent detachment from her subject. She wrote
as one writing of times past, and so avoided the temptation to

draw her characters too closely from her contemporaries. But in this device, she was making use of what later novella writers would call memory: a lucidity which makes possible the writing about desire when desire has passed. In April 1678 – shortly after the publication of *The Princess of Clèves* – she was asked her opinion of it; she replied that it was not so much a novel as memoirs, adding that she understood the word had once been used in the title of the book. The tone of her novella – familiar and objective – has more in common with a reconstruction in memory than with a historical romance; and she brings to it an objective understanding of the differences between sexuality in men and women which has more to do with a mind reflecting upon its own experience than with the distinctions between present and past. Whatever the nature of her relationship with the Duc de La Rochefoucauld over twenty years of intimate friendship, her devotion to him seems to have inspired much of the feeling which made it possible for her to write a novella of passion; but she used the perspective of history to make possible an analysis of relationship and feeling in a novella which she described as memoirs.

After the death of her husband, Madame de Chartres brings her innocent, young and beautiful daughter to Paris. She is sixteen years old. Coming from one of the oldest and noblest families in France, she makes an immediate impression in the Court. 'As soon as she arrived, the Vidame came to see her. He was astonished by the great beauty of Mademoiselle de Chartres, and with good reason. The whiteness of her skin, and her golden hair gave her an exceptional appeal; the proportion of her features, her face and her bearing were full of grace and charm.'[4] Almost at once, two suitors appear, the Chevalier de Guise and the Prince of Clèves, the younger son of the Duc de Nevers. Madame de Chartres has educated her daughter to believe in virtue, which will prove especially necessary once she starts living in Paris. 'The Court revolved around ambition and love; both men and women were preoccupied by them. There were so many different factions and interests; and the ladies were so much involved in them that love was always mixed up with intrigue, and intrigue with love.'[5]

The Prince of Clèves falls deeply in love with Mademoiselle de Chartres, and longs to marry her. Aware of his nobility of char-

acter and his wisdom beyond his years, Mademoiselle de Chartres agrees to marry him, even though she is 'not particularly
drawn to him';[6] and her mother, although realising this, has no
fears about marrying her daughter to a man she cannot love. The
Prince knows he has failed to arouse her deeper feelings, and
tries to express his misgivings to her. She cannot respond to him:
not only does she lack the feelings he longs for her to have, she
does not understand what they are. After their marriage, the
Princess of Clèves does all that is expected of her; but she does
not change her feelings with her name.

The Duc de Nemours has just returned from Brussels to Paris:
preparations are in hand to arrange a marriage between him and
Elizabeth I of England. He is 'Nature's masterpiece' ('un chef
d'oeuvre de la nature'). As well as being the best-looking and the
bravest of men, he has a mental distinction and charm that set
him apart from his fellows. 'His vivacity charmed men and
women equally; he excelled at all kinds of sport; his manner of
dressing set the fashion, but could not be imitated; and his whole
personality made it impossible to look at anyone else when he
was present.'[7] Prompted by the King, he dances with the Princess
of Clèves at a ball, and develops so violent a passion for her that
he quickly forsakes his former pursuits and mistresses, as well
as losing his ardour for the throne of England. The Princess of
Clèves also becomes aware of feelings towards the Duc de
Nemours which she did not know she possessed; and is bitterly
ashamed that she could have such feelings towards a man who is
not her husband. Goodness of heart, loyalty and belief in her
mother's advice that nothing can make a woman happy except
loving a husband and being loved by him compel the Princess of
Clèves to do all she can to avoid the company of the Duc de
Nemours. But her husband insists that she is too young to give
up her social obligations at Court. 'She could not prevent herself
being troubled by his presence or feeling pleasure at seeing him,
but when he was not there and she thought that the origin of her
love lay in the attraction she felt in his presence, she almost
believed that she hated him, because of the anguish this thought
gave her.'[8] Her mother, now dying, confronts her daughter with
the nature of her feelings for Nemours, and warns her against
the unhappiness of love affairs. 'You stand on the edge of a
precipice,' she advises, 'and to draw back you will have to make

a tremendous effort. Compel your husband to take you away.'[9] On her death-bed she fears above all that her daughter might fall as other women do.

Although it is widely known at Court that Nemours is in love, no one except the Princess of Clèves realises that she is the object of his love. Her certainty of his attraction to her is confirmed when she catches him removing her portrait: a loss which also alerts her husband to the possibility that, as he knows she does not love him, she loves someone else.

The loss too of a love-letter belonging to the Vidame de Chartres which the Princess of Clèves mistakenly believes to have been written by Nemours to another woman increases her anguish, adding jealousy to the violence of her existing feelings of love and hate.

At last the Princess gains her husband's consent to go to their estate at Coulommiers. While there, she takes the risk of revealing the danger she feels herself to be in; she confesses the strength of her attraction for someone else, but insists that she has never been unfaithful, and refuses to tell him the name of the man for whom she feels love. Their conversation takes place in the pavilion in the grounds of Coulommiers; and by one of those coincidences which reflect the recurrence of chance in human affairs and which great art succeeds in making plausible, Nemours is present unseen to overhear her confession: a confession that he knows expresses the depth of her love for him.

A burning jealousy is now added to the unhappiness of the Prince that his wife does not love him, at not knowing the name of the man she loves. Although she never gives away her secret, his suspicions settle upon Nemours; and when he sets a spy to follow his movements, he discovers, as he thinks, that Nemours has passed two nights with his wife in the country. In fact, Nemours has no more than glimpsed her because at the first suspicion of his presence she has secluded herself from the danger of his company. Overcome by grief at his wife's falseness in pretending that she has never succumbed to her lover, the Prince of Clèves falls dangerously ill. Not until shortly before his death does his wife succeed in convincing him of her innocence.

With her husband's death and the passage of time, the Princess of Clèves begins to think once more of Nemours. When she re-encounters him, her sleeping passion is violently aroused once

more. Duty and virtue no longer seem an obstacle to their marriage, until she recalls that they have both been partly
responsible for 'murdering' her husband. When for the first time
they are left alone to speak of their feelings, she tells him: 'You
inspired feelings in me which were unknown to me before I met
you, and of which I had so little idea that the shock they gave me
increased the agitation which they always bring.'[10] Further reflection convinces her that she dare not expose herself to the
misery of seeing their present love grow cold, nor to the likeli-
hood, if they were to marry, of his being attracted to someone
else. She had been married to the one man capable of being
faithful to her; but it was her misfortune that this passion of his
brought her no happiness.

She decides not to see Nemours again, while admitting to him
that she is making a sacrifice to a duty which exists only in her
imagination. She retires to her estate near the Pyrenees, and
after an inner struggle with herself succeeds in overcoming what
remains of her passion. She has renounced the world for her own
peace of mind and her continuing sense of duty. Only the years
heal the grief of Nemours, whose passion for her was 'the most
violent, the most natural, and the best founded that has ever
been'.[11] When the Princess of Clèves dies without returning to the
world, the narrrator comments: 'Her life, which was short
enough, left an example of inimitable virtue.'[12]

The rejection of the Duc de Nemours involves a fear that once
the obstacle has been removed desire will fade: a realistic view
that extreme forms of feeling cannot always adjust to marriage,
or that those who undergo them cannot necessarily live together.
As a woman the Princess of Clèves recognises too a difference
between the sexes, which social convention endorses. Nemours is
well-known for his numerous love-affairs, and for the indifference he shows to all those whose hearts he has won. After her
husband's death she rejects him partly because she knows that
for such a man the sexual passion, once consummated, will not
last for ever; and then in spite of all she has suffered for him, she
will have to endure his infidelity to her. 'Every woman, whether
from vanity or attraction, desires to make a conquest of you,' she
tells him. 'There are very few who do not feel your charm. I know
from my own experience that there is hardly anyone who would
not succumb to you. I should always think of you as loving and

being loved, and should not often be mistaken, and then there would be nothing for me to do but feel pain; I do not even know if I should dare to reproach you.'[13] The Princess of Clèves has known the extremity of sexual passion; and she also knows the jealousy to which it can give rise. She does not want to suffer like that again, because in the end her passions affront her; she does not wish to be in thrall even to Nemours. 'I can be led by my passions,' she confesses, 'but they have never been able to blind me.'[14] She would overcome them if she could.

Nemours comes to no such rational view of the matter, nor does he find any such practical solution as retreating to the country and devoting himself to good works. The death of passion involves for him a loss of all appetite for life, while for her it leads to a withdrawal from life, which does not last long. The structuring of desire, like its death, leads to different ends for men and women. At its simplest, the narrative suggests a lack of appropriateness in the relationship between all three of them (something basically ill-adjusted and ill-suited) which creates a personal hell that cannot be overcome; at a more complex level, the passion between the Princess of Clèves and the Duc de Nemours enacts that myth which can only be completed in death, when the estrangement of this world has been overcome. About that Madame de Lafayette has nothing to say. Her imagination is untouched by the Catholic culture in which she lived. Her interest lies this side of the grave.

'L'on n'est pas amoureuse par la volonté,' was among the maxims of Duc de La Rochefoucauld. Passionate love, as opposed to mannered love – to use Stendhal's distinction – is something which happens but is not chosen. The passionate desire which Prince of Clèves feels for his wife is turned to torment by the recognition that it is not returned. (The narrative does not suggest that the marriage is not consummated; but simply that she cannot reciprocate what he feels for her.) In the absence of her desire for him, anguish becomes jealousy and hate when he learns of her 'violent inclination' towards someone else. Nemours, practised in the arts of sexual conquest, sees her husband as no more than his most deadly rival, who increases his desire to win what he does not possess. Desire is intensified by the presence of the husband, and jealousy is aroused by the presence of an unknown lover. For all three, strength of feeling feeds on absence.

Although Madame de Lafayette gives fewer insights into the feelings of Nemours than into those of the other two characters, she sees the degree to which he, like other men, is capable of calculation, and the male vanity involved in his love of conquest. When he discovers for certain at Coulommiers that he is the object of the Princess's passion, he feels a momentary joy; but the mood does not last long, because he soon realises that the incident by which he has discovered that he is the object of her passion means also that he cannot hope to receive any sign from her. 'He felt however a keen pleasure at having reduced her to such an extremity.'[15] After her husband's death he still argues his chances with himself, reproaching himself for his lack of initiative: 'Is it possible that love has robbed me of reason and boldness; and that I have become completely changed, as with none of the other loves in my life? I had to respect her grief, but I have respected it for too long, and have given her the time to let her feelings for me lose their intensity.'[16] The Princess of Clèves has good grounds for suggesting that his constancy was created by the obstacles to the fulfilment of his desire.

And it is in relation to the Princess that Madame de Lafayette's analysis of the nature of desire becomes most penetrating. The intensity of her emotion conflicts with her belief in virtue and with her mother's precept that the greatest happiness for a woman lies in loving her husband and being loved by him. She is utterly shaken by the discrepancy between what she feels she should feel, and what she does feel. She is overwhelmed, she reflects, by an emotion she is powerless to resist in spite of herself. Her resolutions are useless. She thinks today what she thought yesterday; and she does the opposite today of what she resolved yesterday. As she will discover, the determination to go to the country, and never see Nemours, however prudent, does not alter the strength or nature of her feelings for him. Rather the reverse: the strength of her will not to have anything to do with him intensifies the passion she feels for him. As for him, in a different sense, the obstacle makes the predicament worse.

Madame de Lafayette's view that the will is not capable of controlling human feelings points to her recognition of the precariousness of the human condition. Man is a reed – as Pascal observed – shaken by the wind, but a thinking reed. Thought enables us to determine on a course of action, as the Princess of Clèves does consistently in rejecting Nemours; but thought does not alter or diminish the passions. She recalls her mother's advice that it is better to do anything rather than embark on a love-affair; and her husband's insistence on the importance of sincerity. But contemplation only intensifies the tension within her. When finally she does confess to her husband her fear of her feelings for someone else, her anguish manifests itself physically. 'Very well,' she cried, throwing herself at his knees, 'I will make a confession which no husband has ever heard before; but the innocence of my behaviour and my intentions gives me the strength to make it. It is quite true that I have reasons for leaving the Court, and that I want to avoid the dangers into which people of my age sometimes fall.'[17] The Princess's ideal of virtue embraces steadfastness, loyalty and duty, but her loyalty cannot discourse with her passion, just as, after her confession, the Prince's esteem for his wife cannot assuage his jealousy. The anguish of their personal predicament derives from feelings which cannot be overcome, or given way to. In the illness of the Prince, Madame de Lafayette portrays how the suffering of the mind can result in the sickness of the body, and how the desire for a union which can never be fulfilled can in particular circumstances prove to be fatal.

The trap in which they are caught has however been sprung by the conventions of the time, and by life at Court. As in later novellas, the economy of the form suggests rather than explores this relationship, indicating the pressures which can cause emotions to remain concealed and become subversive and explosive. The prevailing code of *galanterie* does not permit an admission of love between the Princess and Nemours. For fear of being humiliated a woman will never admit that she loves, while the man only permits himself to do so after a long wait, for he knows that his declaration will be taken at first as an insult. They both observe this code. No open discusssion of their feelings for one another occurs until after the Prince's death. In the absence of any declaration, their feelings are manipulated by rumour and intensified by secrecy. The change in Nemours' way of life is the subject of Court gossip. No one doubts that he is in love, but the object of his affections remains unknown. The Princess's own uncertainty about his feelings for her inflames her jealousy, even at times her hate of him, while what cannot be spoken of increases its power over her. As for Phèdre, though for different reasons, desire feeds on its own denial.

The rituals of love-making at Court serve ironically to undermine what in the Princess at least is loyalty to her husband, and a wish, which shows the continuing moral influence of her mother, not to live as other women do. As often happens with deep feelings (and temptations), the more strenuously they are resisted in secrecy, the more powerful becomes their hold. The subtlety of Madame de Lafayette's writing owes a great deal to her interweaving of the contrasted reasons for which secrecy is desirable and destructive.

Life at Court mirrors and intensifies this life of hidden uncertainty and repressed feeling. Madame de Chartres has warned her daughter that at Court nothing is as it seems. Secrecy and subterfuge become neccesary where openness is full of danger (the fate of the Vidame de Chartres is sealed by his betrayal of the Queen); they also make possible the sexual duplicity in which the courtiers engage. The story of Sancerre, Madame de Tournon and Estouteville, which the Prince of Clèves tells his wife before he knows about her feelings for Nemours, serves understandably to confirm her in her strictness. The widowed Madame de Tournon has been regarded at Court as inconsolable at the death of her husband. She is cured of her grief by the love of Count de Sancerre. She insists to him on secrecy, on the grounds that she wishes to continue to pretend that she has withdrawn from the world. Sancerre is violently in love with her and expects to marry her. On her sudden death he discovers that she had secretly been planning to marry Estouteville, with whom she had been deceiving him for some time. Sancerre's hatred of both of them reduces him to a desperate state. As a woman writer, Madame de Lafayette never loses sight of the duplicity which can exist in both sexes in affairs of the heart.

The Prince of Clèves, in telling this story to his wife, also uses it as a pretext for expressing, and ensuring the perpetuation of, his good fortune in being married to her; and at the same time cunningly puts fear into her so that she will remain faithful. To step outside the limits of legitimate relationships is to enter a quagmire where no assurances exist; and even where 'true' feelings seem to exist, this leads to behaviour which is excessive and unbalanced, as happens to Nemours. Not only does he give up his hope of the throne of England (which is sensible enough), but his attitude to his former mistresses and his way of life are transformed: 'The passion of Nemours for Madame de Clèves was at first so intense that it simply obliterated the memory of all the women he had loved and with whom he had remained in contact during his absence.'[18] As well as becoming isolated from his previous way of life, he embraces subterfuge: his theft of her portrait, his concealment in the Pavilion at Coulommiers, his repetition of the Princess's confession, lightly disguised, and his nocturnal visits to the forest illustrate an extremity of behaviour brought about by the conventions of *galanterie* and intensified by the power of his feelings. He continues for a long time to pay the price of his feelings, and of the Princess's loyalty.

After her husband's death, Nemours takes a room in the neighbourhood of her house so that he can continue to watch her windows. When at last she re-encounters him by chance in the park, she discovers him in a trance-like state. 'When she had gone through a little wood, she discovered in the most secluded part of the garden, at the end of an alley, a kind of summer-house open at the sides which she approached. When she was quite near it, she saw a man sitting on one of the benches, who appeared lost in deep reflection, and realised that it was M. de Nemours. At the sight of him she stopped at once, but the people with her made some noise which aroused M. de Nemours from his thoughts. Without looking to see who had disturbed him he got up to avoid the people who were approaching and *with a low bow* [my italics] which prevented him from seeing whom he greeted, turned up another alley.'[19]

This image of Nemours, forlorn and unreconciled, comes as close as Madame de Lafayette does to a moral comment on the disintegrating effect of the passions, or the conventions by which the Court lives. The low bow itself is a gesture, both courteous and fashionable, which conceals what the body feels, and is an image of that façade behind which the Court conducts its real life. In the case of Nemours, it may also be read as a gesture of ironic humility from a man who has been defeated by his feelings.

As a story-teller Madame de Lafayette almost never intrudes. Towards the beginning she once uses the phrase 'je vais nommer'

to introduce a description of those historical figures who had been
an adornment of their times. Otherwise she uses a familiarity of
tone, combined with a historical detachment, to describe the
different ways in which desire affects the lives of her central
characters. As a woman novelist she understood the predicament
of a young girl whose sexual feelings have been made inadmissi-
ble even before she experiences them, unless she is to break faith
with the other standards by which her sense of identity is secured. Ironically, she becomes like the women from whom she
flees: her virtue cannot save her from the control of her feelings
by her social environment. And for them she must pay with her
husband's death. The 'lacrymae rerum' or 'tears of things' are
never distant from Madame de Lafayette's inscription of desire.

Anatole France once wrote of her that she kept her secret. She
does not judge her characters, or pronounce on the nature of their
feelings. Whether or not she approved or sympathised with the
Princess of Clèves's decision to withdraw from the world remains
as uncertain as whether she believed the passion of the Duc de
Nemours to be the most violent, natural and best founded in the
world. What is clear is that her novella illustrates how sexual
morality whether as practised by the court or by the Princess of
Clèves involves dangers, once the passions have become involved, and that virtue, however strong, may not be able to
overcome them. The difficulty lies in living in the human world
at all.

But she certainly showed no inclination to follow in the footsteps of the Princess of Clèves. After the death of the Duc de La
Rochefoucauld she remained in Paris, attempting to promote the
career of a boorish son. She was attracted by the corruption of
power, by the intrigues and amours of the court. When she died
in 1693, an autopsy showed among other things two growths in
her heart, the tip of which was all withered and desiccated. We
may see something emblematic in this fact. Whatever the desire
which had caused her to write *The Princess of Clèves*, she had
paid for it dearly; but the revisiting of that desire had created her
one lasting monument.

3

Abbé Prévost: *Manon Lescaut*

'In its immoral and pernicious class, *Manon Lescaut*,' continued
Madame de Fervaques, 'occupies, so I am told, one of the highest
places. The frailties and well deserved afflictions of a guilty heart
are, so people say, depicted there with a truth that is in some ways
profound ...'   Stendhal, *Scarlet and Black*

Dresses, cashmeres, jewels were all sold with incredible rapidity.
None of that appealed to me, and I went on waiting. Suddenly I
heard a voice say: 'A volume, perfectly bound, gilt-edged, entitled
Manon Lescaut. An inscription on the first page. Ten francs.'
                              Dumas *fils*, *The Lady of the Camellias*

The pleasure of love lies in loving, and the passion one feels brings
more happiness than the passion one inspires.
                                            Stendhal, *Scarlet and Black*

'Monseigneur the Lieutenant of Police is humbly entreated by
the Superior-General of the Congregation of Saint-Maur to cause
to be arrested a fugitive monk of that congregation .... He twice
left the Jesuits, and has been for eight years with the Benedicti-
nes. He is called Antoine Prévost ... is a man of medium height,
fair, deepset blue eyes, rosy complexion, full face .... He walks
with impunity every day in the streets of Paris. He is the author
of a little novel which has for title *The Adventures of a Man of
Quality*. He is about 35 or 36: is dressed in clerical garb ....'[1]

The order for Prévost's arrest and imprisonment in the Bas-
tille was never carried out. The monk escaped. And in 1731 the
Histoire du Chevalier des Grieux et de Manon was published in
Amsterdam. It formed the seventh book of the *Mémoires et
Aventures d'un Homme de Qualité*, withdrawn from the world.

A little more than half a century had passed since the publication of *The Princess of Clèves*. Prévost's life, like Madame de
Lafayette's, had considerable bearing upon his masterpiece,

without making it in an obvious sense autobiographical. Many of
the adventures his hero encounters had been his. He knew what
it was like to be wanted by the law, to flee, and be arrested. At
times he lived close to the underworld of crime; at others he took
refuge from his love of women and want of money in the contemplative life. Like Cholderlos de Laclos, who wrote a much more
extensive fiction fifty years later on sexual treachery, *Les Liaisons Dangereuses*, Prévost gained much of his early experience
through life in the army. He knew its violence and crudeness, and
its alleviation of boredom and penury through gambling, all of
which are reflected in the character of Manon Lescaut's brother.

Love of women determined too the course of his life, as it does
for the Chevalier des Grieux: both men being swayed by the
double pull of life in and out of the world. As a young man Prévost
gave up his novitiate in the Jesuits to join the army; later, the
end of an affair led him to seek refuge in the Benedictine order.
He was later to write of his decision to withdraw (temporarily, as
it turned out) from the world, that the unhappy end of a too
tender relationship brought him to the tomb: 'the name which I
give to the worthy order where I buried myself and where I lived
for some time so really dead that my friends and relations were
unaware what had become of me'.[2] About the same time as
Manon was written, Prévost started a prolonged liaison with
Lenki Eckhardt whose character and way of life had much in
common with Manon's. She seems to have entered his life too late
for any direct influence on the novella; more probably the fiction
reflects a recurrent sexual fantasy which he lived out in some
ways with her.

On 5 October 1733, all copies of *Manon Lescaut* were seized by
the French authorities. It had been acknowledged in Paris for
three months that the book was written with such art and in so
interesting a fashion that decent people were to be seen melting
for pity over a card-sharper and a whore. Even worse, the author
was in holy orders. A contemporary wrote to his friend in the
provinces: 'This ex-Benedictine is a madman who has just written an abominable book called the "History of Manon Lescaut",
and this heroine is a street-walker out of the Hôpital, and sent to
the Mississippi in chains ... there is only one good phrase in it,
that she was so beautiful that she might have brought back

idolatry to the universe.'[3] Like much bad publicity, *Manon Lescaut* brought the Abbé Prévost fame and money.

In the same year he started to publish a periodical, *Le Pour et le Contre*, which he wrote almost entirely himself, and which reflected his interest in English literature. During the next twenty years he was to translate the major novels of Richardson, as well as works by Addison and Fielding, and several of the plays of Shakespeare. He spent laborious days working in libraries, writing a history of voyages, and compiling a dictionary of unusual words in the French language. He was caught up in the Encyclopaedic spirit of his age, and his output was prolific. Of all the labour in those library hours, little is now remembered.

In Prévost's life we can see the recurrent attraction of an ordered and rational account of things, of a dedication to knowledge and its dissemination. His early training with the Jesuits left its mark on him permanently; he was drawn to austerity and hard intellectual labour. He used his reason to contribute generously to that wider project in his time, which saw in Reason the great power and majesty of the human mind, and an instrument for controlling and ordering human life. But ironically his lasting monument is a work which recognises how deeply uncontrollable and irrational are the impulses at work in human character, as deaf to counsel as they are blind to the consequences of particular actions. The revisions and alterations which Prévost made in 1753 to *Manon* reflect his view of how men ought to live, but his less meditated work expresses how they do.

At the age of seventeen, Des Grieux is studying philosophy at Amiens; his life is good, virtuous and happy. If he had fixed his departure from the town for one day earlier, he would have avoided the gulf into which his passions plunged him. By chance he and his friend, Tiberge, happen to watch the coach arrive from Arras: Manon is travelling on it. A 'fille de plaisir', she is being sent by her family to a convent against her will and as a punishment for her sins.[4] In what Stendhal later described as a 'coup de foudre', Des Grieux is at once deprived of his reason and his self-control: she becomes the mistress of his heart. Although Manon is of humble birth and Des Grieux possesses no more than 50 crowns, they conspire to escape the vigilant eye of Tiberge and run away to Paris together. Their mutual and uncontrollable love deprives the Church of its rights; they become man and wife

without giving it a thought. But within twelve days of their
arrival in Paris in a state of passion that they make no effort to
conceal, their diminishing resources have led Manon to take an
elderly lover. Although Des Grieux is aware of a new source of
money, his sexual innocence and his background protect him
from imagining its source until a servant informs him of M. de
B.'s rapid departure down the back stairs. Before he can confront
Manon with her infidelity, his father's servants arrive to arrest
him and drag him off home to the country.

Des Grieux's father ridicules his son's credulity and dullness.
When he at last accepts that she has only been faithful to him for
twelve days, his extreme emotion causes him to fall on the floor
senseless, rave about returning to Paris, refuse food, and
threaten to burn down the house in which Manon and M. de B.
are living. Under the influence of his friend Tiberge's contempt
for the world, he determines at once to enter into holy orders and
live a life which is both peaceful and retired. A life divided
between study and religion will leave him no time for love. 'I liked
the idea of a retreat hidden in a wood, with a clear stream of
running water at the end of the garden: a library, with carefully
chosen works; a limited circle of virtuous and intellectual friends;
a well served table which was frugal and modest.'[5] (A vision
which Prévost substantially realised towards the end of his life;
and which often reappears as a version of the earthly paradise,
and a reprieve from emotional burdens. What Noël Coward
described as retiring to bed with a book and an apple.) But Des
Grieux soon realises that this vision of contentment would only
be complete if he could share it with Manon.

When his father believes him cured of his passion, he with-
draws his objection to his son's return to Paris. There he becomes
the Abbé des Grieux, and has to submit himself to a public
examination in theology at the Sorbonne. More than a year has
passed since he has set eyes on Manon; but when he sees her
again at the Sorbonne, he at once falls into the abyss which he
lacks the power to resist.

For the sake of frugality, Manon agrees to live with Des Grieux
at Chaillot, only visiting Paris for the opera and the theatre. But
she quits Paris with regret; and when winter comes, they also
take an apartment there. Two events now hasten their ruin: the
start of an acquaintance with Manon's brother, who lives by

card-sharping and other forms of petty crime; and the loss of all their money in a fire at Chaillot. As before, when the money that provided for a life of pleasure has gone, Manon deserts Des Grieux; and to his love for her, he now finds that hate, jealousy, shame and greed have been added.

In the life of crime and procurement of money from Manon's lovers in which they now become involved, Des Grieux realises the immense space which separates him from honour and virtue. Fate rescues him from one precipice only to lead him to another. As Des Grieux explains to Tiberge, virtue itself has no power against the passions, any more than family, society or religion: the heart has its reasons which reason knows not.

Arrested for theft of her new lover's jewels and money, Manon is now incarcerated in the Hôpital, a reformatory for criminal prostitutes, while Des Grieux is committed for his part in the theft to the prison at Saint Lazare. When he discovers where Manon has been put, he attacks her accuser G. de M. with frenzied physical force, overwhelmed by the gulf between her as the Queen of his heart, and the degrading place to which she has been sent. He determines to rescue her even if it means burning down Saint Lazare.

When with the help of Manon's brother he succeeds in effecting an escape for both of them, he returns to a life in which his feelings oscillate from subdued tranquillity to ungovernable fury, making him capable of warming his hands with the heart's blood of Manon and her lovers. (George Poulet has described this as 'instant-passage' from greatest joy to greatest sorrow; and it gives to Des Grieux's narrative a neurotic lack of control, like an emotional roller-coaster ride.)[6] What Des Grieux finds increasingly hard to tolerate is the discrepancy between his idea of Manon's love for him and its actuality. He needs to 'ennoble' what is 'flawed'.

But Manon equally is unable to resist the attractions of the demi-monde, to which she is instinctively drawn. She enjoys plotting with Des Grieux to outwit her old lover and his son. But their unscrupulousness is not matched by their ingenuity, nor blessed with good luck. Once again Manon is arrested and condemned this time to be transported with other 'filles de joie' to New Orleans. When Des Grieux hears of this, he once again falls into an 'apoplexy' which induces a swoon, leaving him as if dead;

he recovers from paralysis only to be overcome by violent feelings
of vengeance. Once again the world is confronting him with an
image of Manon which he cannot accept because of its inconsis-
tency with his own.

Manon is condemned to leave Paris the following day; and Des
Grieux determines to accompany her. He feels no regret at
quitting Europe which, without Manon, would become a savage
and deserted abode: ironically, an accurate description of the
place where she will die.

In New Orleans fate turns the knife once more. Manon and Des
Grieux decide to get married, but before they can do so the
Governor there succumbs to pressure from his son, who having
formed a passionate attachment to Manon, claims her as his
bride. Des Grieux and the Governor's son fight a duel, and the
latter is left for dead (though he is in fact not even badly
wounded). Manon and Des Grieux flee into the surrounding
desert, and there Manon dies. Even as she dies, he receives the
purest assurances of love. 'I lost her: even as she died she gave
me expressions of her love. I have no strength to tell you any
more of that fatal and unhappy hour.'⁷ For two days and nights
Des Grieux remains with his lips on the corpse. After burying her
he loses consciousness, and some days later is found in the desert
and brought back to the city.

His resentment at not having died too and hatred of life leave
him dangerously ill, until through the operation of grace, peace
returns to his soul. His friend, Tiberge, comes to accompany him
back to France, where he determines to make amends by an
ordered life for the scandal of his past behaviour. And to begin
with at Calais, as an exorcism of the experience he has lived
through, he tells the man of quality his story.

Prévost sets his tale in a double frame. The first takes the form
of an 'Avis de l'Auteur', provided by the man of quality. 'The
public will see in the conduct of M. Des Grieux a terrible example
of the strength of the passions. I have to depict a blind young man
who turning his back on happiness plunges of his own free will
into the most terrible misfortune.'⁸ The invocation of moral choice
in the phrase of his 'own free will' ('voluntairement') is clear
enough; but Des Grieux in telling the story refers on a number of
occasions to the destiny which controls him (a reflection perhaps
of the then prevalent Jansenist belief in predestination): a des-

tiny which leads him to disaster through his powerlessness to
control his passion for Manon. The Greek view of man as bewildered by the gods seems closer to the mark here than
Renoncour's moral disapproval: the interest of Des Grieux's narrative does not derive from its representation either of destiny,
or of the freedom to choose between good and evil, both of which
offer a rationally comprehensible account of human behaviour.
In his narrative, passions are seen without reference to any
preconceived principles. Quite simply, they blow up; and Des
Grieux's story is concerned with the consequences of that seismic
shock. The 'Avis' seems more like an attempt on Prévost's part to
dampen the moral indignation which he rightly suspected his
story would arouse.

The second frame is also provided by the man of quality,
Renoncour, to whom Des Grieux tells his tale on his arrival in
Calais, and who writes it down exactly as he hears it. This
Renoncour is a very different character to the author of the
foreword. He has previously helped Des Grieux by lending him
enough money to allow him to accompany Manon to America,
and on his return wishes to record his story exactly. The complaisant friend and listener appears to have little in common with
the moraliser of the foreword. However, the Renoncour of the
foreword is like Des Grieux himself reflecting on the nature of
passion, after it has ended, and so also distances the reader from
it, while Renoncour as scribe conveys the excitement of a tale in
the telling, with a relish for hearing how things are going to turn
out.

Like the *Princess of Clèves, Manon Lescaut* is concerned with
the torrents of spring, the arousal of sexuality. The Princess of
Clèves is only sixteen when her mother brings her to Paris; and
the Chevalier Des Grieux seventeen when he first meets Manon.
But while the Princess of Clèves will only find unhappiness in the
discovery of these feelings after her marriage, the Chevalier Des
Grieux will initially at least discover the ecstasy and fulfilment
of requited love. And this whole tale will be told from his point of
view, with none of the balanced consideration shown by Madame
de Lafayette to her three central characters. The sudden intoxication of first love, of priapic adventure, of erection and orgasm
(of which the Abbé says nothing, but implies all), the dash of
youth are all characterisitc of Des Grieux's narrative, in which

the young lovers are a kind of eighteenth-century Bonnie and Clyde. Manon is not valued by him as an individual; she exists only in terms of her actions, and for arousing in him feelings which vivify his world. The need to sustain these feelings at any cost either to himself or to others becomes an all-engrossing preoccupation. What he fears to lose more than anything in the world is Manon's love for him; and to retain that love (or his idea of it) he has no qualms about committing robbery or murder. His feelings, once aroused, animate his world with pain and pleasure, with intense self-awareness of himself as the object of Manon's love, but shared or mutual happiness plays little part in his narrative, because that would involve some sense of her as separate from his love for her. His passion is, in the end, 'self-magnification'. Like Narcissus, what he sees is a reflection of himself in Manon; and his desire for her is a form of self- creation, made more necessary once he has dropped out of the social world which has previously given him his sense of identity.

As this is Des Grieux's tale, we see Manon only through his eyes: his happiness is dependent on her fidelity to him: a fidelity unnatural to her. Manon belongs to the life of the city, to adventures sexual and otherwise of Paris, to chance encounters which offer her some new excitement or pleasure. She shares with the Musetta of Puccini's *La Bohème* an ability to enjoy the transient relationships of the city, with the fun and self-gratification they involve. Unlike Dumas' Marguerite, she is never really happy without pavements under her feet.

To Des Grieux, who comes from a very different world of family life in the country, all this is implicitly an affront from which he protects himself by his idea of Manon's love for him, which he learns to buy back through a life of crime. As he moves further away from his innate standards of virtue, Manon continues to live in a way that is natural to her. He is determined that her 'love' for him should be something other than it is. (This discrepancy between rural and urban love will recur many times in the literature of the nineteenth century, and only begin to dissolve in our own time when the values of the city become predominant everywhere.)

The weaknesses in Manon's character are weaknesses as they appear to the eye of her lover, and are seen only from his subjective point of view. His male vanity, hurt by her infidelity to him, robs him of his moral sense about the nature of their actions. When Des Grieux suggests jokingly how they might revenge themselves on one of Manon's elderly lovers, she insists upon it putting it into practice. 'You will take his place at supper; you will sleep in his bed; and tomorrow morning early, you will go off with his money and his mistress.'[9] In spite of his misgivings, Des Grieux gives in to this fantastic plan. In so far as his account is to be trusted (he is recalling these events as seen from his own perspective) he presents them as children playing a game in an adult world. To Manon games have no consequences. While he participates in them, he grows in awareness of the catastrophe they are invoking; but she remains scornful of, or indifferent to, it. Manon is isolated from the real world by her moral blindness, while he is isolated by the idea of himself (the man whom Manon loves) which his obsession with her has created. Whether or not this represents the real Manon we have no means of knowing because she is seen only through his obsession.

In his narration Des Grieux keeps returning to his sense of 'honte' (shame) at the manner in which he and Manon are living, while at the same time he sees her as an idol, a goddess whom he wishes to treat with appropriate reverence. He adores Manon as one of Heaven's most perfect creations – a perfection sullied only by her infidelity. Even the house where she lives with another lover, he approaches as though approaching a temple.

The nature of Des Grieux's passion for Manon allows little space for the actual to intrude. His feelings for her do not develop but revolve around the same obsession: his idolisation of her, and her infidelity: a situation which he, but not Manon, regards as fatal. Nothing can remove the mental anguish for him which this distance between them involves, except her removal from possible temptation.

Here, the particular (and peculiar) relationship between Des Grieux as lover and Des Grieux as artist-narrator begins to become apparent. What he wants, and what he finally creates, is for the story to come out right in the end. All he needs to make him happy is for Manon to be faithful to him. This can only happen in a story, and in a story which ends in Manon's death. They are not like Paolo and Francesca, Dido and Aeneas, Héloise and Abelard – a pair of the world's great lovers. Their story involves a twist which brings Des Grieux close to madness; and leads them both to a life of crime involving murder, theft, gaming and violence. As an 'artist' only is he capable of imposing order on his story; for in itself his relationship with Manon is based on the irrational and false. The image which Des Grieux holds in his mind is his image of 'love': not of Manon. In the words of St Augustine, he loves to love. The wholeness which their love lacks does not belong to this world.

Of Manon herself Des Grieux sees little and conveys little to us. She cannot speak directly like a character in a story by Chekov, because all her words are filtered to us through Des Grieux's memory of them, with the exception of one letter from her. In this letter she writes: 'Do you not see, my poor dear friend, what a foolish virtue fidelity is in the state to which we are reduced? Do you think one can be very tender when one lacks bread?'[10]

Des Grieux's words for describing Manon belong to the conventional vocabulary of his time: 'charming' and 'beautiful' on the one hand; 'unfaithful' and 'ungrateful' on the other. But the lack of distinctiveness in describing her is characteristic of the way he sees her, or fails to see her. The origins of this lack of distinctiveness are to be found in his society, his family and his temperament. Des Grieux's temperament veers from an extreme of obsessive involvement, to that of withdrawal. His period of study in the seminary, like Prévost's, expresses a powerful aspect of his personality. His friendship with Tiberge (who sees his relationship with Manon as an aberration and betrayal) reflects this too, as does his intended penitence on his return to France. This taste for contemplative detachment from life cannot be reconciled with the forces within the psyche to which Des Grieux (like Prévost himself) succumbs; and these are activated more often by Manon's absence than her presence.

The influence of family attitudes is also apparent in Des Grieux's view of Manon. The rigour and puritanism of his father, while displaying a genuine concern for his son's well-being, also betray a dismissive attitude to women, especially in their effect on young men, when they happen to be 'filles de plaisir' from the wrong social background. When Des Grieux is first brought home, after Manon's desertion of him for M. de B., his father openly laughs at him for believing that Manon loved him. He has been duped by her and has all the making of a complaisant husband. His father mocks him for his credulity, wishing to educate his son in matters of the heart; but he also reflects a patrician attitude to his son's folly with a girl from a lower social class. Des Grieux, although he never acts on his father's advice, continues to love and respect him. When his father comes to see him in prison, there occurs a scene of dignity and restraint, motivated by reason and enlightenment. His father pleads with him on the grounds of the dishonour he is bringing on himself and his family. He has loved his son tenderly, and spared nothing to bring him up as a gentleman, only to see him live viciously and without any sense of honour. Des Grieux listens to his father silently and with modesty, believing that, as he touchingly puts it, a father's heart is nature's masterpiece. In his own defence he cites a number of other well-born men in Paris who are known to keep mistresses without dishonour, claiming that his weakness lies only in two violent passions he has not been able to control: revenge and love. His desire for revenge is directed at G. de M. for his degrading treatment of Manon; and his love as always is self-justifying. What Des Grieux's father wants him to see, and what he is inevtably blind to, is the mismatch between his idea of love, and the life of crime which he is leading to sustain Manon. What he thinks 'ennobles' in fact debases. Nonetheless, it is notable that in Des Grieux's persistent criticism of Manon as 'ingrate et perfide' there exists a reflection of his father's 'lofty' attitude that women are weak and fickle in their affections; and that a girl like Manon is incapable of really loving him. Des Grieux's desire, which places her on a pedestal, removes her from the world where his father's objections would be valid, and so helps to preserve his obsession.

In addition, society has inscribed on the consciousness of Des Grieux through his education and in the seminary a 'religious' (not spiritual) ideal of what love is like: a dim reflection, but a reflection still, of that love which rules the world, and which it is the job of the seminarist to preach: it may be profane to see Manon as an idol and as the Queen of his heart; but the profanity reveals the source from which such images derive. His passion is 'a change of address of a force awakened by Christianity'.[11]

Des Grieux's 'love' for Manon is not destroyed by her infidelity, but her infidelity is like a wound. His willingness to earn money

by gambling and crime is justified by the need to provide Manon
with the pleasures which will keep her faithful to him. And yet it
is not sexual jealousy which is aroused by her other relationships, as might be expected, so much as an extreme form of
shame, and a desire for revenge on those who have caused this
shame. His deepest rage (leading on at least two occasions to a
catatonic state) originates in the shattering of the image of his
love for Manon: an image not of her purity, but of the purity of
his love for her, which is sullied by other people's view of her and
her behaviour. When Manon first betrays him he thinks of arson
as a means of revenge, as he also determines to rescue her from
the Hôpital by burning down Saint Lazare. Fire suggests his
desire to purify what contaminates the image of his love in the
world's estimate of his mistress.

For Manon to be held up publicly as a 'fille de joie' is to ironise
his feelings about her, and to challenge the sense of identity
which he derives from them. From the moment when he first sees
her in Amiens, Des Grieux derives his sense of his own identity
from his feelings towards her: she becomes the 'mistress of his
heart'. Paradoxically, the arousal of his passion for her leads only
to a view of himself as having a being because of her. This is
comforting because it removes the deepest of all ontological fears.
He can always say, 'I am because of Manon', and believe the same
is true for her. It is not. The importance of fidelity to him papers
over his sense of nothingness without her. Only in death, and by
dying, will she able to give him the security he craves.

The pathology of Des Grieux's desire is reflected throughout
his story in the bond betweeen sexuality and crime: the pursuit
of their pleasure in the underworld of society, in a union un-
blessed by the Church. When Des Grieux becomes a
card-sharper, and abets Manon in stealing her lover's gifts and
money, he is living outside the law, though he rarely notices it.
Threatened all the time with punishment for his crimes, and
sometimes receving it, he also exposes himself, as Tiberge warns
him, to eternal perdition. The reader, like the silent listener,
Renoncour, is drawn to the dangerous edge of things, knowing
that catastrophe waits round the corner. Had Des Grieux lived a
less desperate existence, the drive of his story would have lost its
edge; but he too would have lost that sharpness which comes
from an obsession with a cause, an Idea, or a person. In some men

and women such obsessions are enlarging, providing their lives with a dimension which widens its scope; in others, they become a neurotic disorder, a means of escape from reality, and a desperate attempt to find an identity through someone else.

The reality of the situation is that Manon does not want to live as Des Grieux wants her to; and that his ideal of a country life, with her and their friends, would not suit her at all. Few moments reveal more intensely her need for a life very different to his own than that in which Des Grieux recalls her dismay at the life which they face together in New Orleans, among five or six thousand impoverished exiles. They are taken to a wretched hovel built of planks and clay where they are to live. 'Manon looked appalled at the sight of so depressing a dwelling. As soon as we were alone, she sat down and began to weep bitterly.'[12] Des Grieux is convinced that she weeps for him, and protests that he possesses everything he desires. And now in a sense he does: alone with Manon, and with no one else for her to love. But here Manon cannot be Manon.

Driven out into the desert with Des Grieux, she dies swiftly and mysteriously. At least two figurative interpretations suggest themselves: Manon's life with Des Grieux alone would become a desert; Des Grieux's sense of his own identity is only completed with her death. Only in death will she become faithful to him for ever, and the image he has of her never be sullied by his rivals. Giving him the purest assurances of her love as she dies, she completes the myth he has been living. After her death, what life offers him is neither a return to virtue or his family (as in Prévost's modification of the ending in 1753), but a return in memory to the 'passion of a perfect love'. George Saintsbury was right when he concluded: 'Personally I don't think Des Grieux outlived Manon very long ... because there was nothing more for him to do or be.'[13]

*

Although *The Princess of Clèves* concerns initially the awakening of sexual love in a young girl, it becomes the story of mature and analysed love: passion restrained by human and moral considerations. The Princess of Clèves has power to hurt, and will do none. She rightly inherits heaven's graces, as her reward, though not everyone will agree with what she decides. As the epigraph to the last chapter illustrates, Stendhal believed that the Princess of Clèves should have said nothing, and yielded to Nemours. Pride, as well as loyalty and fear of being hurt, has its place in her behaviour; and when all is finished, her story tells of feelings never allowed expression, and the emptiness of selves not lived. None of this has any place in *Manon Lescaut*. The young lovers are in each other's arms almost as soon as they meet; and are 'enflammé tout d'un coup'. The listener is aroused too by this feverish excitability, expressed in a style simple and direct. 'I was seventeen years old, and had just finished studying philosophy at Amiens ....'[14] (Only with familiarity does the degree of contrivance in the reconstruction of memory become striking.) What Des Grieux refers to as the fate which leads him to disaster can also be seen as the intense nervous energy of the passions themselves: a wound that is always refreshing itself in the mind of the narrator, and which only becomes identified in this self-exonerating way in recollection, when the desire has been transcended.

From the moment when Manon and Des Grieux decide to run away together, their relationship is inseparable from the amount of money which they do or do not possess. Des Grieux possesses about fifty écus at the outset, Manon about twice that sum; and they believe it will last for ever. Within twelve days in Paris, the need for more money has led Manon to take her elderly lover. The theme of money, and the related idea of class (Manon is no match for the Chevalier Des Grieux) marks an essential difference between this novella and that of Madame de Lafayette. Although at the start the Princess of Clèves is brought to Paris for the purpose of making a suitable marriage and the Duc de Nemours is represented as giving up the chance of a throne for her, money as such is not mentioned. The social hierarchy of the Court extending down from the King and his mistress, Diane de Poitiers, is what matters; and the analysis of love takes place in that ruthless and courteous context. In *Manon Lescaut* the environment has become coarser and tougher, and money determines relationships. The man of quality only gives Des Grieux six louis d'or to accompany Manon to America because he perceives that he is well-born, and is repaid on Des Grieux's return with his story. The patrician background Des Grieux comes from saves him from disaster on several occasions, even protecting him from being charged with murder when he shoots a warder on his escape from Saint Lazare. For Manon no such safety-net exists. She belongs to the criminal demi-monde; he does not. Des Grieux's father and his friend, Tiberge, are always around to save him from it. His claims upon Manon's fidelity, for all their idealism, are built on a fantasy which takes no account of the social or economic differences between them. The image of her created by his desire has little basis in reality, and reflects back to him the image he wishes to have of himself as loving.

The coarseness of the narrative (Napoleon pronounced it a novel written for lackeys) which distinguishes it from *The Prin cess of Clèves* becomes more pronounced with the introduction of Manon's brother who initiates Des Grieux into card-sharping and crime. At one point he seriously suggests that he and Des Grieux should be able to live off Manon's earnings from selling herself. Scarcely less offensive to Des Grieux is Manon's sending of a pretty girl to him with the suggestion that he make use of her, when she herself cannot come. The aggressiveness and turbulence in Lescaut's character meet an appropriate end at the hand of a lurking assassin who bears a grievance against him. His death, like that of the warder, is another step downward in the course upon which Manon's and Des Grieux's passion for one another has set them. And it happens without comment or consequence, revealing once more the self-enclosure of Des Grieux's narrative, in which no action counts except in as far as it affects the image of Manon he has in his mind. Even Manon's lovers remain shadowy figures of wealth and power, identified by their initials. Of course, they are also identified like this to preserve the illusion of a true story, of people who cannot be named because they are still alive, towards whom Des Grieux entertains feelings of vengeance for the violence which they offer to that territory which he claims as his own. The only other response which he shows to figures like his father who challenge the autonomy of his impassioned world is hysterical unconsciousness.

In this world, only money, apart from Manon, has value. Lack of money causes him to lose her; regaining of money whether by loans from Tiberge, or by theft from Manon's lovers, or other forms of crime, enables him to set up house with her again. From time to time, Tiberge's generosity towards him makes him aware of the blindness which his love for Manon has caused in him. 'I perceived for an enlightened moment at least the shame and indignity of my chains.'[15] But the struggle does not last long. The sight of Manon would, he claims, make him throw himself from heaven. He is astounded that he could ever think so true a tenderness for an object so charming to be shameful. So he veers between elation and profound dejection. His shame derives from that feeling of violation which occurs when his conception of their love is challenged by a quite different view held by others, as when he and Manon are held captive as common criminals. Des Grieux feels himself to be superior because of the nature of his feelings which separate him from the common herd; and that superiority, as well as his idolisation of Manon, is pushed from its pedestal by the response of society to them.

In the world of crime, passion too becomes furtive and self-deceitful. In *Phèdre*, passion is 'funeste' and baleful because of its incestuous nature: the crime lies not in the passion but in its object. Here, the crime exists in the attempt to sustain a passion on borrowed or stolen money; and in an avoidance of admitting the situation between them. Des Grieux remarks at one point, 'Venus and Fortune had no other slaves who were more happy and more tender.'[16] But this typifies Des Grieux's subterfuge with himself, and his attempt to justify everything he does, even by invoking the gods. He perceives no discrepancy between his image of Manon and their criminal way of life, except during those brief moments when they experience shame. The crystallisation[17] of his feelings around Manon also falsifies her status; and nothing which Tiberge or Des Grieux's father says about Manon can break through the image he has formed of her.

Prévost, aware and with one part of him attracted to reason and enlightenment, was nonetheless conscious that reason was the thinnest of walls against violence of emotion. He sees the turbulence of subjective feelings in their self-deceit, excitement and shame; and that in passion one no longer belongs to oneself.

No other novella registers with such reasonableness the force of the feelings aroused by the discovery of sexuality, and 'the cliffs of fall' which they can open in the mind experiencing them; or how they distance its central character from the values of the rational and enlightened society in which he has been brought up. To this end of compression and enlargement the form of the novella is entirely appropriate, allowing the figure in the foreground to tell his tale without interruption, but setting his narrative against a background of quite different conventions. This disjunction between the self which experiences and the society which observes sustains a tension in the narrative, but a tension which can only be recognised and articulated in recollection.

When others based their work on Prévost's novella, they turned his narrative into something very different and more conventional. Puccini's opera illustrates this well. He, like Massenet, forgot the Chevalier in the title, and let Manon become the centre of the work. After Des Grieux saves Manon from the elderly Geronte in Act One, she is to be found in Act Two living with him, but bored with a life of luxury and the attentions of Geronte's elderly friends. When Manon plans to abscond with Des Grieux, Geronte has her arrested; and in Act Three in Le Havre, Des Grieux succeeds in persuading the Captain of the ship taking Manon to America to employ him as his Cabin Boy. The Fourth Act is set in the boundless plain near New Orleans. Manon is already dying of thirst; and Des Grieux is searching desperately for help in this wasteland. Manon, abandoned by him, sings of her desire to live, and her belief that she would at last find peace in this land. Des Grieux returns to find her breathing her last. She dies with her lover beside her, affirming that her sins will be forgotten but her love will not die.

The opera becomes a story about the redemption of Manon (a kind of Mary Magdalene figure), whose feelings of abandonment and desolation – 'Sola, perduta, abandonnata' – bring her to penitence, and a belief that what will survive of her is love. Des Grieux is left sobbing, like Rodolpho in *La Bohème*, beside the body of the woman he has loved. It is music drama of poignance, and dramatic effectiveness; but in making the story Manon's story, Puccini (and his five librettists) have lost all the emotional complexity of Des Grieux's recollected narrative, with its bolstering of identity and its magnification of self. What matters in the opera is what Manon succeeds in becoming, even as she dies: she represents the triumph of love over death.

By never separating Manon from Des Grieux's idea of her, Prévost created a narrative which revealed the lover not as the human reflection of Divine Love, but as a fugitive who seeks refuge in the image of himself as loving. Like Narcissus, what he sees is always the reflection of himself; and that is an image which can only be held still when death has intervened. His account of her death in the desert, and his behaviour towards her, owes everything to a mythical narrative. While the earlier account of their life in Paris establishes itself easily enough as a true account, their arrival in the desert makes possible the leap to a new narrative mode.

In 1753 Prévost returned to the book which had brought him notoriety, and attempted, as Wordsworth was to do almost a century later in *The Prelude*, to moralise his song, making numerous changes to the style. As in Wordsworth's case, these changes tended to diminish the lyrical intensity of the youthful version; and more crucially in Prévost's case diminished the mythical element in the narrative. In the original version, Des Grieux, after Manon's death, deprived of his 'idol', seeks grace through penitence, redirecting his thoughts to God, while in the revised version he merely returns to a view of things worthy of his birth. Prévost's changes to the account of Des Grieux's vigil in the desert with Manon's body also remove the suggestion of a comparison with the Easter vigil: 'I remained for two days and two nights with my mouth pressed to the face and hands of my dear Manon. My intention was to die there; but at the beginning of the third day I realised that after my death her body would be exposed as fodder for wild beasts. I decided to bury her ... I dug a large pit, and laid the idol of my heart there, after having wound her in all my clothes to prevent the sand from touching her. I did this only after having kissed her a thousand times with all the passion of the most perfect love.'[18] In the revision, Des Grieux only remains a little more than twenty-four hours, and the resonances of the mythical narrative are lost.

4

Benjamin Constant: *Adolphe*

'Pas de phrases!'   Madame de Charrière

There can be no peace of mind in love, since the advantage one has secured is never anything but a fresh starting-point for further desire.   Proust, *Within a Budding Grove*

On est si juste lorsque l'on est désinteressé.   Constant, *Adolphe*

As stories, Constant's *Adolphe* and Prévost's *Manon Lescaut* have certain things in common. Both novellas tell the story of a bondage in life which continues in memory after death. In both cases the woman dies, leaving an impression which cannot be effaced. Des Grieux purports to be telling the story of a love flawed only by Manon's infidelity, while Adolphe tells of a bond which cannot be broken even when love has ceased to exist. In both cases we are aware of the incompleteness of the narrative. But there is an essential difference. Des Grieux is taken in by his own story; he tells it with all the conviction of someone who knows how it was. Adolphe in telling his story reveals increasingly his uncertainty about the truth of his relationship with Ellenore, and the inadequacy of words to represent it. A narration, as we know from contemporary fiction (as well as from Prévost!), is an unreliable thing; the narrator tells his story from a particular point of view (or views). But Adolphe, unlike Des Grieux, is struggling to come to terms with what has happened to him, to see it objectively and disinterestedly; and in the course of his narration Ellenore will emerge as vividly as Adolphe, not least because her dominance and possessiveness lie at the centre of his tale, where passion is represented as a constantly shifting interaction between two people whose fate is that they cannot break the bonds which exist between them.

The image of Adolphe – the first which we have, and the only

external and vivid one – is not of a man who has resolved or
clarified his story by setting it down. He appears as a traveller,
whom we meet in an inn at the start of the story, and who has
lost all interest in life and company. According to the servant who
looks after him, 'he was not travelling out of curiosity, for he did
not go to see ruins or picturesque places, or monuments or people.
He read a good deal, but never consistently. He took walks in the
evening, always alone, and often spent whole days sitting motionless with his head in his hands.'[1] This account of Adolphe
occurs not merely some considerable time after Ellenore's death,
but some time after he has written down his story, which he is
about to abandon in a box with other letters[2] and a portrait of a
woman (presumably Ellenore). So he is a stranger to the world,
still trying to come to terms with what he has lived through, still
obsessed by a story which he cannot 'put down'. The poignancy of
this image of him derives from his perplexity about his story, and
from his inability to foresee the effect of the breaking of a tie
which he will not know how to live without. He embodies a
general human truth, as well as an indivdual predicament. The
knowledge of what it means to lose (the experience of losing) only
comes when the situation is beyond recall, whether through
death, or the final breaking of a tie, or both. The effect of death,
in passion or in life, cannot be known until it has happened.

Constant uses Prévost's technique of telling a story which is
true and and unchanged, within a number of frames. The box
containing the narrative is left by Adolphe at the Calabrian inn
where we first see him, and sent on by the innkeeper to the man
who will decide to publish it when, many years later, he discovers
someone who has known Adolphe and Ellenore. The acquaintance urges publication on the grounds that it might help others
to see that 'even the most passionate emotion cannot struggle
against the order of things. Society is too powerful.'[3] The publisher for his part feels the moral of the tale to be very different:
'Circumstances matter very little, character is everything; it is
useless to break with outside things or with people if we do not
know how to break with ourselves.'[4] Adolphe's fate is not to be
blamed on society; we are all responsible for the disasters we
invite. These two contrasting views open up the reader's response to Adolphe's narrative, suggesting varieties of reading

which are left unresolved, not least because they constitute an important part of Adolphe's own anxiety.

In the 'Preface' to the Second Edition, Constant stresses the dangers of exciting in others, 'transient emotions of the heart .... We start on a course of action of which we are unable to foresee the end: we do not know what feelings we may inspire, nor what we may expose ourselves to experience.'[5] He goes on to stress the suffering which men inflict on women when they are abandoned. 'It is not having started such liaisons which is necessary for the happiness of life; once we have started on that road nothing remains for us except a a choice of evils.'[6] In the Preface to the Third Edition, Constant stresses even more the pain which arises out of bonds which have to be broken, often of a very different sort for a man and a woman. Both in the argument in the Prefaces, and in the narrative itself, the reader is confronted with the difficulty of coming to any certain conclusion about the nature of this relationship and its value to those involved. In this sense Constant is a modern writer. What these various perspectives point towards is an unknowingness in Adolphe, and in the surrounding comments on his life, as to the truth about how he has lived, and so the impossibility of coming to any final judgement about it. As will be seen, this is partly the failure of language in transcribing desire. What causes the problem between the lovers becomes the aesthetic problem for the reader in coming to any certain conclusion about them. As Adolphe attempts through memory to sort out what he has lived through, now that desire has been transcended, so too Constant offers the reader these frames to distance the emotion in an attempt to see what has been involved. His difficulty in transcribing desire reflects the complexity of his own life, and its intricate influence upon his novella.

Benjamin Constant was born in Lausanne, Switzerland, in 1767. His mother died a few days after he was born; and his upbringing became the care of a father ambitious for his son but incapable of either closeness or affection. Like Adolphe himself, Constant learnt from an early age to act for the purpose of concealing his real feelings. This 'dramatisation' of himself helped to form the style of his novella (as the rhetoric of the self does in other novellas); but it also posed the riddle of the discrepancy between what we present ourselves as being, and what we feel ourselves to be, which itself changes all the time, and is most evident in those given to self-dramatisation.

Constant's education was entrusted to a series of tutors 'who were at best incompetent and at worst criminal'; but with them he saw Europe and learned the only true form of education, that of educating himself. He read widely and developed a particular interest in religion, which was to become the basis of his most substantial, though not his most celebrated work, *De la Religion* (1824).[7]

The life of Benjamin Constant, like that of Prévost, was shaped by his relationships with women. By the age of seventeen he had already created a scandal by flaunting his mistress in society's face, although as he later revealed the relationship had never been consummated. 'The delight I experienced from pretending to have a mistress, and from hearing other people say so, consoled me for having to spend my time with a person for whom I had no affection and for not sleeping with a woman with whom I was supposed to have an affair.'[8]

In 1785 his father sent him away to the University of Edinburgh, where he spent two of the happiest years of his life in gaming and debauchery, while at the same time studying hard and gaining a reputation for his intellectual brilliance. But it was the extent of his debts which caused his return to Paris. There, Constant, now nineteen, made the acquaintance of Madame de Charrière, who was then forty-six. She became his close friend and intellectual mentor for the next twenty years, and the inspiration for the portrait of the old woman whose death Adolphe recounts in the first chapter of the novella. 'Like so many others this woman had begun her career by setting out to conquer society, equipped with great strength of spirit and a powerful mind. Like so many others when she failed to adapt herself to the artificial but necessary conventions of her time, she had seen her hopes disappointed, and her youth pass without pleasure, until at last old age had overtaken her without crushing her. She lived in a castle near one of our estates, disillusioned and retired. Her mind was her only resource and she analysed everything with it. For nearly a year we tirelessly discussed every aspect of life, and death as the inevitable end of everything. After having talked with her so much about death, I saw death strike her down in front of my eyes.'[9] Madame de Charrière, the figure of the woman retired from the world through disillusionment with the life of the emotions, and the conventions controlling their expression, recalls the Princess of Clèves, though without her metaphysical solace.

Madame de Charrière's powers of analysis, together with her hatred of cant and hypocrisy – summed up in the famous phrase, 'Pas de phrases' – helped to form the young man's creative personality, enabling him to become the critical spectator of his own actions and feelings, and to analyse their nature. In addition, her attitude to death as inevitable and final pervades *Adolphe* in a more subtle manner. (Despite Constant's interest in religion, his novella is scarcely touched by metaphysical ideas or attitudes.) Human conduct is analysed in terms of its effect on others, without reference to reward or punishment in another world. When Ellenore dies, Adolphe sums up its effect in wholly secular terms: 'I was free, truly; I was no longer loved. I was a stranger to the whole world.'[10] This sense of estrangement comes directly from the loss of a relationship which for all its problems deprived the world of its solitude; and which in its wholeness was metaphysical in another sense. With Ellenore he knew what it was not to be alone.

Constant's first marriage in 1789 to Minna von Cramm was a failure; and he was divored from her in 1793. The following year he was to meet Madame de Staël, daughter of the wealthy German statesman and financier, Gustav Necker, a woman of overwhelming presence and loquacity. Demanding and possessive in the extreme, she ruled the circle of interesting and talented men in her entourage despotically. Stendhal was to describe her as an outrageous blue-stocking and the most brilliant improviser in France. She was able to talk in praise of herself for a whole week without interruption; and on one occasion held forth for a complete day on the beauty of her arms. But her listeners were always enchanted and never bored. Often dressed in a turban, her appearance was as exotic as her character. Constant became and remained her lover (intermittently) for more than ten years. But increasingly he suffered from the 'lien' or bond with her, which not even his marriage to Charlotte von Hardenburg in 1808 was capable of severing. So afraid was he of the scenes and storms which Madame de Staël would create around him when he tried to break with her that he kept his marriage a secret from her for three further years. Much of the tempestuous unhappiness in the bondage between them is reflected in *Adolphe*.

As early as 1798, Constant recognised that he was continuing his affair with Germaine de Staël out of duty or out of weakness. But they also gave much to each other which was irreplaceable. As one of their friends said, Constant brought out the best in her. By a force of character which equalled her own, he awoke in her an eloquence, as well as a profundity of soul and thought, which were only shown off in their true brilliance in contrast to his own: something which is often true of lovers, and which was present, it seems too, in the relationship between the Duc de La Rochefoucauld and Madame de Lafayette.

In the story of Adolphe and Ellenore the positive as well as the negative aspects of the relationship between Madame de Staël and Benjamin Constant have left their mark. But Ellenore is no Madame de Staël; in her passivity she altogether lacks the dynamic, exotic and uncontrollable characteristics of the woman who so much influenced the theme of the book. As with all major fictional creations, she grows out of a number of different sources, including his future wife and Anna Lindsay, with whom he had a brief but intense affair. The mistress of M. de Lamoignon by whom she had two children, Anna Lindsay met Constant in Paris in 1800, and fell passionately in love with him. Constant, following the pattern (repeated in *Adolphe*) began to withdraw, or attempted to, once the conquest had been made. As one of his friends said about his relations with women: 'You always take, and never leave,'[11] a remark which in its acerbity reflects the relationship between Adolphe and Ellenore. But Anna was to take the initiative and leave Paris without him, while Constant went off to Germany with Madame de Staël, where she so terrified Goethe that he feigned illness until she departed from Weimar.

Benjamin Constant started writing *Adolphe* at Coppet on Lake Geneva in 1806, but it was not to be published for a further ten years. Coppet was the family home of Madame de Staël. There she surrounded herself with her friends, who shared a violent antipathy to Napoleon. He represented to them a continuation of all that was worst in the Ancien Régime, together with the ambitions of a tyrant for a world conquest, which offended their belief in human perfectibility and the Enlightenment of the eighteenth century. Constant, as a believer in all forms of freedom, and an opponent of all forms of despotism, was shaped as a creative writer by the tension between these ideals on the one hand, and his submission to Madame de Staël's form of despotism on the other. Her hold over him became more that of a mistress over a servant than a lover; and his servitude to her induced a feeling of being always necessary and never adequate. Comments such as this reveal the process of analysis which their way of life fostered; the scrutiny of their relationship in all its emotional turbulence was part of their continuing life together. Among other things it nourished the epigrammatic style of *Adolphe*. Like Pirandello, Constant was at the height of his powers in rationalising pain, and transmuting emotional distress into a lucidly analytic objectivity. A work of imagination, he believed, must not have a moral purpose but a moral result. It should resemble a human life which has no purpose, but has a result in which morality necessarily has a place. The nature of that morality became the riddle which the novella tried to solve, through Adolphe's attempts to understand his own behaviour. For him, as for Madame de Staël and Constant, aphorism served as an instrument of analysis; but one which for all its sharpness proved inadequate to describe what was occurring. Existence could not be caught in the net of reason; and slipping away it caused an unresolved anguish.

In writing *Adolphe*, Constant reflected his own emotional temperament and his varied experience. In Ellenore he created an image of love which he had known, but which he had only been able to respond to with destructive indecision. Like Goethe's *Werther*, the novella concerns the nature of love when it becomes separated from the world of work and practical endeavour. Ellenore stands between Adolphe and the career which beckons an intelligent and well-connected young man of twenty-two. As his relationship with Ellenore deteriorates, Adolphe becomes aware of a new kind of self-centredness, without courage, discontented and humiliated. Increasingly imprisoned in his own personal reflections, and with eyes turned inward, he loses interest in ideas and becomes concerned only with the relationship between himself and Ellenore. This, however, does not reflect life at Coppet: the brilliance of the company, the concern for the state of France, the opposition to Napoleon, together with Constant's preoccupation with comparative religion, and his involvement with the intellectual vortices of Germaine de Staël's mind vanish into the social and mental isolation which characterises Adolphe's life with Ellenore. As in other novellas, the passions are seen to isolate because they create a world into which others cannot enter, and which they cannot share. Among the most memorable passages in the novella is that in which Adolphe confides to a woman friend of Ellenore's that he no longer loves her. What he violates by the involvement of someone else is that private terrain which makes intimacy possible. 'It is a major step,' he reflects, 'and an irreparable one, when the secret recesses of an intimate relationship are revealed to someone else; when daylight penetrates this sanctuary, it reveals and completes the damage which night had concealed in its shadows. In the same ways bodies sealed in tombs are often preserved, until the outside air reaches them and turns them to dust.'[12] This metaphor is of particular interest. It stands for desire which requires darkness and privacy to survive; the act of breaking it open to the scrutiny of someone else deprives it of this darkness and privacy. Passion in its self-regard harbours the morbid as well as the life-giving. It exacts as the price of its intimacy, and survival, an immurement which excludes the world's scrutiny.

Adolphe was finished in 1807, but not published until 1816 in London and Paris. (It was to have formed an 'episode' in a longer novel which he never completed.) During those years Constant had refrained from exposing to public view what he knew to be an intimate confession; and one which would draw the scribblers to attempt to identify its various characters. As in almost all important fiction, they were composite; and here more than usually so, because of the author's own recognition that the self was not a unitary thing. In expressing itself it revealed the accretions of many different kinds of experience and involvement.

The tale of Adolphe and Ellenore opens in the little town of D., one of those dull provincial towns to which Goethe took exception, and from which Constant suffered in Brunswick. Boredom and insipidity characterise a way of life in which Adolphe cannot bring himself to participate – to the anger of his fellow citizens, who regard him as arrogant and condescending. His first encounter with adult life awakens him to the artificiality of society and the pressures it exerts on the individual: 'It weighs so heavily upon us, and and its imperceptible influence is so powerful that it does not take long to mould us into conformity with it.'[13] Those who rebel are soon characterised as 'unreliable and immoral'. Society, like the gods in the classical world (and with comparable hypocrisy), has its revenge on those who fail to conform.

Even before Adolphe meets Ellenore, we are aware of the conventions against which his future actions will be judged. The pressure under which both will live derives from the social context of their lives, and society's view of what is respectable. In small-town life, unlike Paris, middle-class morality operates with avenging force.

In his listlessness Adolphe observes the joy a young friend derives from being in love, and wants a similar experience for himself. His desire is aroused by rivalry, and his attraction towards Ellenore starts as an act of imitation. She does not exist as a person but as an object. As often, the arbitrariness of the imitation makes even more ironic the tragic consequences of the connection.

Under his father's influence, Adolphe has come to believe that there is nothing wrong with passing affairs, provided marriage is not contemplated with anyone from the wrong social background. There was no harm in taking any woman and then dropping her. 'I had seen him smile with a kind of approval at this parody of a well-known saying: "It does them so little harm and gives us so much pleasure." '[14] Ironically again, Adolphe will take a woman from the wrong background, live with her but not marry her, and be unable to drop her when he does not love her. As he will later be told by Ellenore, he does not know the harm he is doing. Constant's choice of evils does not involve moral choice only, but a psychological choice in which the woman in this society pays more heavily.

The older Adolphe who writes down the story after it is concluded will recognise a problem of another sort: 'Man's emotions are confused and mixed, they are made up of a mass of different impressions which go unobserved, and language, always too crude and generalised, can be used to identify them, but never really defines them.'[15] In the novella Constant dramatises the conflict which arises out of the impotence of language to define the emotions, and Adolphe's discovery of the binding power of words. Constant recognises both that desire needs language to express itself and that language betrays what it attempts to express. The trap which Adolphe springs on himself is one which only silence could avoid; and that means, as Constant recognises, avoiding the course of action which makes him Adolphe.

Out of longing for the affection he has never known from his father, and out of vanity, Adolphe decides that Ellenore is a conquest worthy of him.[16] When he starts to write to her, warmed by his own rhetoric, he begins to feel some of the passion he is at such pains to express. Adolphe's capacity for playing a role (reflecting Constant's relation to his own father) compels him to dramatise himself, and his feelings for her, until he believes himself to be in love. Desire in the absence of any real object invents an object created out of the desire to love and be loved.

In time, and after many attempts at resistance, Ellenore confesses that his love is returned, giving herself to him wholly. And for a time – for a brief time – their passion for each other is mutual, enclosing them in a solitude where they believe the world cannot touch them. As Constant recognises, this time of magic is one which cannot be described: words lack the power to express the complexity of human feeling. Nonetheless, as their relations deteriorate because of Adolphe's resentment at the sway she holds over him, and the sacrifices she has made for him, it will be to this time of shared passion that they will return in memory. This form of remembering will be seen to differ from the memory which causes Adolphe to write down his story, and acts as a frame for the whole.

With the death of Ellenore's father, and her inheritance of an estate, they set off for her native Poland. 'The long familiarity we had with each other, the varied circumstances we had shared together, had given to every word, almost to every movement, memories which suddenly carried us back into the past and filled us with an involuntary tenderness, as flashes of lightning pass across the night without dispelling it. We were living, so to speak, in a kind of memory of the heart ...'[17] This form of memory has less in common with Proust's involuntary memory, dependent as it is on particular stimuli, than with Bergson's, 'where the whole range of the person's past is incorporated in a continuous process operating in the margin of consciousness.

'It is by such deep feelings, developing naturally and organically and without conscious awareness, through the operation of the "memoire du coeur" linking his past with his present in an emotive *durée*, that the individual grows in time and acquires that continuity and sense of continuity of experience which is the basis of personality and sense of personal identity.'[18] For Adolphe this memory of the heart is not a self-sufficient thing, because it conflicts with his idea of the life he would have lived without Ellenore. The wife he dreams of would not separate him from family or society or career, as she has done, but would provide a bridge between his adult life and the hopes associated with his youth. In a night-time reverie, he sees the castle where he has lived with his father, with its woods and mountains, and imagines a young wife who would animate them and fill them with hope: all of which urge upon him the necessity of separating from Ellenore. Only Ellenore's death will bring this about; and with it the impossibility of fulfilling his dream, now that he has become a 'stranger to the world'. With Ellenore's actual death, another kind of death occurs in Adolphe's soul at the loss of a wholeness he can now never recover, except in the aesthetic emotion of the account he writes.

In this story of the mutual destructiveness which a bond can create, Constant never loses sight of the tensions created by the outside world, and the impossibility for Adolphe and Ellenore of living outside the conventions of their time. The subtlety of Constant's recognition of the different pressures exerted on each of them, as man and woman, provides a major part of the work's fascination.

Ellenore's position in society is insecure from the outset, as she lives with Count P. to whom she is not married, and by whom she has had two children. She endures a way of life repugnant to her by temperament and by upbringing, fostering in herself a spirit of contradiction which makes her deeply religious because religion sternly condemns her way of life. When Adolphe, more out a desire to imitate what he sees others doing than from any deep feeling, makes his conquest of her, he deprives her of the tenuous security she has known, alienating her from her 'family' and from society. She is made miserable by solitude, and ashamed by society. At the same time she cannot share her worries with Adolphe, because she has made a sacrifice he did not ask of her.

Adolphe's father uses all stratagems to attempt to bring an end to a liaison which he sees as ruining his son's chances of a successful career. When Adolphe goes back to Poland with Ellenore, Baron T. (a friend of Adolphe's father) exerts even greater pressure, attempting to persuade Adolphe to end his life of enforced isolation, and at the same time reminding him that some women can only be seen in their own homes. By such comments, Constant does not allow the reader to forget how the nature of private relationships is determined by their social context, and the hopeless illusion of trying to live without reference to one's surroundings.

Ellenore's need for Adolphe is intensified, if not created, by the sacrifices she has made for him and the exile into which their relationship has driven them. As a woman who has lost her social status, Ellenore endures the full stress of this isolation, in the same way, and for the same reasons, as Anna Karenina. The Baron proves an able diagnostician of Adolphe's situation: 'You are doing harm to yourself by your weakness, and you are doing no less harm by your harshness; and to make the absurdity worse, you are not even giving happiness to this woman who is making you so unhappy.'[19] Adolphe succumbs to his persuasive powers (not least because they cunningly sound a note in his own conscience), declaring in a letter that his connexion with Ellenore can now be regarded as over. Baron T. responds by sending this letter to Ellenore, who had until that moment regarded their lives as indissolubly bound together. Words as usual in this fiction prove misleading. As Adolphe observes, she has read in his own hand promises to leave her, dictated only by the desire to stay with her. But external pressure has won. Ellenore falls ill, and will not recover.

On her death, he finds a letter written to him after one of their violent quarrels, in which she reproaches him for the pain he inflicts on her for loving him. He is haunted, she claims, by the thought of her grief if he leaves; but does nothing to assuage the grief he causes while he stays. What she lacks is the strength to leave him herself. As she has already told him, 'love was the whole of my life: it could not be yours.'[20] Ellenore lucidly sums up one of the differences between them; but this generalising power in language also reveals a defect in words themselves. Seeing the situation does not alter it, because of the fracture which exists between articulation, and those other parts of the self, or other selves, which remain unexpressed. As Adolphe finally recognises, the image of Ellenore matters more than anything that can be said; she stands for a love that is greater than self.

In the letter to the publisher printed at the close of Adolphe's narrative, his acquaintance expresses the view that Ellenore's tragedy proves that even 'the most intense emotion cannot struggle against the order of things. Society is too powerful ....'[21] In the narrative, society expresses itself in disapproval of Ellenore's relationship with the Count, as well as of her relationship with Adolphe. When Ellenore leaves Count P. for Adolphe, she becomes an outcast, losing all the devotion and loyalty she has built up over ten years, while Adolphe is regarded quite simply as a seducer. As she is a woman with no settled home or position, Adolphe's father can even attempt to have her driven out of town. And back in Poland, the land of Ellenore's birth, their isolation is no less intense: circumstances can crush the most powerful emotions. But these circumstances are seen by Constant to result as much from a psychological as from a social inheritance. Adolphe's inability to express his feelings, and act on them, reflects the self-concealment he has always found it necessary to adopt in relation to his father. Subterfuges adopted in childhood as a means of evading the instructions of an authoritative father prove equally serviceable in dealing with the painful reality between him and Ellenore, or failing to deal with it. As Adolphe strives to opt out of the pressures of a conformist society, so he seeks to duck out of the consequences of his involvement with Ellenore, whom he no longer loves. Neither works.

Society exerts its pressure too through the world of work and the ambitions that a young man of Adolphe's class is expected to fulfil. His lack of a useful occupation, and his failure to secure his own advancement, intensify his feelings of 'superfluousness' (shared by several of Turgenev's characters). As a result he comes to resent Ellenore for the wasting of his life and promise, to which his remaining with her leads. Equally, her willingness and ability to support him, while removing the need to work, isolate them with their feelings and the inadequacies of their relationship: '... the confidence with which I had once thought I could command the future, the praises bestowed on my earliest ventures, the brilliant beginning of a reputation I had seen fade away. I repeated to myself the names of those fellow students whom I had treated with such contempt, but who simply by sticking to their work and living a conventional life, had now outstripped me on the road to fortune, respect and glory. I was oppressed by my own inertia. As misers conjure up in the treasures they accumulate, the goods those treasures could buy, I saw in Ellenore the deprivation of all the successes I might have aspired to.'[22] He feels like an athlete chained up in a dungeon, whose efforts to free himself fail before the vision of Ellenore. The image of the dungeon is however telling, since it represents a refuge as well as a prison: a refuge in particular from the conflict with a father who wishes his son to share his own satisfaction in success, and from becoming the kind of man his father wants him to be. Adolphe's relationship with Ellenore puts off the day when he will have to decide whether to follow in his father's footsteps; and cloaks an indecision about his identity in a society in which he feels an exile. Constant's perceptiveness about character reaches down into that area of darkness where the origins of behaviour cannot be clearly identified or revealed.

From the moment when Adolphe decides that his relationship with Ellenore has 'become a tie', his account of it becomes increasingly uncertain, and coloured by quarrels, rages and depressions. As the narrator of his own tale, Adolphe combines analytic penetration and introspection with an awareness that the 'meaning' of the tale is eluding him. In narrating himself, he fails to discover himself. For her part, Ellenore changes (as Adolphe narrates her) from being a woman who has an identity as mother and unmarried wife to Count P. to being a figure who lives only for love. As her obsessive importance for Adolphe increases, so her identity as a separate being is diminished. Adolphe's consciousness – for all its inwardness and power of analysis – remains trapped in its own partial understanding, in its own obscurities and evasions. As Adolphe notes at one point: human beings are not completely integrated. Almost never is anyone utterly sincere or completely in bad faith; a balanced judgement is most likely when one is disinterested, and this can never be the case when the passions are engaged.

The papers which Adolphe leaves behind at the Italian inn are an account complete in itself, but necessarily incomplete, of the experience which has shaped his life. They reflect an attempt to come to terms with that experience, to make some kind of judgement upon it, which proves in the end impossible, because the nature of the experience remains elusive. The answer to the question, 'Why did you write your book?' with the words, 'To discover why had I the desire to write it,' indicates the problem of language which Constant's novella insistently raises.

The act of creativity originates in a profound impulse to resolve the passion which he still feels in memory. Adolphe's narration is obsessed with an attempt to come to terms with a bond which he does not fully understand: a meeting with Another in himself, which he cannot accept and from which he cannot free himself. He is haunted, Ellenore claims, by the thought of the grief he will cause if he leaves, but does nothing to assuage the grief he causes while he stays. Haunting is an appropriate metaphor, because it indicates the obsessive and spectral nature of the 'liens' between them, and the power which they possess to vanish when Adolphe attempts to narrate what they are, or were. In his case memory, like experience itself, vanishes into its own uncertainty, except in his inability to start a new life once Ellenore is dead.

In one sense, this is a problem of words. The desire which he feels for her at the outset is expressed in letters and confessions; but when the desire fails, he is left with an absence which words cannot fill, and anger takes their place. 'Words imply an absence of things ....' And it is this absence with which the narration in memory is concerned, after Ellenore dies. What Adolphe cannot do is to find words which encompass the experience of Ellenore's love for him which he could not return; or the indifference to life which he feels after her death. This is of course not a failure in his narrative from the reader's point of view. Quite the reverse. Words do not fill an absence; they offer a substitute for it. And as a substitute, they provide an account which is always different and never complete. The 'man motionless with his head in his hands' is an image of the artist faced with the insoluble problem of language, as well as the man whose emotions have been spent.

The obsessive but elusive nature of the bonds between Ellenore and Adolphe is an appropriate theme for the novella form. Constant's handling of it shows his especial tact in the tension he sustains between the bewilderment of the relationship between them and the relentlessness of the pressures society imposes upon them. Adolphe's father offers himself as a model for the success which the son should emulate, by using his abilities and pursuing a career which will bring advancement. Ellenore is depicted as the only obstacle to his success. (This theme of the dispensability of the woman has already been seen in *Manon Lescaut*, and will recur again in the future.) Count P. has no compunction in trying to buy Ellenore back if she will leave her young lover, though money proves impotent here against the power of the emotions, as Ellenore possesses a sufficiency. Baron T. has equal lack of compunction in forwarding Adolphe's letter for Ellenore to read as an admission of his intention to leave her. Society lacks scruples about its treatment of those who offend its sense of *amour-propre*, whether by these pressures or the silent pressure of exile. In Adolphe's anger with Ellenore, his offended vanity at society's rejection, and his self-contempt at foregoing his ambition play a substantial part.

Constant's narrative never allows us to forget the circumscription of experience by an engrossing passion, or the limitations it imposes on life outside its walls. In Adolphe's nocturnal meditation, just before Ellenore's death, Constant poses too the problem with which his work on religion confronted him. Religion is like a branch offered in the torrent bearing us all away which none can afford to reject. The novella, however tentatively, questions the significance of the passions in a world where the river sweeps on towards darkness. As Constant wrote elsewhere, 'love takes pleasure in sacrificing for the chosen person all which would otherwise be held most dear'.[23] For both of them the start of their passion involves a religious emotion. 'I looked upon her as a heavenly being, and my love for her was close to a religion.'[24] It is this feeling which he can neither sustain nor forget.

Ivan Turgenev: *First Love*

The passion for destruction is a creative passion.   Bakunin

... to part from her would be like parting from life itself.
     Turgenev, *A Month in the Country*

... during some moments of her impassioned performances, especially when she opens wide her large mouth with its dazzling
white teeth and smiles with such savage sweetness and delightful
ferocity, you feel as though the monstrous plants and animals of
India or Africa were about to appear before your eyes, as though
giant palms festooned with thousands of blossoming lianas were
shooting up – and you would not be surprised if a leopard or a
giraffe, or even a herd of young elephants were to stampede across
the stage.   Heine, on hearing Pauline Viardot sing in 1844

Turgenev's place in the art of the novella is a special one. The
form was especially suited to his talents and to his manner of
writing, with long periods of gestation and sharp concentrated
bouts of creative activity. In Russia in the 1840s no settled
tradition of novel writing had been established: a cultural and
literary situation far removed from that in England or France.
The influence of Pushkin, who had been killed in a duel in 1837,
was still paramount; and his *Eugene Onegin* (1831), though
written in verse, provided a model for narratives of lyric intensity, of the kind to which *First Love* belongs.

    Turgenev's *First Love*, like Dumas' *The Lady of the Camellias*,
was based on personal experience: rivalry in love between father
and son. Turgenev described it as the most autobiographical of
his stories. He wrote it in 1860, describing events which had
taken place in 1831, when Turgenev was twelve and his father
thirty-eight. In the actual story he modifies this slightly, so that
the son becomes sixteen, enabling this too to become a narrative

of the torrents of spring. 'Reason by itself is fatal,' he wrote in 1865. 'Truth, however powerful, is not art ... truth is the air without which we cannot breathe; but art is a plant, sometimes even a fantastic one, which grows and develops in this air.'[1]

The man who wrote the story down in 1860 recollected these events of thirty years previously with the understanding of someone who had suffered, and continued to suffer, the torments of obsessive and largely unrequited love with Pauline Viardot. Rivalry in love did not cease for Turgenev with the events recalled in his novella; and its recurrence in his later life has also affected the telling of the tale.

Memory here operates in a different way to that in earlier narratives. The middle-aged man recalling the experience of first love brings to it the lucidity of long-meditated reflection; and the awareness that no other memories are so fresh and clear to him as those of that 'brief storm that came and went so swiftly one morning in the spring'.[2] This is neither an account of an experience with which he is still attempting to come to terms, nor the story of a loss he is still trying to overcome. It involves a turning-point of a different kind: an initiation into the pathology of passion, and a view of love which continues to resonate in his life as it did in Turgenev's. This initiation derives from rivalry in love between father and son, with the Freudian implications that such a conflict involves. But being set down after a long interval, it reflects what Proust was to write about love, using Turgenev's own idea of 'delicious poison'. 'For a single malady goes through various evolutions, and a delicious poison can no longer be taken with the same impunity when, with the passing of the years, the heart's power of resistance has diminished.'[3] In the early and sudden death of the narrator's father, this warning is borne out.

Turgenev had first met Pauline Viardot when she was singing at the St Petersburg Opera in 1843, and her effect on him had come as a *coup de foudre*. She was already married; and after what may have been a brief affair, Turgenev became a recurrent member of the Viardot household – a situation which Pauline's husband, who was twenty years older, accepted with complaisance. Pauline Viardot, it is clear, was not attracted to Turgenev sexually, and when she fell in love, which happened not infrequently, Turgenev became the pained observer of a relationship with her he had never known. He noticed the change in her which new relationships brought about; and though, especially in 1856, this caused him to become deeply depressed, he could not free himself from his enslavement to her. This continuing state of bondage is reflected in the novella he was shortly to write. When the young boy, Vladimir, in *First Love*, realises that Zinaida is in love, but does not know who his rival is, his anguish reflects what the older Turgenev continued to suffer in the Viardot household. This present pain kept open the wounds he had first suffered at the hands of his father, and perhaps compelled him to make a work of art from what appeared to belong to the past, like the persistent irritant causing the oyster to secrete its pearl.

Although Pauline Viardot did not respond to his passion for her, her music and singing inspired him. In her singing she became 'higher than any transient, any temporal thing – you are a thing apart. This is your moment, and it will never pass.'[4] This art of catching the unique moment and turning it into something which did not pass lay close to the heart of Turgenev's genius and his craft in the use of the novella. What Pauline Viardot could not give him as a woman, she gave him in a different way as an artist, making him aware of those moments which galvanise a life, providing a sudden revelation and often crystallising a feeling in such a way that it comes to dominate the future. Turgenev was to use these sudden, implosive moments in the structure of his fiction; but they also reflect the creative moment itself, the celestial fire which burns and destroys.

The feeling of enslavement in love ('I belonged to her just as a dog belongs to his master') was not one which Turgenev enjoyed. The father's advice to his son in *First Love*, to beware of the love of women as of a slow poison, reflected Turgenev's dislike of any form of tyranny, which his own mother's savage thrashings of him, and cruel treatment of her serfs had formed in his childhood. Love was associated in his mind with cruelty; and this view played some part in shaping his view of passion as pathological.

A fierce and isolated upbringing in a culture Asiatic in its excess, where cruelty had long been evident, formed a very different background to the writers brought up in France, Germany or England. The Turgenevs were descended from Khan Turga who left the Golden Horde in the fifteenth century, was baptised and served under Prince Vassily the Blind. Continued violence and improvidence had bankrupted the family by the nineteenth century. When Varvara Petrovna, the owner of a vast estate, then unmarried and twenty-nine, made known to a cavalry officer of twenty-three who came to buy horses for his battalion, her attraction to him, Sergey Turgenev succumbed to his father's pleas to save the family's fortunes by marrying her, despite her looks. Turgenev's father seems to have disliked his wife intensely from the outset. As he had no role in running the estates, he devoted himself to his one real passion, which was women. A brilliant horseman with dashing good looks, he was well-suited to his chosen career. Like many successful Don Juans, Turgenev's father displayed an aloofness and coldness – 'pour discourager les autres' – which figured prominently in the portrait of him in his son's novella. For his mother, in spite of her sadistic thrashing of him, he seems to have retained a good deal of love; and the portrayal of the wife and mother in *First Love*, though never filled out, is of someone attempting to maintain her self-respect by holding her family together, and arguing with her husband against his involvement with the girl who is twenty years younger. Although unsuccessful, she will show generosity to Zinaida after her husband's death, by sending money for their child. In this, Turgenev has not so much portrayed his mother, as portrayed the feelings of affection he retained for her, and his belief in the values of family life, as he experienced them in the Viardot family when his own illegitimate daughter by a peasant woman in Russia was taken in and brought up by them.

In his lonely childhood on his mother's estate, Turgenev absorbed a deep love of the Russian countryside, and a knowledge of Nature which he was able to use in that instinctive way which comes to a writer from his childhood experience. In *First Love* it cannot be separated from the rendering of those feelings of awakening desire which forms the theme of the novella. But life in Russia was far from secure; and partly because of the separations which distance brought about, lacked that sense of social and family continuities to be found in Western Europe and reflected in its literature.

In 1831, the year of the events described in *First Love*, Asiatic cholera began to scourge the population. Moscow was cordoned off by troops, and Turgenev's mother had a special sedan chair built in which she was carried through the streets, as a protection against infection. Turgenev developed a life-long fear of the disease, which infected too his idea of love. 'Love is a disease, a certain state of mind and body, it does not develop gradually; it is impossible to be in any doubt about it ... it usually takes hold of a man without asking, suddenly against his will   just as if it were a fever or cholera ....'[5] The imagination of the artist not only reflects things personal to him but mirrors the cultural pressures of his time in the images which occur to him. For Turgenev, the poisoning of river water by disease was akin to the poisoning of life through passion. Both led to mute suffering in the stillness of the night.

First Love is the tale of a young boy's awakening to the experience of love, and his coming to understand what passion means in the adult world. As in *The Princess of Clèves*, *Manon Lescaut*, *Adolphe* and *Cousin Phillis*, the youth of the central character or characters allows an investigation of feelings unexpectedly aroused; and here, as in them, the narrator's perspective determines the insight of the tale told. Vladimir Petrovich and his friends pass an evening amusing each other with reminiscences of their 'first love'. Vladimir Petrovich refuses to tell about his, impromptu; he insists on writing it down, and reading it out when they next come together. The effect on the reader (as well as on the listeners, presumably) is to suggest that this is a meditated and organised account of an experience the narrator knows to be of special importance to him, not just a casual way of passing an anecdotal evening with middle-aged friends. This fictional device serves to convince the audience of the veracity of what is being told, by combining a personal confession with a carefully structured account of what has occurred. Of course this might have the opposite effect in suggesting that memory or self-interest have modified the original experience; but in fact the narrative convinces that it is like a plant which has grown in the air of truth: one of those 'real events' which Goethe identified as being characteristic of the novella form, where memory revives feelings of an earlier time.

The narrator does not interfere in the telling of his tale; but his manner of telling it is marked by the assurance and urbanity of the mature man (and artist) who knows now what the experience was, how it affected him, and how it formed his understanding of the nature of love. He tells his story with an urbanity of style, and an understanding of human feelings which comes with reflection upon them. So much his audience perceives. But his story is about the incomprehension and hurt which occurred in the sixteen-year-old boy when confronted with his father as rival. Through his sureness in not recalling what the boy would not have known, Turgenev succeeds in investing his story with the feeling of a mystery or puzzle which has to be solved: an exploration increasingly fraught with psychological danger, and leading to unexpected perils and revelations. Turgenev shows how the mind is forced to open to new experiences and come to terms with them. He recalls what the wound was like when it was inflicted, and how much in psychological experience is felt as cruel, but also misty. (We are not sure at the time what we have been hurt by.) When Vladimir thinks of himself as Othello, he reveals an adolescent love of self-dramatisation, but also an early sophistication. The boy shows himself as father to the man who sees his life as a literary construct, in which feelings develop and clarify, whereas in life they often become more complex and confused. In defining a particular kind of experience, he holds it up to be compared with other kinds of experience, revealing both its strangeness (its unrepeatability) and its admonitory power. This comes about through the transcription of a lived experience into a written narrative, and the detachment which turns what has been lived through into an account of it, inevitably not the same thing.

At the same time as the boy is learning about himself, through his awakening feelings, he is also learning about his father's life and character. With the death of his father at the age of forty-two, and the death of the girl they have both loved in childbirth, Vladimir reaches at the close of this tale a point of perilous perception: that only in death is this slow poison of love transcended.

In the work of a lesser writer, the ending might have struck a falsely melodramatic note; Turgenev succeeds in making it an exemplum of how cruel and unpredictable life can be, but also, more circumspectly, of how the slow poison in love of women against which his father warns his son works its fatal effect. The brevity of his father's life shows how little time is offered to human beings to come to an understanding of themselves, or to fulfil their desires. 'Before, and above everything, my father wanted to live and did live. Perhaps he had a premonition that he would not live long.'[6] Affairs of the heart, like the affair of life itself, share transience: a brief illumination followed by darkness. Early in the novella, Turgenev suggests this analogy; and in its close shows its justness.

'Several days before his [i.e. his father's] death he had received a letter from Moscow which upset him greatly. He wanted to beg some sort of favour of my mother and, so they told me, actually broke down and wept – he, my father! On the morning of the very day on which he had the stroke, he had begun a letter to me, written in French. "My son," he wrote, "beware of the love of women; beware of that ecstasy – that slow poison."

'My mother, after his death, sent a considerable sum of money to Moscow.'[7]

Looking back when the shades of evening are beginning to close upon his life, Vladimir recalls no memories fresher or dearer than those of that brief storm that came and went so swiftly one morning in the spring. But its recollection is associated with that of another death: a poor old woman whose whole life had been spent in a bitter struggle with daily want; and yet who struggles to the last breath in her body against the coming of the dark. Her terror of death arouses his fear for his father, for Zinaida, and for himself; and for the way they have spent their briefly passing moments. Memory of the brevity of the storm cannot be separated from awareness of the storm which ends in death. Turgenev uses the novella form to reflect and to express this suddeness and brevity, of desire and of life. Memory is a memory of death, but also through the creative life an awakening, and a movement in search of completeness.

The affair which brings first love and rivalry with his father to Vladimir occurs during a summer spent outside Moscow in a rented house. 'The house we had taken was a wooden building with pillars and had two small, low, lodges.'[8] The lodge on the left was used as a tiny factory for the manufacture of cheap wallpaper; that on the right was taken by Princess Zasyekin and her family. 'The house she had taken was so decrepit and narrow and low that no one of even moderate means would have been willing to live there.'[9] The Princess, the daughter of a minor official, has risen in status by marriage; her husband, now dead, was an empty and ridiculous man who ruined himself by speculation.

The Princess speaks French badly and is engaged in endless law suits over her debts. She is uncouth and tedious, and uses her daughter to attract men to her household. The worldly-wise Dr Looshin will warn the as yet undiscerning and vulnerable Vladimir against it. 'You have a tender skin. The atmosphere isn't healthy for you here. Believe me, you might become infected …. Hot-houses smell sweet too, but one can't live in them.'[10] The ambiance of an impecunious aristocracy living on the outskirts of Moscow is distinctively Russian, not least in uncertainties about language, which Vladmir's mother feels in responding to the Princess's invitation: 'to write in French seemed inappropriate – on the other hand, her own Russian spelling was not too certain; she knew this and was not willing to take the risk.'[11] Culturally, this world is far removed from the self-assurance of Western Europe and uncertain where its own roots lie. Equally, the metaphor of the 'hot-house' associates the idea of sexuality with disease and death, which will become a central theme of Vladimir's story.

In contrast, Vladimir's own home is seen as ordered and well-run, with his mother attempting to preserve respectability in spite of her husband's infidelities. Of the wider social scene the narrator says little; but these two households suggest the imperfect environment in which the young Vladmir has to find his own orientation. In the sixteen-year-old at the outset, there always rose upwards, 'like the grasses of early spring, shoots of happy feeling, of young and surging life'.[12] The beauty of the Russian landscape, to which Turgenev was always deeply responsive, mirrors this freshness, and stands in contrast to the decayed and corrupt feelings of the adult world. The suitors who surround Zinaida are feckless, idle and seedy. The retired Captain, for example, is described as being 'a man about forty, hideously pockmarked, with curly hair, like a negro's, slighly bowed bandy legs, and wearing a military tunic, unbuttoned and without epaulettes'.[13] They fill their hours playing foolish games and attempting to fulfil their all too obvious lusts. To the young boy from the 'apparently' conventional home, the presence of these unattractive characters around the girl who has become the object of his love is hard to account for. 'Least of all did I understand the relations which existed between Zinaida and Count Malovsky. He was good-looking, clever and shrewd, but something false in him, something equivocal, was apparent to me, a boy of sixteen, and I wondered that Zinaida did not notice it.'[14] On the one hand, we see the awakening of love, and, on the other, what love can degenerate into. But the novella also implies a criticism of the social world in which such degeneration occurs. Money, or the lack of it, is seen as a determining factor in the nature of human relations, as is ageing and decay. Cause and effect are not analysed, nor should we expect them to be in the novella where implication and suggestion are of the essence.

Such comment as there is comes from Vladimir's mother, whose hostility towards her husband's and son's involvement with the Zasyekin family involves a natural desire to protect herself and her family, but also a right judgement. She, not her husband, tries to prevent her son wasting the time he ought to be spending working for his University examination (his father takes no interest in his education) and perceives the danger of their proximity. Nonetheless, after her husband's death, she retains the generosity to send a considerable sum of money to Zinaida – we assume, for the child.

The narrator recalls the experience of first love as the unravelling of a mystery, not least because of his growing awareness of a rival for Zinaida's affection, whose identity he does not know, but which the reader may guess. The father first encounters Zinaida in Vladimir's company. ' "Is that the young princess?" he asked me .... My father stopped, and turning sharply on his heel, went back. When he drew level with Zinaida, he bowed politely to her. She also bowed, though she looked a trifle surprised, and lowered her book. I saw how she followed him with her eyes. My father always dressed with great distinction, simply, and with a style of his own, but never did his figure seem to me more elegant, never did his grey hat sit more handsomely upon his curly hair that was scarcely touched by time. I made as if to move towards Zinaida, but she did not even glance at me. She raised her book again, and walked away.'[15] In these few sentences Turgenev indicates the future course of the relationship: the interest aroused in his father by the sight of Zinaida, reciprocated by her to the immediate neglect of Vladimir. But it also reconfirms the son's admiration for his father, and his acceptance of his attractiveness, which will be sustained even when his father is revealed as his rival, and in spite of his cruelty to

Zinaida: 'My wound healed slowly, but towards my father I actually bore no ill feeling. On the contrary he somehow seemed to have grown in my eyes.'[16] The desire to supplant the father cannot be separated in this tale from the desire to imitate a man whom he sees as 'ideal', and whom he reveres because he holds himself at a distance. This memory of love held at a distance and never expressed before death intervenes gives Vladimir's tale its special poignancy. 'God knows how specially attached to him I should have been if I had not felt constantly the presence of his restraining hand.'[17] Desire has a dynamic structure not confined to one object, and involves as here a desire to be another. As T.S. Eliot wrote in *Burnt Norton*, 'desire itself is movement, not in itself desirable'. Through memory this shifting emotion is translated into the aesthetic emotion of the story.

Almost as soon as he meets her, Vladimir's 'passion' for Zinaida begins: a passion which from the start is inseparable from suffering. Zinaida, who is five years older, guesses that Vladimir has fallen in love, and his passion amuses her. 'She made fun of me, played with me, and tormented me.'[18] (This theme of the woman who loves to command and torture was dealt with more extensively in *Torrents of Spring*, and reflects an aspect of Turgenev's relationship with Pauline Viardot.[19]) But Vladimir's father embodies the male who dominates. He is a superb rider, capable of breaking the 'wildest horse'; and Zinaida, by her own admission, needs someone who will master her. Vladimir's awakening to love proves increasingly an awakening to its potential for cruelty, and the infliction of pain, trivial and serious. Byelovzorov, whom she called 'my wild beast' or sometimes simply 'mine', would gladly have leapt into the fire for her. The sarcastic doctor, Looshin, she tortures by sticking a pin into his hand. These admirers of Zinaida are helplessly in her thrall, but with Vladimir's father the power-game will be reversed.

In his anxiety and self-pity, Vladimir takes to climbing on a ruined greenhouse. When Zinaida sees him, she challenges him to jump. 'Now you always declare that ... that you love me. Well then jump down into the road, if you truly love me.'[20] He falls fourteen feet, loses consciousness, and wakes to find Zinaida bending over him, declaring her love. But the bliss which he feels is also a sensation of delicious pain. Physical and mental suffering mirror each other; and both can only be overcome, as the old woman's story points out, when life is at an end.

Vladimir's submission to Zinaida is mirrored in his father's domination of her. 'They were riding side by side. My father was saying something to her; he was bending across towards her from the waist, with his hand propped on the neck of his horse. Zinaida listened to hm in silence, her eyes firmly lowered, her lips pursed tightly.'[21] Later, when she recovers from being unwell, Zinaida will appoint Vladimir as her 'page'. 'And always remember that pages must never leave their mistress's side.' But the page alone does not yet know the identity of the lover who has changed her whole deportment: 'Her very walk seemed gentler, her whole figure more stately and more graceful.'[22] As in *Adolphe*, passion is seen to involve an enslavement which wants to ignore other bonds and ties.

The bizarre nature of Vladimir's situation extends to the odd way of life in Zinaida's home, where the middle-aged lovers exist more for the pleasure of her mother than for Zinaida herself. Egged on by the malicious Count Malevsky, Vladimir arms himself with a penknife to take his revenge on his rival, only to recognise him as his father. 'Jealous Othello, ready for murder, was suddenly transformed into a schoolboy ... in my terror, I dropped the knife into the grass.'[23] It is one of those moments in Turgenev when a life is transformed by a sudden revelation. But with a part of him Vladimir still does not understand what has happened: he is overcome by a quite unfamiliar kind of sadness, as if something in him was dying. When he tries to confront Zinaida, he only exacts from her an admission of her wickedness and her love for him, which binds him ever more deeply to her. 'I was hers utterly from head to foot. She did exactly what she liked with me.'[24] The acceptance of what has happened does not, however, heal a deeper sense of affront. He cannot understand how a young girl can have brought herself to do such a thing, when she knew that his father was not free. It also serves to develop in the young boy a view of love: 'Yes, I thought, this is it – this is love; this is passion; this is devotion.' And in going to say good-bye to her, he finds his love for her confirmed: 'however much you make me suffer, I shall love you and adore you to the end of my days ....'[25] Equally he feels no ill feeling towards his father. 'On the contrary, he somehow seemed even to have grown in my eyes. Let psychologists explain this contradiction if they can.'[26] The mastery which he knows he can never have over Zinaida, and which his father naturally assumes, has aroused a feeling of unspoken complicity, as though his rival in love assumes the role which can never be his.

Vladimir's perception of love has to suffer one further twist. After the family has left its summer house, he is destined to see Zinaida once more. His father, now riding a vicious English mare called 'Electric', takes Vladimir out with him, and leaves him for a while to look after the horse. When he does not return, Vladimir goes in search of him, and sees him talking to Zinaida at a window. 'My father seemed to be insisting on something. Zinaida would not consent ....' And then the listener hears the words, ' "Vous devez vous separer de cette ..." '[27] Turgenev does not attribute these words to one or the other.[28] It may be that Zinaida is telling him to leave his wife, or that he is telling her to break with her lover, Byelozorov. Either is possible, but what matters is what happens. Instead of shaking her hand in parting, his father strikes her with his whip across the bare arm; in response, Zinaida raises her arm slowly to her lips, and kisses the scar which glows crimson upon it.

What the boy still cannot understand is Zinaida's lack of resentment at being struck by a hand, however dear. But it modifies his understanding of love and passion, transforming his earlier and childish excitements into 'that other unknown something which I could hardly begin to guess at, but which struck terror into me like an unfamiliar, beautiful but awe-inspiring face whose features one strains in vain to discern in the gathering darkness'.[29] In vain has this passion between an ageing man and a young girl tried to become something more than a meeting of two fantasies, and two solitudes. Soon after, his father dies of a stroke.

The narrator, recalling these events, knows that the shades of evening are beginning to close in upon his life, but also that no memories are fresher and dearer to him than those of this first love. Time has brought with it detachment, and also the power to recollect the intensity of feelings which are no more, in their complexity. First love does not initiate Vladimir into sexual love (actual physical love plays little part in the tale, apart from kisses and the indication at the end that Zinaida has become pregnant by Vladimir's father) but into the psychopathology of passion. In the love between the forty-year-old man (determined to live for and belong to himself alone) and the girl of twenty-one, herself attracted to the boy of sixteen as the young image of his father, Turgenev writes of feelings more complex than those of Adolphe, unable to free himself from a woman he no longer loves. In that we may feel something of a tragic dilemma; here, no dilemma exists, only an experience which, profoundly shocking as it is, has to be absorbed by the understanding, in the process of coming to terms with the nature of the passions. Turgenev has no message to deliver. The notion of love of women as a slow poison is not offered as a general truth. It comes as the perception of a man, not unlike Turgenev's own father, whose life has little to fill it other than the pursuit of illicit loves, and it comments on that way of life, which involves belonging only to oneself. The novella offers too a more modern view of what love may involve – not as a romantic ideal, but as a fever which affects the whole body, colours perception, and exacts as its price an awareness of the incompleteness which cannot be healed: a meeting of two solitudes.

The desire for revenge, which can become obsessive in adult love, is here only touched on as part of the boy's awakening. Turgenev does not dwell on this; nor does he more than hint at the corruption of relationships in the Princess's household. The brevity of the novella becomes an instrument for perceptions only glancingly realised; and this is appropriate for the boy's partial understanding of the adult world. Parents are those we know best, and in another sense do not know at all. The adult narrator remains true to the experience at the time (except in style); and tells his story as it affected the developing consciousness of the young boy. The form of the novella demands this sharpness of focus, and contains the narrative within the limits of Vladimir's perceptions and feelings.

V.S. Pritchett describes Turgenev as 'hearing his characters, as if they were the notes of a haunting sonata, passing from one movement to the next'.[30] This acute observation, with its awareness of how glancingly Turgenev writes here, indicates also why the form of the novella was so appropriate for his art.

Elizabeth Gaskell: *Cousin Phillis*

An English Interlude

> In the long fifteen- or twenty-roomed suites, very cool and dark,
> where Italian women pass their lives reclining languidly on low
> divans, they hear talk of love or music for six hours a day. In the
> evenings, hidden in their boxes at the theatre for four hours, they
> hear talk of music or love.
>
> So besides the climate the very pattern of life in Italy and Spain
> is as conducive to music and to love as it is discouraging for them
> in England.
> Stendhal, Love

In his book, *Love*, Stendhal uses his European travels, and his
experiences in them, to characterise the differences between
forms of love in European countries, which he also relates to
differences in 'government or national character'. He divides love
into four kinds of which the first is predominantly, but not
exclusively, the subject of this book: passionate love, mannered
love, physical love and vanity-love. (Mannered love is a matter of
gallantry; physical love, of an unexpected encounter in the forest,
and vanity-love of the feelings of a bourgeois for a duchess, who
will never be more than thirty in his eyes.) Italy is the only
country, he states, where the plant he is describing can grow
freely. In France, vanity stifles or drives it into the strangest
paths: 'I seem to see a man throwing himself out of the window
but trying nevertheless to land gracefully on the pavement below.'[1] In Germany, there exists a so-called philosophy so crazy
that it makes one die of laughter: 'The Germans regard love as a
virtue, a divine emanation, something mystical. It is not eager,
impetuous, jealous and tyrannical as it is in the heart of an
Italian woman. It is deep, visionary, and utterly unlike anything
in England.'[2] He confesses that he is too fond of England, and has

seen too little of it to be able to discuss it, but nevertheless does so, using the observations of a friend. He describes the two great English vices as cant or hypocrisy in morality (undimmed today – witness the persecution of politicians by journalists) and bashfulness: a proud, agonized shyness. Scotland scores rather higher than England in the league table of the tender passions, in spite of the dreadful Scottish sabbath (compared to which the London version is a real picnic). The Scots at least compensate for Sunday on Monday. 'In Scotland, the Lord's Day is strictly observed, but on Monday they dance with a joyous abandon utterly unknown in London.'[3] The ruling sin of English society is exemplified by something he is told in Croydon, near the statue of a Bishop (the Bible looms large in his recollection of this country): 'No man here wants to press forward, in case he should be disappointed in the attempt. Judge for yourselves what laws such men will impose, in the name of modesty, upon their wives and mistresses!'[4]

Quite so, and we shall see, in the case of Mrs Gaskell's novella, on their daughters too.

Before crossing the Channel to Protestant and puritanical England, it seems a good moment to pause and reflect briefly on the differences in the representation of desire and feeling in the literatures of different countries, however little human nature varies between them. In so far as desire is structured by imitation, it remains true to a pattern prescribed by cultural context and language, by codes of behaviour approved or disapproved by particular commmunities. In Russia, the representation of passion never floats free of the great existential questions: what is involved in the love of women, how does it affect the way we live, and the meaning of our lives. This is as true for Pechorin as for Vladimir, and for Raskolnikov, for whom Sonya's love offers the promise of a new life, and of redemption.[5] At the other extreme, the debate in the railway carriage in Tolstoy's *The Kreutzer Sonata* as to whether it is necessary and desirable to beat one's wife to ensure her submissive obedience indicates a widespread social acceptance of what would be regarded elsewhere as pathological behaviour. The question asked at the end of Chekov's *Three Sisters*, as to why things are as they are, remains unanswered, but the differentiating thing is that it is asked.

In France, the representation of desire raises moral questions, not just in relation to sexual morality, but to the effect on character of falling into an abyss where no handholds exist. As Stendhal recognised in his own fictions, once restraint is abandoned, identity is threatened, character transformed and loyalty destroyed: 'a passionate man is only like himself, and not like other people, and this in France is the source of all ridicule.'[6] Ridicule offends the vanity of its object, but also expresses the affront to the vanity of the person who ridicules.

Tiberge scarcely recognises in Des Grieux the friend he once knew and respected, once his 'love' for Manon turns him into a card-sharper and liar; and the vanity of each is offended. Adolphe by refusing to leave Ellenore after the sacrifices she has made for him preserves his vanity at the cost of their mutual happiness. Society always exacts a price for the rejection of its conventions, so that the challenge to identity from within is magnified by the rejection of society from without. (In *The Princess of Clèves*, the image is reversed: virtue can only be held on to by the rejection of a society based on conspiracy and deceit.) Once passion has been given way to, no escape from its consequences offers itself, except in death. The extremity of feeling which is structured by desire is perceived as being a dangerous fall, to which anyone may succumb: a cliff in the map of the human heart, which may equally result in eternal damnation or a mystical union outside Time. Such extremes are characteristic of a Catholic culture.

What Stendhal described as English bashfulness involved not just a fear of disappointment, but a more general fear of wading in too deep, of getting out of the shallows that were regarded as decent. The nonconformist temperament buried even deeper what the puritanical revolt against indulgence had begun. The spirit of thrift applied equally to the feelings. Denial did not lead only to repression, but to an unawareness, a form of innocence, about what could occur as a result of human desire. Awareness, when it happened, gave rise not just to moral shock, but to an emotional horror of excess, no different to the dislike of excess in all its forms. Bashfulness concealed far deeper waters than a mere lack of forwardness or even sophistication and *savoir-faire*. Mrs Gaskell as a woman writer understood what these were and wrote about them in *Cousin Phillis* with particular understanding of the effect on a young girl of feelings in herself which her upbringing had taught her to suppress, scarcely to acknow-

ledge, and which equally went unacknowledged in the lives of
those round her. Phillis's mother would have lacked even the
vocabulary to speak to her daughter as Madame de Chartres did
to hers. Mrs Gaskell writes of a rural family whose feelings and
beliefs would be affronted at the deepest level by the social and
sexual mores of the society in which Madame de Lafayette lived.
Two hundred years are as nothing compared with the distance in
values which separate them. And yet both novellas are concerned
with sexual awakening in contexts where fulfilment is doomed.
In Mrs Gaskell's myth of desire, the death of a way of life will
substitute for death as conceived in other novellas; and this may
still be seen as involving a kind of evasion in the puritan temperament: that passion can dominate and destroy.

Mrs Gaskell's *Cousin Phillis* (1864) is a rare example in English fiction of the 'novella of passion' and also a tale of 'first love'.
One of Mrs Gaskell's most perfectly executed works, it reveals
the depth of feeling running beneath the cool and moderate flow
of English rural life. Like sap which leads to the profusion of
spring, the passion is present but almost concealed. Rhythms of
human life still correspond quite closely to the cycle of seasons;
and those fresh shoots which Vladimir feels have not yet begun
to degenerate in the hot-house against which he is warned.

Cousin Phillis was published in the *Cornhill Magazine* in
1863-64, just three years after *First Love*. In her novella, Mrs
Gaskell recalled memories of her childhood visits to Sandlebridge: a house to which she returned later in life with her own
family, and which was especially associated in her mind with the
timeless peace of the countryside. A place, she once said, where
one cannot think anything but poetry and happiness. This perceived and harmonious relationship between man and Nature,
which is itself another form of wholeness, is seen in the course of
the narrative to be under threat.

Her grandfather, Samuel Holland, who owned Sandlebridge,
provided the model for Farmer Holman, as farmer and preacher;
in the Hollands' house her father, at that time a dissenting
preacher, met her mother. Memory (and memories, renewed by
subsequent visits) deeply influenced *Cousin Phillis*; but they are
mediated through the narrator, Paul Manning, whose story begins when he is seventeen, and who sets it down when he is
middle-aged and married. (The perspective of the novella is

similar to Turgenev's in *First Love*, but the preoccupation is
wholly different.) As happens with great art, experiences of
different sorts, occurring at different times, are integrated in the
act of imagination. The coming of the railways which is central
in the novella reflects the opening of the railway at Knutsford,
Mrs Gaskell's childhood home, on 12 May 1862, just a year before
the story was begun. Although the time-span of the narrative is
only a few years (and as with all novellas of this sort the time-
span is telescoped to reflect the intensity of what occurs) the
experience which went into its making covered more than half a
century, and is set in the 1840s.

Cousin Phillis is a deeply meditated account of life in the
English countryside, under the influence of the nonconformist
tradition, where ministers earned their living five days a week
on the land, and exercised their ministry for two. (This way of
life, without hope of preferment, would hold no attractions for
Obadiah Slope, or appeal for Dr Grantley!) But Mrs Gaskell did
not see any form of life as static; and her eye contemplates the
changes which are beginning to touch life on Hope Farm: changes
in ways of life, attitudes, beliefs, as well as changes brought
about by the industrial revolution and the coming of the railways. Like Forster's *Howards End*, *Cousin Phillis* depicts a way
of life just before it begins to disappear, and records rural simplicity without sentimentality or condescension: an example of
what Schiller described as naive art in which feeling is expressed
directly, without being mediated through ideas. Mrs Gaskell
perceives the deep human qualities of life on Hope Farm, but
recognises too their blindnesses and limitations (blindnesses
which are by no means peculiar to their environment); and the
inevitability of change as another generation with different pri-
orities and aspirations begins to take the place of one untouched
by the profound social transformations starting to occur.

This is made possible by Mrs Gaskell's creation of a narrator,
Paul Manning, who tells the story of what happened to his
Cousin Phillis when she was seventeen, and he about eighteen
months older. The narrative belongs to the period of life about
which Madame de Lafayette's, Prévost's, Goethe's and Constant's tales were told. But how totally different to these
European cousins Mrs Gaskell's work proves to be! The intense
self-involvement has vanished, as have the powers of analysis

and emotional percipience: not, one hastens to add, on Mrs Gaskell's part (she understands far more than she ever gives away), but on the part of the somewhat callow, naive young man who tells the story. We find in him something of the undeveloped heart which Forster disliked so much, but not seen here as part of some wider failing of class. Paul is more simply the young man who lacks knowledge of the world, and particularly of women: practical, straightforward and naive in much that touches the emotional life, of which he has little experience or understanding. He becomes destructive because he lacks any conception of the ground upon which he has entered. More surprisingly – though here Mrs Gaskell's restraint is at its most telling – when he comes to set down the narrative he feels no compulsion to analyse what was happening to him then, or to comment upon it, nor does he attempt to rewrite it with the benefit of hindsight. Like earlier narrators, he writes it as it happened, so it comes as a surprise at the end of Part Two when we are confronted with the length of time which has elapsed between the occurrence and the narration, when Paul comments: 'It is many years since I have seen thee, Edward Holdsworth, but thou wast a delightful fellow!'[7]

The style of *Cousin Phillis* is made possible by Paul's role as observer and friend: directness typifies Paul's character, and suits the unembellished tale he wishes to tell. Nonetheless, in the restraint of the narrative, an artistic maturity which conceives Paul in a particular way is apparent. Paul's father warns him at one point that he lacks much in the way of inventiveness which might enable him to go far in the engineering line; but this defect is part and parcel of his emotional blindness, an inability to analyse feelings, either his own or other people's, which characterises his English phlegm, both as a young man and an author. Behind Paul, in other words, stands Mrs Gaskell shaping the work of art in which he participates and which he relates, but always relating it as might be appropriate for a man of his temperament, who sees and recalls without much insight. That is left to the reader.

Memory here is far from memory of the heart, of the kind which Adolphe experiences, not least because the passion recalled is Phillis's, not Paul's. In so far as his own feelings are involved, they are those of the friend who has been betrayed by a man more worldly wise than himself. And even that does not, as the quotation given above indicates, blemish his feelings for Holdsworth permanently. Nonetheless memory does make him write about Cousin Phillis rather than anyone else. 'It is about Cousin Phillis that I am going to write, and as yet I am far enough from even saying who Cousin Phillis was.'[8] Although muted and oblique, like so much in this narrative, his tone reveals the same obsessive need to recall and come to terms with the past.

Cousin Phillis opens with the narrator recollecting his first day of independence, at the age of seventeen, when he finds himself in lodgings and about to start a job as clerk to the engineer responsible for building the branch railway line from Eltham to Hornby. His father has introduced him to the family of the Independent Minister in whose home Paul spends Sunday evenings of intolerable boredom and solemnity, when the day of chapel-going and sermonising is concluded by further devotions with the servants. (Whatever Stendhal may have thought about the English sabbath, it was not exactly a picnic either, and Mrs Gaskell knew it!)

Paul quickly develops a hero's admiration for his boss at work, Mr Holdsworth, but one which may perhaps not be altogether well founded: 'he had travelled on the Continent, and wore moustachios and whiskers of a somewhat foreign fashion.'[9] As Russians were suspicious of those who had been Westernised, so here in middle England foreign fashions suggest moral dubiety. In this way, Mrs Gaskell establishes the tension, central to the novella, between the narrowness of the old way of life and the thrusting vitality of the new. In the narrative's development, the values of each will prove complex and unreliable as change ushers in a new instability.

By the time Paul gets to know Cousin Phillis, he is nineteen and she seventeen; it strikes him at once that she still has many of the attributes of a child. 'I thought it odd that so old, so full-grown as she was, she should wear a pinafore over her gown.'[10] And she still possesses a child's simplicity of feeling; lack of sophistication is the hallmark of both clothes and emotion.

From her father, though, she has inherited an enthusiasm for learning, which includes Latin, Greek and the reading of Dante. (Mrs Gaskell, if not Paul, recognises the distinction between cultivation of the mind and education of the feelings.) Sharply aware of her physical presence, Paul also senses the incompatibilities between them. 'A great, tall girl in a pinafore, half-a-head taller than I was, reading books that I had never heard of, and talking about them too, as of far more interest than any mere personal subjects – that was the last day on which I ever thought of my dear cousin Phillis, as the possible mistress of my heart and life.'[11]

Although the French word *maitresse* does not invariably imply a sexual relationship, its English usage here lacks any conceivable connotation of impropriety, suggesting little more than respect and consideration of her as a marriage partner. The portrait of life at Hope Farm, in which simplicity and education of the mind go together, does however have its European parallels. Werther is most happy when reading Homer while shelling peas. The importance of the classics in the reading which goes on at Hope Farm indicates too a European continuity, a common heritage of civilisation, in which desire is confined to a desire for knowledge about a common past. As for the Abbé Prévost, books do furnish a room, creating a haven secure from the passions outside. (In her marriage, Mrs Gaskell was to experience the tension between her own need for a social life and her husband's preference for spending his evenings in his study preparing his lectures; in writing *Cousin Phillis* she reflected some of that tension between the attractions of a reflective life and the deeper emotional needs of living life to the full.)

As can often happen, the putting away of the idea of love strengthens the friendship between Paul and Phillis, giving the young boy a degree of detachment from what ensues. The incompatibility between them is reflected in the relationship between Phillis's mother and father. 'She was completely unable even to understand the pleasure her husband and daughter took in intellectual pursuits, much less to care in the least herself for the pursuits themselves. I had once or twice thought that she was a little jealous of her own child, as fitter companion for her husband than she was herself; and I fancied the minister himself was aware of the feeling, for I had noticed an occasional sudden change of subject, and a tenderness of appeal in his voice, as he spoke to her, which always made her look contented and peaceful again.'[12] Their relationship has mellowed into an acceptance of difference, permeated by tact and consideration; and altogether lacking in the competitiveness and 'condescension' which Paul acknowledges in his relationship with Phillis, because he can never be cleverer or taller than she. Unlike other novellas, intense feelings of the sort which will erupt are seen in relation to tolerance and affection which endure. And in this recognition of the strength of bonds rooted in moderation Mrs Gaskell's Englishness also expresses itself. In *Manon Lescaut,* by contrast, Des Grieux's father acts out of a sense of family pride, just as in *The Lady of the Camellias* Germont will attempt to prevent his daughter's betrothal from being ruined by his son's relationship with Marguerite; but these feelings are peripheral to the excess in the main story, whereas Mrs Gaskell's moderation permeates the whole work.

When Paul's manager, Mr Holdsworth, falls ill, he goes to recuperate at Hope Farm. As Paul percipiently tells him before he goes there: 'I think you are good, but I don't know if you are quite of their kind of goodness.'[13] It is a doubt shared by Farmer Holman, who tells Paul: 'I have almost been afraid lest he carries me away, in spite of my judgement.'[14] His cautiousness, which proves justified, comes not from a difference of class, but of temperament and generation. He lacks 'gravitas', affronting Mr Holman's sense of what is decent and proper and offending the vanity on which his conception of himself as walking in God's way is based. 'I listen to him till I forget my duties and am carried off my feet. Last Sabbath evening he led us away into talk on profane subjects ill-befitting the day.'[15] In Mr Holman's rigour, there exists a firmness of purpose, and seriousness of intention, absent in Holdsworth, for all the attractiveness which Paul communicates; but it exists at the expense of those powerful emotions to which his daughter will succumb, and which the structure of his desires prudently excludes.

The relationship which develops between Holdsworth and Phillis is suggested but not analysed. Paul's narration is characterised by a reticence which the older (and married) story-teller has not lost; but it also occurs largely in Paul's absence, making possible the speed necessary for the novella form. On one of his weekend visits, he finds Holdsworth sketching Phillis, and his stare discomposes her: 'her colour came and went, her breath quickened with the consciousness of his regard; at last when he said, "Please look at me for a minute or two, I want to get in the eyes," she looked up at him, quivered, and suddenly got up and left the room ....' With characteristic obtuseness, Paul comments: 'So all things went on, at least as far as my observation reached at the time, or memory can recall now, till the great apple-gathering of the year.'[16] There, the one moment of reciprocated intensity occurs, when Phillis offers Holdsworth a nosegay: 'I saw their faces. I saw an unmistakable look of love in his black eyes; it was more than gratitude for the little attention; it was tender and beseeching – passionate. She shrank from it in confusion, his glance fell on me; and, partly to hide her emotion, partly out of real kindness at what might appear ungracious neglect of an older friend, she flew off to gather me a few late-blooming China roses.'[17] Passion, as always in this novella, is observed from without. Memory is also incomplete, and while it revives past experience, offers no comment upon it. As in *First Love*, the turning-point is witnessed by the young boy, though not as a traumatised participant, whose own emotions and attitudes are developed by it.

Then, at once, Holdsworth accepts the offer of a job in Canada, where advancement beckons. The mobility and impermanence of the modern world has touched the rural stillness of life at Hope Farm. So sudden is his departure that it falls to Paul to break the news of his going and witness its effect on Phillis. Before he goes, however, Holdsworth has told Paul of his love for her, and his intention to return in two years and marry her. During the next two months Phillis begins to show all the signs of a neurasthenic illness; but not until Paul discovers her poring over Holdsworth's notes does he realise the source of her distress.[18] This leads him to make the fatal and intrusive mistake of telling her what Holdsworth has told him.

When the following year Holdsworth writes to tell the family of his marriage in Canada, Phillis, already deeply affected, develops a dangerous brain-fever. (Like Prévost in his account of the unconsciousness into which Des Grieux falls twice, Mrs Gaskell is interested by the body's reaction to the emotions with which which the mind cannot deal.) 'Her face was brilliantly flushed, her eyes were dry and glittering; but she did not speak; her lips were set together, almost as if she was pinching them tight to prevent words or sounds coming out .... Once my eyes fell upon her hands, concealed under the table, and could see the passionate, convulsive manner in which she laced and interlaced her fingers perpetually, wringing them together from time to time, wringing till the compressed flesh became perfectly white.'[19] Only through these physical manifestations can Phillis express the repressed nature of her intense feelings, for to her father and mother she is still a child. When she admits her love, it is only to be reproached: ' "Have we not loved you enough?" She did not seem to understand the drift of the question; she looked up as if bewildered, and her beautiful eyes dilated with a painful tortured expression.'[20] Then she loses consciousness. When she begins to recover from the ensuing illness, the family expresses its thanks in prayer; but the return of her bodily strength does not put an end to her lassitude or her weeping.

In all the novellas considered so far, parents understand, though they do not approve, the intensity of their children's emotions. Here, the misunderstanding in the use of the word love is heavily ironic, in revealing how little the Minister is capable of differentiating between parental love and sexual desire. The failure reflects too the possessiveness of the father towards his only daughter which again goes unrecognised by the narrator. Part of the Englishness of this narrative lies in its attempt to brush aside or disregard the powerfulness of the emotion from which Phillis suffers; but the triangular structuring of desire between parents and child also reflects a deliberate evasion.

Betty, the family servant, who has long since been critical of Paul for his failure to understand what has been going on, now confronts Phillis with her reality: 'We ha' done a' we can for you, and th' doctors has done a' they can for you, and I think the Lord has done a' He can for you, and more than you deserve, too, if you don't do something for yourself.'[21] The servant understands more, but is also dismissive of weakness or self-indulgence, as an affront not just to good sense but also to the modest decency to be expected in a god-fearing life. Phillis's response is to ask to go and stay with Paul's parents for a couple of months. Then – 'we will go back to the peace of the old days. I know we shall; I can, and I will!'[22]

So, Mrs Gaskell ends this narrative with a return to English stoicism and pragmatism, different enough to the despair and retreat which closes the novellas of the European past. Convents and monasteries do not offer themselves as alternative ways of life to the non-conformist wounded by passion. Nonetheless, a return to the peace of the past would mean a return to life in which feelings are held in check, and the vicarious life of books becomes a substitute for a life fully lived. Vergil or Theocritus may walk again, but scarcely Catullus. Betty, the uneducated servant, alone understands the life of the emotions; and what she has to offer is not the moral advice of Tiberge, but the practical good sense of the country-woman, which for all her talent and involvement with the London literary world, Mrs Gaskell rightly believed herself to be.

At one point Paul compares Phillis to Wordsworth's Lucy,

> ' "A maid whom there were none to praise,
> And very few to love."

And somehow those lines always reminded me of Phillis; yet they were not true of her either.'[23] So why does he quote them?

Both Lucy and Phillis belong to the landscape in which they live. When Paul first sees her, 'the westering sun shone full upon her, and made a slanting stream of light into the room within'.[24] She is associated with the weather, the changing seasons, the flowers of the passing year, as in the nosegay she gives to Holdsworth, and which he takes with him to Canada. Both Lucy and Phillis, though, are perceived as isolated, and in some way independent of the reciprocity of human feeling. Phillis does right in her parents' eyes, out of her natural goodness and wisdom; and their devotion to her is amply revealed in her illness. But Paul notices what they do not. 'I could not help remembering the pinafore, the childish garment which Phillis wore so long, as if her parents were unaware of her progress towards womanhood. Just in the same way, the minister spoke and thought of her now, as a child, whose innocent peace I had spoiled by vain and foolish talk.'[25] Paul knows better than that. He perceives at last the intensity and depth of feeling of which she is capable. But Paul – like Phillis's parents, and like the poetic 'I' which observes Lucy – is distanced from the object of attention, as though she lives on the other side of a glass-screen. Neither possess the skill or tact to break through her inarticulacy. The strange fits of passion which the lover knows in

Wordsworth's poem he can tell to another lover: Phillis has no
such relief; and the effect of this silence on her becomes the more
severe.

The detachment of the narrative perspective (both because
Paul is not Phillis's lover, and because he is transcribing her
story in later years) enables Mrs Gaskell to write more discursively and less obsessively than in other novellas by other
writers. A frame for the story is provided by Paul's relative
detachment, and the unquestioning nature of his intelligence.

The domestic and religious life of Hope Farm embodies a
traditional continuity, close to that of the seasons. The only
disturbance of its calm and continuing surface is caused by
Timothy Cooper, the labourer not worthy of his hire, who offends
the proper ordering of things. 'There's but little he can do; and
what he does do, he does badly.'[26] When, in a fit of displeasure,
Holman tells him to go, the labourer takes up a post at the bridge
leading to Hope Farm, during Phillis's illness, to prevent the
carts crossing it and disturbing her. Phillis's restoration to health
is associated with the renewal of balance in the life of Farm,
where Timothy is only given work carefully adjusted to his
capacity. No such continuities or forbearance are likely to be
found in the world of work, of railway engineering, to which Paul
and Holdsworth belong. At Hope Farm 'great creating Nature'
still holds sway; its values are those of the country, not of the
town.

In Betty, the faithful servant who epitomises the wholesome
good sense of the country, Mrs Gaskell depicts too the value of
loyalty, and the stability on which the life of rural England is
based. Neither for master nor servant are there riches or plenty;
but no actual misery either (though the threat of starvation
exists for Timothy and his family on his dismissal). Betty understands instinctively too what is wrong with Phillis, and what the
cure must be. Storms in human life, like storms in Nature, are
things that pass. How Phillis will deal with Betty's advice
remains a matter of speculation. But in her departure, albeit only
to Paul's parents, Mrs Gaskell perhaps suggests the need for her
too to live outside the restrictive bounds of Hope Farm and its
way of life, as she herself had found the need to encounter a wider
world than her upbringing had encompassed. Phillis in her
awakening embodies the necessity of not staying on. If her eyes

do not turn yet as far as the sea, to which her creator was always drawn, she will not return, we may surmise, to the 'peace of the old days' which has gone for ever.[27]

'Hope Farm', Paul is told when he goes to find it, 'is an old place, though Holman keeps it in good order.'[28] Enduring, se-cluded and unpretentious, the house reflects the values of the Holman family, not yet quite threatened by the railways as Howards End will be about seventy years later by the encroach-ment of London and the appearance of the motor-car. 'The many-speckled fowls were picking about in the farmyard beyond, and the milk-cans glittered with brightness, hung out to sweeten. The court was so full of flowers that they crept out on the low-covered wall, and horse-mount, and were even to be found self-sown upon the turf that bordered the path to the back of the house.'[29] In this place the continuities of Nature and the changing of the seasons create a seamless way of life upon which passion intrudes. When Paul first introduces Holdsworth to Phillis, he does so in a world from which care seems to have been removed, where flowers border the gravel paths in the productive kitchen garden. This is an England of sunshine and harvest, of devotion and thanksgiving. 'After the one thunderstorm, came one or two lovely serene days, during which the hay was all carried; and then succeeded long soft rains, filling the ears of corn and causing the mown grass to spring afresh.'[30] Much of the harshness and drudgery has been removed from this portrait of farm-life: labour is God's work, and is not associated with the dreariness of body and spirit which Tess of the d'Urbervilles will find in the turnip fields. In this well-tended and orderly way of life, disorder of feeling cannot be assimilated and has no place. Passion becomes quite literally a brain-fever: an expression of the body's refusal to endure any longer the mental pain which has no outlet.

The implication of what is happening cannot be lost on the reader, but at the same time it is not dwelt upon or spelt out. What appears in Paul at nineteen as failure to understand the dangers of meddling in the affairs of other people's hearts ap-pears too in Phillis's parents as a blindness to the emotions in their own daughter's life. While Constant offers an analysis and critique of the passions, Mrs Gaskell offers something much closer to a critique of our reticence about them, and our inability to acknowledge their potentially convulsive force. It remains an irony of the work (and a tribute to Mrs Gaskell's artistry in writing it) that the calmness of Paul's narration is scarcely ruffled by the tale he has to tell.

Paul's style owes most to a special quality in Mrs Gaskell's imaginative use of memory, as though by returning to the past she has drawn out from her childhood the peace and radiance which belong to communion with nature, and to the identification of people with it. A state of mind, now gone, is restored by imaginative memory; and with it an understanding of the things – both personal and social – which fractured it. Phillis's idea that she can go back to the peace of the old days expresses the illusion that life at Hope Farm has not been overtaken by new values. The death involved in overcoming an obsession is that of a way of living and feeling.

Alexandre Dumas *fils*: *The Lady of the Camellias*

> Armand and Marguerite do not belong socially to the same world and there can be no question between them of tragedy in the manner of Racine.
> Roland Barthes, *Mythologies*

> A public prostitute ... coughs her way through three acts and finally expires on stage in a manner which, however true to nature, ought to be revolting to the feelings of spectators .... Next season we trust to hear no more such abominations.
> *The Times* (1856) on the first London performance of *La Traviata*

The Lady of the Camellias brought success to Dumas *fils* at the age of 24, in 1848. The following year he turned it into a play. As with many novellas the subject was inherently dramatic; but until 1852, and the coming of the Second Empire, its performance was censored. In that year the play became a theatrical hit. Verdi saw it and at once set his librettist, Piave, to work. He referred to the new opera as *Amore e Morte*, indicating that it was partly the mythological theme which appealed to him. *La Traviata* was first performed in Venice in 1853, and was a fiasco. On its revival fifteen months later it became a triumph, and has remained central to the operatic repertory ever since. The interpretation of the role of Violetta has brought fame to the great sopranos of the last hundred years, from Adelina Patti to Maria Callas and Angela Georghiú.

In 1937, Dumas's story also became the basis of one of Garbo's most celebrated films, *Camille*. Garbo's enigmatic beauty suited the doll-like role of the courtesan, but failed to suggest the innocence in the character of Marguerite Gautier, or her underlying humanity. In 1963 Frederick Ashton created the ballet, *Marguerite and Armand*, for Fonteyn and Nureyev: roles which they alone have danced with the required intensity of feeling and personal involvement.

The figure of the courtesan dying alone of consumption which Dumas created in this novella of passion has never lost her power to touch hearts. As a narrative of passion between the young son of a tax-collector and a courtesan, her death was needed to complete a myth which has no other ending, for a relationship which cannot be fulfilled in this world, and to which death gives permanence. The autobiographical experience on which it was based did not differ in the fact of death, but in the way in which that death was narrated in the creative imagination.

Dumas was the natural son of a famous father, the author of *The Three Musketeers*, and Catherine Labay, a seamstress. Brought up in a household animated by talent and love of pleasure, Dumas learned quickly the attractions of his father's life-style. His formal education ended when he was seventeen, and from then on he frequented the world of Bohemian Paris, of cafés and theatres, which was his father's. Although he lived in a Catholic culture, his upbringing taught little restraint, and he threw himself into what he described as the 'paganism of modern life'. Debts drove him to write; and what he wrote about was based on his relationship with Marie Duplessis.

Marie Duplessis came from the rural poor. At the age of fifteen, she was taken by her drunken father to work in Paris, where her striking beauty and intelligence led quickly to her becoming 'une femme entretenue'. In addition to her beauty, she had 'an inborn tact, and an instinctive elegance', and soon she received huge sums of money from her admirers. In 1842, the eighteen-year-old Dumas, who met her in the Place de la Bourse, fell passionately in love with her; they had a brief, but intense affair. But her need for money, and the difference in their social circumstances, brought their relationship to an end. In a farewell letter to her probably dating from 1845 (which Dumas himself bought back in an autograph sale in 1884, and presented to Sarah Bernhardt) he claimed that he was 'not rich enough to love you as I would wish, nor poor enough to be loved as you would wish. Let us forget each other – you a name which must be almost a matter of indifference to you, and I a happiness beyond my reach.'[1]

Life and literature (even in letters) are, however, never the same thing. Words are inevitably a form of self-dramatisation.

The young Dumas did not need to blot out the memory of her by new liaisons; the following year he accompanied his father to Spain where he seems to have pursued his 'rage de vivre' and returned in high spirits. Marie did not give him up to save his sister's marriage. She became for a time the mistress of Lizst, but her health was deteriorating. When she died the following year at the age of twenty-three, Dumas was in Marseilles; she was buried before he returned to Paris. But he did go to the sale of her effects (as did Dickens), and the sight of her possessions aroused in him the memory of her as a person, which the following year provided the starting point for his novella. Objects as a means of inscribing desire contribute much to the originality of Dumas's style: a device used earlier by Shakespeare in the famous handkerchief of *Othello*.

Dumas had already begun to reject the self-indulgence of his father's way of life. As he observed, the comedy of pleasure all too often ended in tragedy, especially for the women around whom it revolved. His novella, like Verdi's opera, was inspired by anger at the waste of life and the self-serving lusts of the demi-monde, where women became a commodity. In both works, the sentiment evoked by the passion between Marguerite and Armand has tended to obscure the unpleasantness of the grasping and cold-hearted society which used and destroyed Marie Duplessis. She was the victim of her class and her poverty, and of a degeneration in Parisian society where male lusts were justified by being paid for. The romantic image of dying of consumption (not of course romantic in any way except in an aesthetic death which enables one to sing very movingly about it) has also diverted blame from its proper goal.

Nonetheless, the transformation of life into art reflected Dumas's growing conviction that art had a moral and reforming purpose. His intention was to draw attention to the lives led by women like Marie Duplessis, and the inevitability of their early death. His view of art as being a kind of court of appeal influenced his future writing and helped to form his increasingly conservative attitudes. In the revival of *The Lady of the Camellias* in 1884, he instructed the actor who was playing Armand's father to keep his hat on during his scene with Marguerite. As it had been performed in 1852, he spoke to her with his hat in his hand. The member of the Academie Française was conscious, as the young man had not been, of the proper way to behave in the presence of a courtesan. What he *felt* as a young man for Marie Duplessis had become overlaid by ideas of social decorum: some women still had to be treated as being beyond the pale.

Dumas reread *Manon Lescaut* before starting to write his own novella, which he completed in a month. While 'the man of quality' claims to be publicising Des Grieux's tale as a warning against the dangers of violent passions, the narrator of *The Lady of the Camellias* (the person to whom Armand Duval tells his story) is driven by a desire to reform a society which accepts the use and abandonment of women such as Marguerite Gautier. The romantic introspection of *Werther* and *Adolphe* has been replaced by a more circumspect view of society; the roles of women in it are determined largely by their possession of wealth or their need of money to survive. Later in the century, Zola and Tolstoy will explore the abyss into which women with no secure position in society can fall. Dumas, like G.B. Shaw in *Mrs Warren's Profession*, conceals some of the unpleasantness of his tale by papering it over with a drama of sentiment and allowing his central characters a temporary escape from the vice and corruption of the city into the continuing peace and tranquillity of the countryside. Unlike Manon, Marguerite can be happy returning to a way of life familiar from childhood, which also frees her from the agitation her health can no longer tolerate. Feelings which express themselves naturally in the country are turned into corrupted emotions in Paris, identified with the hot-house flowers that Marguerite wears.

Dumas uses narrative techniques already familiar in the novella, but he gives them an added complexity. The narrator – and the man who writes down the story of Marguerite and Armand – is telling a story he knows to be true, and which could be confirmed by other participants; his position is unique because he alone possesses the final details which conclude Marguerite's story. Unlike the narrator in *Manon Lescaut* he does not simply write down what he hears. As an investigator whose curiosity has been aroused, he wants to find out the whole of Marguerite's story. Only in its completion can his obsession with her, though not Armand's, be transcended; and for him that inevitably is an act of memory.

In some ways (though not in structure) the narrative may

usefully be compared with *The Princess of Clèves*. The difference between the 'Princess' and the 'Lady' (itself ironic in English) indicates the transition in setting from the Court to the *haute bourgeoisie*, reflecting a change in the representative cultural context. In both, Paris, its codes of behaviour, its social and sexual mores, presides over individual destiny like a goddess of the classical world. In the Court of the seventeenth century, sexual intrigue went hand in hand with the struggle for power and influence; by the mid-nineteenth century the pursuit of pleasure in and for itself predominated. Power in the public world does not concern the inhabitants of the demi-monde in their search for private gratification. Like the majority of the children of the rich, reality exists for them only in private worlds, and not in the world of work.

On 12 March 1847, the narrator sees a yellow placard announcing a sale of furniture and curiosities the following week at 9 Rue d'Antin. He calls to preview the sale and realises at once that he is in the home of a courtesan, whose opulent way of life is now being exposed to the scrutiny of respectable society women. He is fascinated by the details of the kept woman's bedroom, with its gifts engraved with coronets and the initials of the French nobility. These objects, so personal and now up for sale, fill him with a sense of regret for the ephemerality of human lives, at once detailed and unique (these were the very combs she used) and quickly abandoned, leaving behind a kind of detritus, the few remaining signs of how this life was lived. These objects – memorably observed in Zefirelli's film of *La Traviata* – also initiate the reader into a kind of fetishism in the novella, which reduces people to objects which are acquired and discarded. Consumption, and being consumed, are one and the same for the courtesan; and the love she is capable of feeling is doomed by a social milieu from which she is for ever excluded. Dumas's sense of things includes the materiality of persons. It would be better, he reflects, to pass over such things in silence if it was not essential to reveal from time to time the martyrdom of those who are condemned without a hearing and scorned without a proper judgement. He asks to whom the possessions have belonged, and learns the identity of the owner whom he has known.

Her sudden death has brought about the need for the sale to pay off her creditors. (The crimes which supported Manon and

Des Grieux, and the jewels which they stole, were petty indeed
compared with the sums now needed to support a woman like
like Marguerite Gautier.)² The necessity for the sale also reminds
him that Marguerite was a woman who only had friends when
she was well and able to serve their purposes. Dumas's contempt
for the hardheartedness of the rich is matched by his dislike of
the deceits and evasions through which society preserves its own
image of respectability.

The sight of Marguerite's possessions laid out for sale recalls
to the narrator's mind all that he knew of her, her association
with the camellias which she always wore – twenty five days in
the month they were white, and the rest red – an enigma about
her which he still cannot explain.³ As in Proust, the instinctive or
involuntary memory aroused by the association of objects engen-
ders the narrative, and a curiosity about completing the tale.

At the auction, the narrator bids for a copy of *Manon Lescaut*,
in which he discovers the words: 'Manon to Marguerite, Humility.' It is signed by Armand Duval. He can then make little of the
inscription, but he knows *Manon Lescaut* in detail; and he finds
in the heroine's life a comparison with Marguerite's which
touches him deeply. Manon dies in the arms of her lover in the
desert; Marguerite dies in the desert created for her by a society
without pity or kindness.

Marguerite's sister, a fat country girl who has never before left
her village, comes to Paris and collects, to her astonishment,
50,000 Francs from the proceeds of the sale. The immensity of the
sum symbolises the divergence of family life, and the degree to
which Marguerite has become estranged from her roots in the
country. She has become quite literally déracinée, estranged
from her past, valued only for the price which men will pay to
support her.

The copy of *Manon Lescaut* which the narrator has bought
becomes the link between him and Armand Duval, who comes to
ask it of him – reinforcing once more the supreme importance of
objects in Dumas's world.⁴ While there, he starts to tell the story
of his love for Marguerite by showing the narrator her last letter
to him. We are thus again hearing the end of the story before the
beginning, a technique which makes us view the following narrative, as in *Manon Lescaut*, through the perspective of an
irreparable loss. In addition to confirming that Armand has

given her the only happy moments in her life, Marguerite reveals she has kept a journal for Armand to read after her death. This journal forms the final section of the novella, which the narrator copies without adding or omitting a syllable (again a token of its authenticity), while Armand sleeps, worn out by his recounting what has occurred. The story is gathered from various narrative sources; each of them reinforces the vision of a society, cruel and indifferent to those it makes use of. In this way Marguerite assumes a symbolic force, not just as the woman who is forgotten as soon as she is not desired, but as the woman sacrificed to the desires of those whom she serves.

Although some time passes before the narrator meets Armand again, his curiosity about Marguerite leads him to make his own inquiries about her. While he feels pity for Armand, his real interest lies in the courtesan's life; and the nature of the feelings which her way of life arouses in her, and others. According to the conventional view, 'love' is beyond them; Dumas's depiction of such a woman as being capable of deep and generous feeling caused much of the indignation aroused by his work.

When the narrator meets Armand Duval again, he has become so obsessed by Marguerite's death that he has arranged for her body to be moved from the cemetery where she is buried so that he can see her once more. The narrator accompanies him on this bizarre expedition which reveals the remnants of a familiar beauty eaten away by mortality. 'The eyes were only two holes, the lips had disappeared, and the white teeth were clenched against one another. The long hair, black and dry, was pressed on the forehead, and partly concealed the green hollows of the cheeks; and yet I recognised in this face, the joyous white and pink of the face I had seen so often.'[5] The possessiveness of desire is consummated in this graveyard scene; in death she belongs to him as she has never been able to do in her life.

A psychosomatic illness overwhelms Armand, as it had Des Grieux. When he recovers he starts to tell his story in earnest. This reconstruction in memory serves as an exorcism, and also as a re-enactment of the myth of passion which is fulfilled in death. In the graveyard scene, with its suggestion of necrophilia, Armand attempts to cheat death of its victory, only to prove more conclusively its triumph. The fragility and impermanence of life is contrasted with the 'testament' of art in which desire is re-

newed, each time the tale is read or the opera performed. In
Verdi's musical transcription, the farewell to Paris ('Parigi, o
cara, noi lasceremo') becomes a promise of eternal return to the
happpiness they have known. But we are also aware that in the
social perspective of this tale there exists the foetid air of corruption and decay.

When Armand is first introduced to Marguerite in her box at
the theatre (ironically, in the light of the play's success, she never
shows any interest in the performance), he reacts with anger to
the mockery with which he believes he has been treated. His
companion explains to him that behaviour like this is to be
expected from such women. 'They do not know what style and
politeness are. It is as if you were to offer perfumes to dogs – they
would think they smelled bad, and go to roll in the gutter.'[6]

Armand's character derives its sympathy not just from his
rejection of such attitudes, but from his being untouched by
them. It enables him to establish a relationship with Marguerite,
different to those with her other lovers, which exists (or attempts
to) without reference to the social environment in which they
live. The isolation which he attempts to create around his passion
for Marguerite is born partly from jealousy, but also from the
desire to distance her from that milieu in which she is used.
Marguerite is touched by his act of kindness when he calls
anonymously to ask after her when she is ill. As she admits, 'from
the moment we can no longer serve the vanity or the pleasure of
our lovers, they abandon us. Long nights follow long days, as I
know too well. I was in bed for two months, and after three weeks
no one came any longer to visit me.'[7] As Roland Barthes has
argued, what Marguerite needs is not love but recognition; as a
'femme entretenue' she is permanently excluded from the class
of her masters.[8] But when illness keeps them away she loses the
only identity she possesses which is conferred by their recognition of her. Armand's kindness is not altogether disinterested.
His desire for her is 'appropriative' in that while he is capable of
being her companion as well as her lover, he cannot remove the
social barriers which keep them apart. His desire for her is
aroused by a desire to save her from a way of life unworthy of her
and at the same time to claim her for himself. The obstacles to
his desire also inflame it. 'I felt almost sad seeing this beautiful
creature of twenty, drinking, talking like a docker, and laughing

the more loudly the more scandalous was the joke.'[9] As for Des Grieux, the vanity in his love is offended by the role Marguerite has to play. Marguerite is more realistic. Unlike Manon, she is seen from within, and her otherness, although not accepted by Armand, is perceived by Dumas: an otherness created out of her knowledge that she is under sentence of death. 'Come and see me, we will laugh and chat, but don't exaggerate what I am worth, for I am worth very little.'[10] Her terms for accepting him as a lover are that he must be confiding, submissive and discreet. By submissive, she means obedient to her commands, 'because I shall not live as long as others, and I have promised myself to live more quickly'.[11] This 'quickness' of living depends on the money with which her lovers provide her, and a way of life which she despises, but cannot avoid. 'If those who start in on our shameful business only knew what it really was like, they would rather be chambermaids. But no! The vanity of having clothes, carriages, diamonds seduces us … and one fine day one dies like a dog in a ditch, after having ruined others, and ruined one's self.'[12] Her need for recognition is quite literally desperate; but the problem of identity which her role creates is only a foreshortening of the crisis of identity created by her approaching death. Ironically, in the face of this, Armand still believes in the redemptive power of his love to save her from her way of life. Dumas's skill lies in the interlacing of narratives which are on the one hand of social import, and on the other, common to all human lives, as Tolstoy was to realise in his Arzamas nightmare. What is the significance of the 'I' subject to the dissolution of mortality?

Armand's desire to possess her for himself alone overlooks the scale of her need for money. His anger at her failure to give up her other lovers is seen by her as a different kind of failure in him. She is 40,000 Francs in debt, has no money of her own, and spends 100,000 Francs a year. She reproaches him for not understanding this; and even more for what she describes as a failure of 'the intelligence of the heart'. She wanted him to be the man she longed for in her noisy solitude, the man who did not treat her as a thing, and he has failed her.

As a gesture of reconciliation he sends her a copy of *Manon Lescaut*, inscribed from 'Manon to Marguerite; Humility.' It implies his recognition that he has failed in 'intelligence of the heart'; and also his acceptance of a role subject to Marguerite's will. The inscription, with its change of gender and its identification with a figure incapable of fidelity, asserts an acceptance of otherness (and the cash-nexus) which will prove destructive of him. His life, previously so calm, becomes disordered and chaotic, as well as expensive beyond his means. In three and a half months she costs him a year's income, and if he is not to leave her (which is unthinkable) he has to find a new source of money and a way of assuaging his jealousy. Passion always requires new fires on which to stoke itself up. 'Gambling diverted the fever which would otherwise have taken hold in my heart, and fixed it upon a passion which gripped me in spite of myself, until the hour struck when I might go to my mistress.'[13] Unsatisfied desire makes it necessary for Armand to find a way of slaking his emotion through a substitute. Without Marguerite, he would have had no need to gamble, just as Marguerite, free of consumption, would have been free of death. For both of them, Paris acts as the catalyst; and from Paris they attempt to make their escape.

To Marguerite, the country represents the wholly different kind of life she has known in her childhood (here idealised as compared with the real life-story of Marie Duplessis). The happiness she affects to feel for Parisian life conceals an increasing weariness; she longs for the peaceful life she associates with her country childhood. To attempt to relive this idyll she persuades the Duke who is her patron to take a country-house at Bougival, in time installing Armand there too. Like Count P. in *Adolphe*, the Duke offers to forgive her, provided that she will leave Armand. Reading *Manon Lescaut* she notes that when a woman loves she cannot do as Manon does and leave her lover when money runs short. At Bougival they are now enclosed in the privacy which passion requires, but at the cost of pretending that the real world no longer exists. The curtains in the country house remain closed during the day. 'We were like two obstinate divers who only came to the surface to take breath.'[14] Marguerite, though, cannot share Armand's peace of mind. He has taken her away from one way of life, and let her taste another, so that she feels she would die if she had to return to what she previously endured. But while he has succeeded in his desire of 'possessing' her, she knows the falseness of a haven, without money or contact. He lacks the power to break down the iron doors closed against them: their seclusion at Bougival expresses society's rejection of them, as much as their rejection of society. Their relationship, seen as myth, not as personal anecdote, has only one ending.

Armand notices the disappearance of valuables from the house and goes to Paris to find out what is happening to them. Their friend, Prudence a modiste, tells him the extent of Marguerite's debts. She is stripping herself of everything she owns, rather than be unfaithful to him. Prudence advises Armand not to try to borrow the 30,000 Francs which are necessary, but to let Marguerite return to Paris. He has lived with her alone for four or five months, and that is enough. 'Shut your eyes now, that is all that is asked of you.'[15] Armand rejects this advice, with all its urban sophistication and venality. But the world outside will not leave the lovers alone. Armand's father summons his son to see him, and orders him to leave his mistress. At the age of twenty-four he is in danger of risking his whole career.[16] His love will not last, and news of his scandalous way of life has already reached the quiet countryside where the family lives. As in *Manon Lescaut*, the tradition of family life and its values are associated with the countryside, while Paris is associated with corruption and waste. Armand's father appeals to his son's common sense, practicality and honour. When he is rejected he leaves, believing his son to be mad.

As the narrative is being told by Armand, the reader does not discover, until Marguerite's own journal is revealed at the end of the narrative, how Armand's father achieves their separation. When Armand goes back to Bougival and finds the house empty, he assumes that Marguerite has gone to Paris, and taken a lover. But at the Rue d'Antin he finds only emptiness. 'I listened at the door, trying to detect a sound, a movement. Nothing. The silence of the country seemed to be present there. I opened the door and entered. All the curtains were tightly drawn.'[17] This transference of the attributes of the house in Bougival to Paris indicates the fixity of Armand's perception of their relationship as something outside normal experience, closed against the world, but now emptied of its significance. 'The curtains opened, a pale light made its way in. I rushed to the bed. It was empty. I opened the doors one by one. I visited every room. No one. It was enough to drive one mad.'[18] And mad is what Armand nearly becomes – like des Grieux – when he receives Marguerite's note telling him, without explanation, that she has left him. Once again, he takes refuge in the country: this time with his father, who, though Armand does not yet know it, has brought about their separation. The spareness of Dumas's style in the scene of Armand's return has much in common with a film-script, and its dramatic effectiveness is at once apparent. More interestingly, the fixity of emotion, associated with sexual obsession, is reflected here in the expectation of permanence, and permanent presence, in the now empty apartments. Armand is maddened by the recognition that where he relied on fixity, change has occurred.

The breaking of a 'habit' which has formed the centre of his life interrupts all life's other functions for a time; he becomes 'decentred', until the obsession to see her again revives. Marguerite has returned to her old way of life, with money given by the Comte de N. His desire for revenge upon her prevents him from seeing that her frenzied existence is an attempt to stamp out the memory of him and her former happiness, as well as to obliterate the knowledge of her rapidly approaching death. As his revenge, Armand takes a new mistress, flaunting her in Parisian society and in Marguerite's eyes. Olympe discovers that she can get whatever she wants from Armand by insulting Marguerite at every opportunity, and she does so with relish. As Armand knows, his cruelty to Marguerite is a form of madness and self-bewilderment which must burn itself out; it is proof of his continuing obsession with her. Memory becomes too painful to bear and needs itself to be rewritten, or at least overlaid with new experience.

In these later chapters of the novella, passion is seen in its destructive aspect, as containing a great deal of hate. Rejection arouses the desire for revenge and the enjoyment of humiliation. Ironically for Armand, his hate arises from a misconception of Marguerite's motive in leaving him, which he will only come to understand after her death.

Marguerite reveals in her journal how Armand's father has visited her, pleading that she should sacrifice her love for Armand's future: a future and a career which would be ruined if they stayed together. Even more irresistibily, however, he pleads on behalf of his daughter. The family of the man to whom she is betrothed have made it a condition of the marriage proceeding that Armand give up his present way of life. 'She enters an honourable family which requires that all should be honourable in mine.'[19] The claims of middle-class morality and respectability are set against whatever claims Marguerite might make for her own happiness and well-being. Nothing can alter the fact that she is a kept woman and, as such, feels no right to dream of a future. Neither society's views nor her past can be changed. To participate in securing the happiness of Armand's sister gives her a pride in herself, which for the moment obliterates the memory of her own happiness with him. It is another way of achieving the 'recognition' she so much desires; and of identifying herself with that 'respectable' society from which she is for ever excluded. She is also continuing to serve her masters by flattering their sense of what it is decent to do. In acting as she does, she turns Armand's love to hate and sets up a barrier between them which will only be overcome with her death. The tragedy cannot resemble that in Racine because it has not been determined by character or fate, but only by money and class; and desire is being structured or restructured by the pressures of convention. The act of self-sacrifice nonetheless is illustrative of a generosity of feeling in Marguerite, which is held separate in the novella from her way of life, as though her body and mind can be violated by society, but not her soul.

As death approaches, Marguerite's 'friends' continue to bring her presents in the hope that one day she will become their mistress. Only Armand's father continues to show her generosity, in Armand's absence, revealing how even the usual parental disapproval of such relationships can be transformed by a recognition of the discrepancy between the social role and the person within it, and the inadequacy of labels (and language) to define personality.

The account of Marguerite's last hours is written down by her companion, Julie Duprat, in the place where she died so that she can give it to Armand, on his return, in all its 'melancholy exactitude'. Once again, the appeal is to the reader's sense of the accuracy and truth of what is being told. And this is further underlined by the narrator, who writes down Armand's account of his relationship with Marguerite just as it has been told him, claiming, as its merit, the fact that it is true. He justifies his relation of it on the grounds that it exemplifies how a woman like

Marguerite was capable of experiencing a 'serious love' for which
she suffered, and in the end died. Her breaking with Armand,
and her subsequent return to the excesses of Parisian life, hastened her end. Unlike many narratives in contemporary fiction,
the fragments from which the portrait of Marguerite's life and
death are built up confirm each other, and Dumas's obsessions:
the indifference of a society which uses women like Marguerite
as long as it is flattering and pleasant to do so, but has no interest
in them beyond self-gratification; and his desire to explore those
feelings in Marguerite which survive her way of life. Although
these are largely mediated through Armand, and are to be read
as his point of view, they are also confirmed by her journal, and
by the response of Armand's father and the narrator to her. The
force of the novella comes from its desire to change society, so
that the abuse of women as courtesans may come to an end; but
also from a deeper intuitive sense of what Marguerite is like, and
a recognition of the generosity of which she is capable.

The objects which Marguerite collects, and which are so
quickly disposed of at her death, represent a personal life which
has no true 'personality' other than that which is conferred by the
vanity of others. As these objects adorn her rooms for a time, so
she as an object adorns the lives of her lovers for a time. When
Armand finally leaves Bougival, he notes: 'At last I left the room,
where the smallest object was invested with that melancholy
appearance which the anxious loneliness of the heart gives to all
which surrounds it.'[20]

*

The Lady of the Camellias is not without its faults of sentimentality, and rather surprisingly ends on a note of pietism (Marguerite dies a Christian, after receiving the last rites). It also depicts
a way of life and a society now passed. At the same time it
dramatises an increasing estrangement brought about in the
urban society of the nineteenth century by money and class,
which particularly affects the role of women once they move
outside the position in the hierarchy to which they are born: an
estrangement equally from themselves and from their background. Marguerite can never belong to the high bourgeoisie of
Paris, except as a courtesan. Her chance in life derives from

playing this role as extravagantly and exuberantly as possible; but she can only be alienated by it from herself, her family, and from society too. Playing her role means ironically an increasing alienation, a kind of inner wasting, of which her consumption is a metaphor. Armand's situation, like that of the Chevalier Des Grieux, is entirely different; he has no need of recognition because he belongs to society, and while his actions are wayward (like those of all young men having their fling) his social position is never imperilled. (His father's appeal to Marguerite is significantly on behalf of his daughter whose position in society is threatened not by her brother's behaviour but by his association with her: in this society the women are more vulnerable at every move than the men.) In all these representations of passion, the burden of guilt and disapproval is seen to fall more heavily on the woman, whatever her role in initiating the relationship, as, for example, Ellenore certainly is not.

Armand's desire to possess Marguerite for himself alone – to appropriate her – is symbolised by the move to Bougival, and their way of life there; for her, the move means something quite different. It signifies an attempt to return to the security and tranquillity of childhood, to eradicate her adult past, and to recover an identity buried by the role she has been forced to play as a means of survival. It is an attempt to recover from a violation of herself in a situation which can only superficially mimic the past.

Marguerite's consumption provides an escape-route from a social situation where reconciliation is impossible. Death was needed to poeticise their love, and to complete the myth of passion embodied in it. Armand's obsession with her can only be transcended when she is dead, and through the figure of the surrogate narrator reconstructed in memory. In this novella, as in others, the narrative retains its dramatic intensity by focussing on an obsession; but also through the figures of Prudence, the ageing and discarded procuress, and Marguerite's wealthy lovers, observing the power exerted by this society over its young lovers.

The novella reflects the uneasiness of Dumas's position. As the son of a famous and lionised father, he was in society; as a young man he revolted against what he saw. His position was not unlike that of Oscar Wilde, who warned, 'Never speak disrespectfully of society; only those who cannot get into it do that'; but who also recognised from the inside its hardness of heart, its cruelty, and its power to destroy. The more rigid the boundaries of caste, the less Eros can act as a free agent; and the greater are likely to be the disruptions when he tries to do so. Barthes is right to see such a situation as being not tragic, but the product of a difference between the direction in which instinct leads, and the restraints which society places upon its fulfilment. Society intervenes between the psyches that Eros has joined together, and only beyond death can that intervention be transcended. Or in its reconstruction through memory.

Leo Tolstoy: *The Kreutzer Sonata*

After the mind has been poisoned, it needs physical antidotes ....
Stendhal, *Scarlet and Black*

As long as mankind shall endure, it has an ideal to strive for and
its ideal is certainly not that of rabbits and swine, which is to
multiply as often as possible, nor that of apes and Parisians, which
is to enjoy sexual pleasure with the highest possible degree of
refinement.   H. Troyat, *Tolstoy*

And when Raymond of Rousillon heard the song that Guillaume
had made for his wife, he made him come and talk to him far from
the castle, and cut off his head, and put it in a game-bag; he took
the heart from his body and put it with the head. He returned to
the castle, and had the heart roasted and brought it to his wife at
table, and made her eat it unawares.   Stendhal, *Love*

On 3 July 1887 Tolstoy listened to a performance of Beethoven's
Kreutzer Sonata, given by his son playing the violin and his
teacher from the Moscow Conservatory. Tolstoy was deeply
moved by the music, the scherzo of which reduced him to tears.
It also aroused in him the sensuality which he objected to in the
effect of art on others. His wife recorded in her diary for that
night that he had become the 'affectionate and tender Lyovochka
of old'.[1] A few weeks later she discovered she was pregnant, with
her thirteenth child; and in September of the same year the
couple celebrated their silver wedding anniversary. Tolstoy recorded in his notebook of his long marriage: 'It could have been
better!'[2]

The novella was sketched out between March and May of 1888,
and after a further period of gestation completed and revised the
following year. The storms which it caused in his life and marriage were only just beginning. As usual he gave it to Sonya, his
wife, to copy from his almost illegible manuscript. What she read

as a silver-wedding present was a passionate denunciation of sexual love, of marriage and procreation, as well as an argument for the chastity her husband showed no inclination to practise. She also recognised much in the story, with the exception of the murder, as being autobiographical. With her husband now revered as a sage, surrounded by disciples, sycophants and parasites, visited by pilgrims, sought out by the famous, she faced the prospect of their marriage becoming the object of ridicule. While he advocated chastity, she continued to bear him children and saw marriage proclaimed as no better than 'legalised prostitution'.

As soon as Sonya had finished her copying, the book was taken to Moscow, and within a short time a further eight hundred lithographed copies[3] were in circulation: numbers which rapidly grew as the work circulated round the country, provoking intense discussion. 'How are you?' it was said, was replaced by 'Have you read *The Kreutzer Sonata?*' Sonya's sense of humiliation was profound: 'Deep in my own heart, I always felt that the book was directed against me, mutilated me and humiliated me in the eyes of the whole world, and was destroying everything we had preserved of love for one another. And yet never once in my entire married life have I made a single gesture or given a single glance for which I need feel guilty towards my husband.'[4]

In 1890 *The Kreutzer Sonata* was banned from publication. Sonya, although still infuriated by the discrepancy between how her husband lived and what he preached, defended him fiercely from outside attack. She also resented the financial loss if Volume XIII of the Collected Works, which included *The Kreutzer Sonata*, could not be published, invoking Tolstoy's further condemnation for her mercenariness.

Sonya decided to seek an audience with the Tsar to plead for the ban to be lifted. When she was received by him in St Petersburg, she pleaded in spite of her personal humiliation for the story's moral conviction – a plea that resulted in her being authorised to publish the work. She received little thanks from her husband other than the revival of his sexual desire after her fifteen days' absence. Meanwhile her husband continued to record his low opinion of women: 'To say that a woman has as much strength of character as a man, or that one can find in women what one can expect to find in men, is to deceive oneself.'[5]

Tolstoy's hostility to marriage was nothing new in his work. In War and Peace, Prince Andrew warns Pierre fiercely against marriage: 'Never, never marry, my dear fellow! ... Marry when you are old and good for nothing – or all that is good and noble in you will be lost. It will be wasted on trifles.'⁶ Pierre's marriage to Natasha, when it eventually occurs, turns out to be less than perfect. The same is true of Levin's and Kitty's marriage in *Anna Karenina*. Not only do the bad marriages turn out to be very bad, but the good marriages turn out to be pretty bad too! As in Tolstoy's life, the demands of family and home remain incompatible with the man's inner and spiritual needs. 'Pierre was greatly surprised by his wife's view, to him a perfectly novel one, that every moment of his life belonged to her and to the family ....'⁷

The discrepancy between Tolstoy's views and his own life, shocking though it is, has never obliterated the extraordinary power of *The Kreutzer Sonata*, as Chekov recognised at once. He thought it hardly possible to find anything of equal importance, for its conception or beauty of execution, being written either in Russia or abroad. Apart from its artistic merits, the story was thought-provoking, and even when reading it made one exclaim, 'That is the truth!' or 'That is absurd!'

The sacrifice of women to male lust and vanity in *The Lady of the Camellias* was portrayed as part of the corruption of Parisian society. What a 'pagan' society permitted led to disease and death; married love had no place in its critique of the passions. Tolstoy's denunciation is more radical, subversive, and in one sense modern, because it centres upon what happens within marriage, when the only bond is the satisfaction of desire, and where passion requires new stimulation to remain alive. Tolstoy prefigures the twentieth century in that his critique of passion derives not from moral laws – although he always claimed to be pursuing a higher ideal – but from his awareness of its psychopathology, its obsessiveness and fixity, of which he himself was the victim throughout his long married life. Although Tolstoy's ideas are rooted in nineteenth-century beliefs and practice, his obsession with the relationship between sexuality and violence has remained central to Western literature, and is among the most common preoccupations of contemporary cinema. The overcoming of passion frequently involves the murder of the person who is its object.

Tolstoy believed that the solution to the 'disease' of his marriage, with its recurrent sexuality, lay in abandoning his wife, which he was still trying to do when he died. Then, as in *The Kreutzer Sonata*, the memory of desire caused him to wrestle with the problem of passion which had so long obsessed him. In the novella, unlike life, he was able to transform the desire into an aesthetic emotion. His hero becomes capable of telling his own story. For his creator there was only the silence of death.

Long train-journeys produce odd bed-fellows. In Russia, as in India, they provoke conversation between strangers. Some remain till the end of the story and the journey; others comment and are gone. 'It was early spring, and the second day of our journey. Passengers going short distances entered and left our carriage, but three others, like myself, had come all the way with the train.'[8] Tolstoy's voice, 'like Nature itself ', begins a story which will contain much that is unnatural, with a realism that cannot be argued with. The 'I' is only part of that corporate 'we' travelling together, amongst whom a dispute about women and marriage will arise. The 'I' is also the observant eye, who notices the differences between his travelling companions, and in particular singles out the prematurely grey man, with his glittering eyes, who emits a sound 'something like a clearing of his throat, or a laugh begun and sharply broken off '.[9] In time, this first 'I' will also become the attentive listener to Pózdnyshev's tale, the one traveller who in the long reaches of the night is held enthralled by his terrible confession, as we are. The coming of fresh passengers, the closing of the window, the entry of the conductor who in the first light of dawn snuffs out the candle which has burnt down, the snoring of the clerk, keep reconfirming the ordinariness of the circumstances against which the central narrative is told, vouching once again for its authenticity.

Pózdnyshev's own story involves two railway journeys. On the first, when he decides to return home unexpectedly because he suspects his wife of being unfaithful, his jealousy turns his love to hate, as his mind is filled with terrible images of what has occurred in his absence. On the second journey he relives that experience in memory, re-enacting and intensifying his fantastic aberrations as though the journey itself helps to recall its full horror to him.

When his story is done, he will lie down on his seat, covering himself with his cloak, only to be woken at eight in the morning by the companion who has watched and listened throughout the night as he leaves the train. 'I touched him with my hand. He uncovered his face, and I could see he had not been asleep.'[10] He attempts a smile so piteous that the listener is ready to weep. In saying good-bye he also repeats his plea that he may be forgiven.

Unlike other novellas, no indication is given as to how Pózdnyshev's tale comes to be written down and published. We must assume that the listener gripped by the tale wants also to make a plea for the lessons it seems to teach; and so of course it was with Tolstoy. But the great artist and story-teller has not forgotten also how to fix his reader with his glittering eye. What might have been a piece of moral preaching becomes an impassioned plea born out of the 'suffering' from which passion is by definition inseparable. The hero who has overcome his desire comes together with his creator in the conclusion of the tale, and becomes capable of writing his story. To quote René Girard, 'the inspiration always comes from memory and memory springs from the conclusion'. The final image of the narrator is not however of someone who has found a new beginning in the conclusion of his tale. The breadth of vision which he has discovered is based on a largely imposssible rejection: not of the world as in *The Princess of Clèves* but of marriage and sexuality as he believes it to be. The man travelling on in the train resembles no one so much as the Tolstoy who will attempt to flee from his own family, his problems and his conflicts with them unresolved. The Other whom he created in his novella is like Oedipus calling down curses upon his own head.

The conversation in the railway carriage which acts as a prologue to the main narrative asserts in a variety of ways the distance between Russia, in its still feudal and often Asiatic attitudes, and Western Europe. A lawyer who has returned from the West announces that Europe is preoccupied with the question of divorce; in Russia too it is becoming more common. To the old man in the carriage this illustrates the socially subversive effects of education; a view which prompts an outburst from the lady against the continuing practice in Russia of arranged marriages, where the bride and bridegroom do not even see each other before the wedding. To the old man what matters in marriage is that the woman should fear her husband and love him as a matter of course. A woman's infidelity only occurs because the husband has not pulled her up properly from the first, beating her if necessary. The lawyer admits that in Russia people are still a long way from the European view of marriage; but the lady's view that a marriage is no marriage without love provokes Pózdnyshev to enter the conversation with a much more subversive question. Love involves a preference for one above everyone else – but preference for how long? 'A month, two days or half an hour?' To the man of glittering eyes, a preference for one above all others for a life-time only occurs in novels; and if it happened to one partner, it would not in the real world happen to both. People go on getting married, appearing to believe in marriage as a sacrament; but because they don't, marriage results in deception and coercion. When the worst happens, they undertake to live with each other all their lives, and begin to hate each other after a month. This leads to that 'terrible hell which makes people take to drink, shoot themselves, and kill or poison themselves or one another ...'.[11] The lawyer admits that there are critical episodes in any married life. Pózdnyshev then claims they must have realized who he is, that man who in a critical episode killed his wife. The embarrassment of the travellers causes the lady and the lawyer to seek another compartment, and the clerk to fall asleep. Only the first 'I' remains to listen, if the tale is not too painful to tell; for Pózdnyshev, on the contrary, 'it is painful for me to be silent'.[12]

In this narrative, more than others, we are aware how the rhetoric of confession and self-justification is being added to the rhetoric of passion. The earlier part of the narrative is concerned entirely with this, as neither his wife nor any other character enters his tale, except as the abstract personification of what marriage involves. But in the lithographed version Tolstoy had written a passage, later deleted, of acute observation about the effect of such a confessional narrative on the human face. 'During his narration his face completely changed several times so that nothing resembling the former face remained: his eyes, his mouth, his moustache and even his beard were all different – it was a beautiful, touching new face. These changes occurred suddenly in the dim light, and for some five minutes there was one face and it was impossible to see the former face, and then, one did not know how, another face appeared and again it was impossible to see it otherwise.'[13] In this passage, suppressed perhaps because Tolstoy wanted the power of the narrative to speak for itself, he nonetheless observed the transformations which can occur in a human face wrestling with the drama of inner emotions, and the pain involved in attempting to exorcise a passion by reliving it. It is this which the close focus of the novella presents.

Pózdnyshev begins by saying that he must tell his tale from the beginning; but what he tells is a generalised account of the lives led by young men of his class, and background. His story begins in adolescence, when he is not quite sixteen, an age which has been seen to recur in these novellas of passion, concerned with awakening desire. Two years earlier he has been 'depraved' by other boys, and he is tormented by erotic fantasies; but he has not laid hands on another human being until with his brother he visits a brothel. That starts a life of debauchery – which still enables him to think of himself as quite a moral man, and no more dissolute than his contemporaries – by removing the moral considerations involved in sex with a woman, through paying her money. (As in *The Lady of the Camellias*, the commercialisation of sex is instrumental in causing disaster; but Tolstoy offers no touching sentiment to soften the perspective.) He believes this kind of sex to be good for his health and not to involve the risk of disease, for a paternal government has seen to it that the women are regularly examined and not permitted to continue with their trade when infected. In a ballroom, young men who live like this are thought to be emblems of charm and purity; and the daughters of the wealthy are released into society for the purpose of attracting a husband from among such young men.[14]

Pózdnyshev continued with this life of debauchery until he was thirty, always intending to marry eventually and live an elevated and pure family life. The excess and normality of this way of living is, as Tolstoy sees it, distinctively Russian and peculiar to the military, aristocratic caste to which he belongs, where the ability to drink heavily and visit brothels proves manliness. In *War and Peace* he shows this as being as normal for a sensitive and intelligent man like Pierre Bezukov, as for rakes like Kuragin and Dolokhov. The spirit of this way of life informs *The Kreutzer Sonata* and distinguishes it from the novellas of Western Europe. The shaping of desire reflects once more the social conditions in which it occurs.

When Pózdnyshev becomes engaged, he shows to the young girl (as Tolstoy had to Sonya the night before their wedding) a journal in which he has recorded how he has lived. 'I remember her horror, despair and confusion, when she learnt of it and understood it. I saw that she then wanted to give me up. And why did she not do so?'[15]

His whole way of life, he claims, has been organised so as to stimulate desire: an excess of food, combined with physical idleness; young girls dressed up and paraded so as to intensify their allurement. Seen like this, the life of the upper classes is no better than that in a brothel, and all too often involves a form of jousting with death.

Falling in love is brought about by excesses of sensuality. The girl is no better than a slave in a bazaar, or the bait in a trap, engaged in catching a husband. Spontaneity of desire has been reduced to the slaking of an appetite. The goal of desire becomes a passionate iteration to which the most frequent obstacle and stimulus becomes a quarrel.

Even on his honeymoon with the girl whom he had married out of love, the abyss between them opens up. 'Amorousness was exhausted by the satisfaction of sensuality and we were left confronting one another in our true relation; that is as two egotists quite alien to each other who wished to get as much pleasure as possible each from the other. I call what took place between us a quarrel, but it was not a quarrel, only the consequence of the cessation of sensuality – revealing our real relations to one another.'[16] After love-making, the simplest things become the pretext for quarrelling, until the quarrelling comes to an end in further love-making. At the time Pózdnyshev believes that this hellish cycle from which they cannot break free is true of his own marriage only. 'I did not know then that it is our common fate, but that everybody imagines just as I did, that it is their peculiar misfortune ....'[17]

As he reveals at the end of his story, only during the eleven months spent in prison awaiting trial does he begin to *understand* what has happened to him – how irrelevant the knife was with which he killed his wife on the fifth of October; and how he killed her much earlier. Pózdnyshev here approaches close to the view of love which Oscar Wilde was to express only a few years later in *The Ballad of Reading Gaol*:

> Some love too little, some too long,
> Some sell, and others buy;
> Some do the deed with many tears,
> And some without a sigh:
> For each man kills the thing he loves,
> Yet each man does not die.[18]

In Pózdnyshev's view the killing comes about through their swinish behaviour with each other, and his own excesses which take no account of her spiritual or physical life. He singles out as particularly unnatural the continuation of sexual relations during pregnancy or when the woman is nursing her child. To this practice he attributes the numbers of women being treated for hysteria. Here, Pózdnyshev expresses Tolstoy's own ideas, which are themselves neurotic; and cast his narrative in a new light. The autobiographical element remains raw; and what Pózdnyshev remembers in trying to come to terms with what he has done fits uneasily with Tolstoy's desire to promulgate his own unbalanced ideas.

Pózdnyshev's reconstruction of his experience, his way of coming to terms with the murder he has committed, involves a persistent self-dramatisation, as the rhetoric of passion often does; in his case it involves his relations not just with his wife, but with his life and the world. Women are reduced to the role of slaves, men become prisoners of family life, doctors earn fees by giving advice about how not to conceive, which increases a woman's love of being a coquette, and so intensifies a man's feeling of jealousy. Modern theories about the psychopathology of emotions are not only dangerous but repulsive. 'Charcot would certainly have said that my wife was hysterical, and that I was abnormal, and he would no doubt have tried to cure me. But there was nothing to cure.'[19] The problem lies in the way we live in a perpetual fog, not seeing the condition we are in. He would have remained like that until his death if it had not been for what had happened, thinking he had led a good life. 'We were like two convicts hating each other and chained together, poisoning one another's lives and trying not to see it.'[20] The poison is only

released through the sacrifice of his wife's life – a crime for which
he will be acquitted in law on the grounds that he was a wronged
husband defending his outraged honour.

It is easy to read Pózdnyshev's narrative as a platform for
Tolstoy's stranger obsessions; but the debate he conducts with
himself ranges over many of the issues with which artists like
Ibsen and Strindberg were equally passionately concerned: the
struggle for power and dominance within marriage, the problem-
atic relationship between woman as mother, wife and human
being with needs different to her husband's – all of them leading
to incompatibility of viewpoint. 'The views I maintained were not
at all so dear to me that I could not have given them up; but she
was of the opposite opinion and to yield meant yielding to her and
that I could not do. It was the same with her.'[21] This fatal failure
to understand, and wilful desire not to, which leads to hatred and
violence, contains, as Pózdnyshev knows, reason and unreason,
clarity and confusion. After the murder he sees things differently
and wants to express them; but what he expresses in his recollection contains little more clarity than the confusion he claims to
have expelled. Like the man with his head in his hands at the
start of *Adolphe*, the final image of Pózdnyshev weeping himself
to sleep – or the appearance of sleep – suggests neither a mind
clarified, nor a conscience stilled. Desire as he has been taught to
experience it has come to its inevitable end in death. The obsession transcended in murder leaves memory with the burden of
trying to forgive himself, or at least accept what he has done.

His narrative moves from the general to the particular when
the family move from the country to the town for the purpose of
the children's education. Unlike previous novellas, the country
has proved no emollient. In Pózdnyshev's neurasthenic state of
mind, only his obsession affects him; but equally, his narrative
only concerns his attempt to come to terms with his obsession;
and this is intensified by the move to the town where desire is
transformed into hate by the proximity of a rival. His wife (she is
never named) has been advised by the doctors to have no more
children; and she begins to develop her other interests. 'She
again enthusiastically took to the piano which she had quite
abandoned and it all began from that.'[22] To begin with, the other
man, Trukachévski, is also anonymous, a worthless fellow, a
violinist, a semi-professional and semi-society man. As in

Chekov's story, *The Butterfly*, the dislike of the true artist for the dabbling Bohemian and philanderer is apparent; he has also recently turned up from Europe, with that softening of moral fibre, associated by many Russians, then and now, with the contamination of the West. (The figure of the lover in Paris in *The Cherry Orchard*, who wantonly uses Madame Ranevskaya, and spends all her money, exemplifies this too.) His sexual ambiguity – or at least Pózdnyshev's contempt for him as a man – is suggested by the description of his physical appearance: 'His figure was weak, though not misshapen, and he had a specially developed posterior, like a woman's, or such as Hottentots are said to have.'[23] Pózdnyshev's jealousy works by trying to emasculate his rival, and associating him with an inferior racial type.

During the trial, Pózdnyshev recalls, the case was treated as one of jealousy. In fact Trukachévski and his music were the cause of the murder. The terrible abyss into which Pózdnyshev and his wife have fallen as a result of a relationship sustained only by sexual passion has exposed them to less visible dangers. The inflammation of one kind of passion has led to another; and music by demanding a special kind of attentiveness in both performers and listeners has intensified feelings which are latent. Passion is seen as reducing the subject to a kind of tunnel vision, a state of intense subjectivity, on which the agitation of the music plays.

Once again we, with the listener in the train, are aware that this is no simple recollection, but an account of the labyrinthine ways in which an obsession, in its literal sense a bewilderment, can lead human beings to disaster. Even before the appearance of the musician they have been living in a state in which murder or suicide seem the only ways out; and where already the wife has resorted to taking opium. And perhaps perceiving Trukachévski unconsciously as a way of solving his problem (which he turns out to be) Pózdnyshev presses him to come to the house to perform with his wife, persuading himself that he does so to prove that he has no fear of his proximity to them. But Trukachévski's presence inflames his jealousy the more, as he recognises between them the flickering of that animal passion which he knows so well. He also knows how Trukachévski's talent on the violin, and the influence of music on impressionable natures as an unspoken communication, is capable of giving him the power to do whatever he likes with her. The more the presence of Trukachévski distresses him, the more he flatters him and treats him amiably, in order not to give way to his desire to kill him. In the intensity of his unsatisfied desire he has somehow to disarm his rival.

He attempts to admit his feelings about Trukachévski to his wife; but the rage which this provokes in both of them releases a terrible desire to beat her, kill her, which he assuages by smashing a glass paper-weight while she is reduced to hysterics.[24] When they are reconciled by the usual love-making, she claims that no decent woman could have any other feeling for such a man than the pleasure of his music. But it is just 'that accursed music' which Pózdnyshev sees to be working against him, by drawing them together, and by the effect on them both of playing the Kreutzer Sonata.

He dramatises, however, the effect of the music on himself, not on them. Music does not exalt the soul, according to Pózdnyshev: it has an effect, neither exalting or debasing, but producing agitation. The condition which caused Beethoven to write the Kreutzer had a meaning for him; but he does not know what that meaning is, and so it produces only agitation until it reveals something to him. 'What this new thing was that had been revealed to me I could not explain to myself, but the consciousness of this new condition was very joyous.'[25] An aesthetic emotion has for the time being taken the place of the emotion he thought that music prompted, as the narration itself does for him. Jealousy no longer torments him; he believes himself to feel what his wife is feeling, thus transferring the alleged communication from Trukachévski to himself. His new high spirits (which suggest the swings in mood of a manic depressive) are confirmed when Trukachévski, in saying good-bye after an evening's recital, says that he will not be returning to the house because of Pózd-nyshev's absence for a while at the Zemstvo meetings.

But on the second day of the meeting a letter comes from his wife in which she mentions that Trukachévski has called, and once again the 'mad beast of jealousy begins to growl in its kennel'.[26] In the night he begins to imagine them together, and to remember their faces as they played together. His thoughts go round in a circle of insoluble contradictions; and by morning he has set out for Moscow. His journey should have been completed by seven in the evening; but on account of a breakdown it takes him till midnight. During the train-journey – and this is repeated in the actual train-journey of the narration – his agitation increases, obsessing him with fantasies of what has occurred in his absence. His hatred of her is deepened by his feeling that he has a complete right to her body. 'I wanted her not to desire what she was bound to desire. It was utter insanity.'[27] His imagining of her desire is heightened by his prohibition upon it; the fruit which becomes more attractive because forbidden also becomes more deadly when he who denies sees himself as the owner. The appropriative nature of passion is intensified by the desire to cheat the rival; and desire is heightened by the presence of an obstacle to its fulfilment.

Here, as often in the recollected experience which is meant to clarify, darkness begins to descend. Pózdnyshev cannot recall what he thought or felt as he approached his home, except a premonition of something dreadful about to happen. The lights are still burning, and the footman tells him that Trukachévski is there. He feels himself become as cunning as a beast, takes off his boots, and arms himself with a knife. When he opens the door upon them eating, he relishes the terror upon their faces – and on his wife's as he interprets it, a look of irritation that love's raptures had been disturbed. As he rushes towards her, Trukachévski sees the dagger and tries to intervene. He makes for the door, and Pózdnyshev would have pursued him, had it not been ridiculous to pursue his wife's lover in his socks. In his recollection he knows he did not wish to be ridiculous but terrible.

In spite of her protestations of innocence – and because of them – he plunges the dagger into her side, realizing what he is doing with extraordinary clearness. Or, it may be, recalling what he did with the clearness which memory bestows on the chaos of an event. 'I felt, and remember, the momentary resistance of her corset and of something else, and then the plunging of the dagger into something soft ....'[28]

In prison he dwells upon that sensation, which mimics the rekindling of desire, and the knowledge that in killing a defenceless woman, he was also killing his wife. It is the horror of that realisation which comes back to haunt him, compelling him to retell his story, as though by reliving the event he can attempt to exorcise its power over him.

When he is taken to see his dying wife, he sees for the first time the human being in her, and asks to be forgiven. To her, that is rubbish. 'You have had your way ... I hate you.'[29] In the completion of his desire love has been turned irreversibly into hate. Only when he sees her in the coffin does he begin to understand what he has done, and that it cannot, as Othello also discovers, ever be remedied. If he had known what he now knows nothing would have induced him to marry her. 'I should not have married at all.'[30] Such forgiveness as there is can only come from his forlorn attempts to forgive himself. In this, as in many other respects – though not in his conclusions – Tolstoy reveals himself as a modern. Lying alone on the seat in the railway compartment, Pózdnyshev seems not far removed from Fowler in Graham Greene's *The Quiet American* whose last words are: 'How I wished there existed someone to whom I could say that I was sorry.'[31]

The many similarities between the narrative and the continuing rows and torments of Tolstoy's own marriage have led many readers to see *The Kreutzer Sonata* as a slice of autobiography and a platform for many of his more extreme ideas on sex, as well as his dislike of women. Seen like this, its achievement as a fiction is diminished. Read as a novella of passion, it traces, as Strindberg does, the catastrophe into which sexual love can lead, through a desire for possession which can never be satisfied, and an incompatibility of temperament which living together can only exacerbate. Memory renews the feeling, with the intention of coming to terms with it, explaining it away; recollection provides a way of ordering it, narrating it, even providing a measure of self-justification (he is 'legally' acquitted), but does not assuage it. Seen like this Pózdnyshev's arguments are interesting not as an expression of Tolstoy's views, but as attempts to come to terms with the suffering which he must continue to live through, and his failure to do so. Why else would he tell his travelling companion at the outset how painful it is to be silent?

As we have seen in previous novellas, the rhetorical declamation, the renewal though memory and the re-enactment are means of trying to live with what has occurred. The listener, not Pózdnyshev, leaves the train: Pózdnyshev's journey will continue until he finds some way of transcending his obsession. For the time being, as he says, it is more painful to be silent. The liberation of creativity arises out of its ordering, of forming a story, of attempting to make sense; and this is what Pózdnyshev does, creating an aesthetic emotion out of suffering in the past. It must have been doubly hard for Tolstoy's wife that she could not have that joy.

What distinguishes this novella and defines an important aspect of its Russianness is to be found in its concern with the essence of things, with a revolutionary desire to see things as other than they are, or they are deemed to be. Pózdnyshev's critique is only partly of the way society has taught him to live (his wife, in spite of not sharing his earlier sexual permissiveness, behaves no differently). The problem for both of them lies in a maladjustment in human nature, which makes them live by what is lowest in them (as he sees it), and without reference to their higher spiritual needs. This was characteristic of Tolstoy, and Tolstoy as a Russian. Stendhal saw things in a different perspective. The quotation which stands at the start of this chapter is truncated. It should read: 'After the mind has been poisoned, it needs physical antidotes, and a glass of champagne.'[32]

Thomas Mann: *Death in Venice*

To Thomas Mann, writing about human experience was incompa-
rably more important than participating in it. Between the
experience he wrote about and his own personal experience there
was an almost inconceivable disproportion, without parallel in the
history of literature. To over-simplify: he experienced next to
nothing and wrote about almost everything.
Marcel Reich-Ranicki, *Thomas Mann and His Family*

The Germans regard love as a virtue, a divine emanation, something mystical.   Stendhal, *Love*

In Thomas Mann's *Death in Venice* (1910) European art reaches
a new self-consciousness, and with it an irony directed at the
writer himself, his way of life, and the decadence of the passion
out of which his art is created. Turgenev's *First Love* purports to
be written by chance – the result of an after-dinner conversation:
and in spite of its polish and urbanity retains the spontaneous-
ness and informality which prompted it. In *Death in Venice*, the
act of writing is seen as a lifetime's dedication, wearing out body
and spirit: authoritative, controlled, intent on fame and ironically dependent on the indulgence of feelings which all who
praise the artist would condemn in the man. The notes which
Aschenbach is making for his next work at the time of his death
are surely notes for *Death in Venice* itself: for the work which
with all his self-reflecting skill he would have forged out of an
illicit passion, creating, as Mann does for him, a narrative preoccupied by, and conveying an image of, spiritual beauty. All that
Narcissus loves in the reflection of himself is transformed into a
distant Echo, as passion is translated into creativity.

We have often seen how 'the conclusion is always a memory'.
Here, the conclusion and the memory are contained in the title.
The whole novella is a memorial reconstruction of the last weeks

of Aschenbach's life, made possible by the intense intimacy with which the narrator understands the darkness of his soul. The narrator is a secret sharer, privy to far more than the previous listeners or narrators; but he simultaneously sits in judgement on the man and his passions. He never exists independently of Aschenbach, or Aschenbach of him, except in so far as Aschenbach belongs to the world which in the final words will receive the news of his death with shock and respect. The narrator who ironically conceives of Aschenbach does so from an Olympian perspective, which Aschenbach shares, as though one god is writing about another, with understanding of the flaws inherent in being a god. As for the heroes of antiquity, Aschenbach's desire is consummated in immortal fame.

Aschenbach's death concludes the novella about him, but his death completes the passion which seeks no other fulfilment, except in art; and here posthumously the narrator who is never entirely separate from him becomes the elegist for him. His narrative begins in the pluperfect: 'Gustave Aschenbach – or von Aschenbach, as he had been known officially since his fiftieth birthday – had set out ....'[1] His account is a 'resurrection', a bringing back to life, of a man whose passion belongs to the past; and as in other novellas a revivification of feelings which summarise the man and his life. Memory in returning to the obsession which has been transcended investigates the nature of the passion and its relation to the creative life which it inspired. Aschenbach's desire is inseparable from his artist life, and his sexual inclination from his creativity. Both are fulfilled in death, which confers completeness upon them; and both are revisited in the narrator's memory, in an act of eternal recurrence, conferring on Aschenbach's death the mythic status he would have wished for it.

Mann's elder brother, Heinrich – who never equalled Thomas in fame or stature as a writer – once referred to Thomas's furious passion for his own ego. And it is this which makes an independent narrator superfluous. Thomas Mann discovered everything in himself and had no need of others. He played tirelessly on the stage of his own life, inventing for himself new roles, new forms of self-dramatisation, with ceaseless attention to his fame, which Aschenbach reflects. What better setting for his death than the grandest, most sensual, beautiful and dramatic of all settings:

that of Venice itself. To walk upon such a scene and be worthy of
it was worthy of Thomas Mann himself, associated as it was with
the artist whom he most admired and envied, Richard Wagner.
A death worthy of him was inseparable from his life-long dedication to his own fame, and to his creation of himself in the eyes of
the world as the artist, like Aschenbach, who dedicated himself
tirelessly to work requiring such sustained concentration. He
believed as early as 1916 that the tragedy of Germany was
symbolised and personified by Heinrich and himself; the death of
Aschenbach symbolises the loss of a writer of equal significance
and centrality for his culture. There is a poignancy and grotesque
absurdity (a sense of which recurs in the novella) in so young a
writer figuring forth his own death in so magnified a manner.
But then the writing of Thomas Mann is nothing if not inclusive.

An Olympian vision of himself – so willingly and happily
seeing himself set up beside Goethe, and conceiving of his place
of residence as another Weimar – has bearings too upon the
nature of his sexuality and the representation of that in his
novella. His diaries and letters make no secret of his homosexual
proclivities; they exist in unresolved tension with that other
image of him as *paterfamilias*, the benign presider over his
actual family and, in later life, over the German community in
exile from National Socialism, well represented in the austere,
proud photos of him as eminent man of letters.

The depth of his attraction to young men from his early youth
until the age of seventy-five, when he once more became obsessed
(with a waiter aged seventeen) is beyond dispute. The male body
fascinated him, as Aschenbach is fascinated by Tadzio's movements, games and physical allure in *Death in Venice*. But there
was in this something unreal or not wholly realised, as Marcel
Reich-Ranicki has suggested in his account of Mann. Speaking of
his enthusiasm at the sight of a male body, Thomas Mann
ponders the 'unreal, illusionary, aesthetic nature of such a pro-
clivity, the aim of which, it would seem, is to be sought in
contemplation and admiration and which, though erotic, has no
interest in fulfilment of any kind, either intellectual or sensual'.[2]

Reich-Ranicki then goes on to ask a number of questions,
especially pertinent to *Death in Venice*. 'Was he here referring
solely to the contemplation of the male body, or was he speaking
of his type of homosexuality altogether? Despite the intensity of

his passion, it seems likely that he rejected "realization of any kind". Or would it be more accurate to say that he shrank from realization? Or perhaps simply that his markedly solipsistic homosexuality had no need of realization?"[3]

These unanswered questions bear directly upon the presentation of desire in Mann's novella; its intensity includes for the reader the awareness that it will not be realised in any way, that such a thing would be wholly inappropriate, not least because Aschenbach has been presented from the start as almost entirely solipsistic, but also because the passion involves that myth which cannot be completed except in death. The narrator's restraint and Aschenbach's contemplativeness are made necessary by the nature of the feelings concerned as much as the individuals involved. Aschenbach's desire for Tadzio, to possess his beauty in this world, has no means of being fulfilled. The poignancy of the narrative lies in the uncrossable distance between them, and its power as an image of the desire and pursuit of the whole, which cannot be realised.

Benjamin Britten's last opera, which takes Mann's novella for its libretto, achieves a parallel, though different effect. Britten's opera becomes a confessional commentary upon the homoerotic inspiration of his earlier work, and itself an inspired account of the artist's anguish. Mann with his strong sense of the inner harmony between the personal destiny of an author and that of his contemporaries in general, was taking up the theme of high bourgeois decadence, equally visible in the work of Henry James, Oscar Wilde and Huysmans. The emptying of the city as news of the plague spreads may be seen as a metaphor for the void which exists beneath the exotic splendours of life as it is enjoyed by the guests of the Hotel des Bains. (In our own 'triumphant' materialism, the pertinence of the metaphor on a planet whose beauty is being daily pillaged remains all too obvious.) In *The Magic Mountain*, Mann went on to explore with far greater discursiveness the causes and nature of the disease which had in the meantime turned Europe into a graveyard.

In the work of Tolstoy and his predecessors, the novella could be concerned with the theme of passion as an aspect of human experience; the feeling mediated through the relationships between the characters was not caught up in the problems of the artist and his work. Rather, the claims of eye-witnesses and of those who wrote down exactly what they had heard were used to sustain the idea that these narratives were veridical. The 'narrator' had no difficulty in confronting the reader with the moral dilemmas which these tales exemplified; part of the purpose in setting them down was to alert the reader to the dangers of passion, and to the disasters which could result from its indulgence. The interest of the narratives depended on the directness and vividness with which powerful feelings were conveyed, while inviting an attitude to them, if not a judgement upon them. This was possible because the feelings, however complex, as in *Adolphe*, were not entangled with the artist's own conception of his work, his awareness of artifice (in the best sense), and his ironic questioning of his activity. He could be concerned with an account of events and liberation of feelings, *tout court*. Of course, art concealed art in this enterprise, but was not 'worried' by itself in doing so!

Thomas Mann at the start of the twentieth century, writing within a few years of the shipwreck of the First World War, had the prescience to know that such 'naïveté' was no longer possible. As we have seen, from the very first sentence (and its aside) he reveals his ironic grasp of the writer's situation: 'Gustave Aschenbach – or von Aschenbach, as he had been known officially since his fiftieth birthday – had set out alone ....' The honorific title, acknowledging his achievement, comes also, as titles do, as a consolation for age. From the title of the novella alone we may guess what his fate will be.

He also embodies the artist as neurasthenic and solitary (a theme to which Mann returns in another novella, *Tonio Kröger*): 'overwrought by a morning of hard, nerve-taxing work', requiring 'sustained concentration, conscientiousness, and tact'.[4] These qualities embody what is demanded of him personally, but also what he will come to offer to a 'grateful' public. They reflect a classical restraint, a moral and aesthetic balance which already is beginning to break down under more demonic pressures. The equilibrium of his authoritative relation to his public, as a *magister ludi*, involves strains which he cannot brush aside. Walking in the cemetery he sights a man standing in a portico who whether real or a fantastic expression of his over-burdened psyche liberates his consciousness from the work in hand, and renews the desire of his youth to travel in distant places. It is as though the stranger has caused a regression to a previous level of feeling and desire, reanimating a state of mind which age and fame have caused to be outgrown, removing the bars imposed by habit and discipline. Appearing in a place of death, he also brings about a form of resurrection. And a visual hallucination, projecting him into a tropical landscape, where the eyes of a tiger glare in the undergrowth. This image imports a new and quivering consciousness, a renewed concentration, energy and excitement, as though by the shift in internal space he has turned his back on suffocation and weariness: on the special tasks imposed on him by his own ego and the European soul. The restrictions of consciousness imposed by the everyday world of work, whatever its nature, are suddenly expanded to provide an adventure in space which is as exciting as it is frightening. This instantaneous fantasy Aschenbach now attempts to live out, at first in what he takes to be the necessity for a journey to the East, and then in his realization that this new place, like nothing else in the world, is embodied in Venice. His previous labouring, at the edge of exhaustion, for which the world has honoured him, as a reflector of its own travails – and which is identified in the narrative with the first Christian martyr, St Sebastian – personifies the old Europe, imperilled by the rigidities of its modes of thought, by a consciousness too limited to enjoy that play of fancy through which new modes of experiencing come into being.

The journey into the forest of the tiger is fraught with unexpected perils, not least in the figure of the unlicensed gondolier who takes him across the lagoon, and then runs off without payment, like the native who takes fright at the explorer who wishes to enter terrain where he does not wish to follow him. Approaching a new kind of self-hood, he is also abandoned in his solitude. Or would be, if it were not for Tadzio, the young Polish boy with the head of Eros, who in common with the tiger cannot be approached but who knows how to lure and to mesmerise.

The recurring figure of the young boy with his family in the Grand Hotel, on the beach, at play with his companions, for Aschenbach conjures up mythologies, 'like a primeval legend, handed down from the beginning of time, of the birth of form, of the origin of the gods'.[5] This image of renewed creativity involves for him too a dangerous decadence – a threat to all those bourgeois values and certitudes on which his fame is based, as though he is obsessed by an image of mortality itself. 'He is delicate, he is sickly,' Aschenbach thought. 'He will most likely not live to grow old.'[6] He does not try to account for the pleasure the idea gives him; but it no doubt takes its origin in the homoerotic desire the boy arouses, and the spiritual beauty which he personifies to the artist.

Myth – its renewal and its play – is woven into the narrative, so that while the man remains a legitimate subject for ironic scrutiny, the artist embodies a dilemma: beauty as the one human manifestation of the divine is created out of the erotic, out of what would seem to Aschenbach's ancestors a degeneracy, and to his own austere stoicism an affront. Passion, like crime, is attractive because it is forbidden, and because it calls to, and from, the abyss to which the artist must travel in search of beauty.

Aschenbach as solitary and devotee recalls the *Phaedrus*, in which Socrates instructs a young boy upon the nature of virtue and desire, telling him that 'beauty is the beauty-lover's way to the spirit'. 'And then, sly arch-lover that he was, he said the subtlest thing of all: that the lover was nearer the divine than the beloved ...', acknowledging an emotion as precise and concentrated as thought, and with that comes the desire to write.[7] In the presence of Tadzio he begins to fashion a page and a half of choicest prose, aware that it is well for the world that it sees only the beauty of the completed work. And when he lays it aside, he is exhausted as though by a debauch. No matter, since beauty is the sole aspect of the spiritual which we can perceive through our senses; and Tadzio arouses in him his fiercest espousal of beauty.

Later, and not long before his death, Aschenbach will dream of Dionysus, and the frenzy he inspires in the Maenads, women who become possessed by the god, and whose emotional excesses he will be compelled to join. 'On the trampled moss there now began the rites in honour of the god, an orgy of promiscuous embraces – and in his very soul he tasted the bestial degradation of his fall.'[8] In his creative persona, the artist discovers in himself the power which belongs to the god. He becomes the instrument through which passion is transformed to a new level of complexity and discovers in frightful excesses a route to self-transcendence. It is as though the imagination which delights in chaos, finds in chaos an order which presents itself as an image of beauty and a mode of expressing the divine. What creativity means in both a human and divine sense is an order where before had only existed randomness and contingency.

Mann, whose artist-nature was formed and disciplined by the classics, invokes the deities of antiquity to suggest the mystery and synthesis of the different levels of cognition at work in Aschenbach: Narcissus, Eros, Dionysus and Semele, agents or victims of daemonic power. But Venice, goddess of the sea – and which he approaches for the first time from the sea – assumes a sway over his mind and emotions no less potent. In Venice, the relaxation of his normal forms of discipline and endeavour, the submission at the very outset of his visit to the criminal gondolier, in the black vessel so like a coffin, opens the gate for feelings which are subversive and voluptuous. The pleasure which lies in the East is discovered in this city to which he returns as a substitute for a journey to the real East. But the East actually comes to Venice in the form of the plague, a fatal and extreme form of the malaise which rises from the foul-smelling lagoon, and which he knows to be inimical to his health. 'There was a hateful sultriness in the narrow streets ... The longer he walked, the more was he in tortures under that state, which is the product of the sea air and the sirocco and which excites and enervates at once .... Beggars waylaid him, the canals sickened him with their evil exhalations. He reached a quiet square, one of those that exist at the city's heart, forsaken of God and man; there he rested awhile on the margin of a fountain, wiped his brow, and admitted to himself that he must be gone.'[9] His sensations of malaise recall Turgenev's comparison of love being like a disease (like cholera, in fact, which also comes to Venice from Asia). He knows that the place makes him ill, that he must flee it for his life and regard it as a forbidden place, to be shunned for ever. But his attempt to leave is thwarted; his luggage is wrongly forwarded to Como instead of the place he has chosen as a substitute for Venice, close to Trieste. And with his return to the hotel which he has so recently left, he experiences the exultation of the truant at returning to pleasures so strictly forbidden. The life of crime in the Parisian underworld to which Manon leads Des Grieux may be seen as an externalisation of the inner decadence which Aschenbach, with equal danger to himself, begins now to enjoy. 'And what a spot is is, indeed! – uniting the charms of a luxurious bathing-resort by a southern sea with the immediate nearness of a unique and marvellous city .... This spot and this alone had power to beguile him, to relax his resolution, to make him glad.' The beguiling, though, is an invitation to crime. 'Aschenbach saw the boy Tadzio almost constantly.'[10]

What the artist, as opposed to the man, sees is perfection of form; and form as an image of spiritual beauty. Eros is indispensable to each. To the man, Eros appears in his obsessive, destructive and selfish guise. He inspires the attraction towards Tadzio, and the desire to be rejuvenated, which the barber hideously affects: 'A delicate carmine glowed on his cheeks where the skin had been so brown and leathery. The dry, anaemic lips grew full, they turned the colour of ripe strawberries, the lines round eyes and mouth were treated with a facial cream and gave place to youthful bloom.'[11] He causes the obsession which leads Aschenbach to follow the young boy through the narrow alleys of Venice, and also of the boy's not-so-innocent observation of this. Aschenbach is lured, enticed, led on, knowing that what he is experiencing is both a passion and a folly. And Eros encloses the relationship in the selfishness of Aschenbach's desire for Tadzio not to leave Venice, even though he knows the city is emptying out of fear of the plague. As in other novellas, Eros is seen to isolate, so that at the close man and boy, observer and observed are left alone on the beach. Then, as previously, their relationship is confined to silent looks, to a secret shared between them and not betrayed, like a crime in which they are both accomplices; and which leads in the older man at least to lawless hopes.

So much for the dark side of Eros. In his positive aspect he tramples on human reason and dignity, so that a new form of beauty can be liberated. Aschenbach's sojourn in Venice, which ends in his death, reawakens his wearied senses and reanimates his inner life so that he becomes responsive again to form as a mode (perhaps the only mode) of perceiving the divine. But Aschenbach dies at the moment of intersection when Tadzio becomes simultaneously the beckoning youth and the Summoner who points towards 'an immmensity of richest expectation'.[12] The novella leaves no doubt, however, that had Aschenbach lived his 'criminal' passion for Tadzio would in some guise or disguise have

fed his power to remain creative, as in the memory of his magus
narrator.

Death in Venice differs from the previous novellas in its preoccupation with passion as a form of degeneracy which leads to a
renewal of the artist's life, and the particular value of spiritual
beauty which the work of art represents. The 'strange god' who
inspires passion also breathes life into Aschenbach the artist. Its
claims, however, are particular rather than general. The end of
the novella, in relation to the artist-life as opposed to Aschenbach's personal life, is open-ended and tentative. It is by no
means clear how that inner harmony between the personal destiny of an author, and that of his contemporaries in general,
would be reflected in Aschenbach's future work.

But in what Mann has written there exists the clearest indication of a consciousness representative of the ills and aspirations
of the early twentieth century, and in many respects still resonant today. Venice – the most astonishing of all human creations
– is swayed by considerations of greed. The city's medical officer
has been replaced by someone more compliant in the face of the
plague. The Venetian authorities have published a statement
reassuring the public that the state of the city's health has never
been better. Corruption at the top, together with fear over who
will be struck down next, afflict the whole life of the city. Gangs
are making the streets unsafe, vice and excess are rampant.
Venice itself will soon be under sentence of death by a blockade.
Or so at least the Englishman in the tourist office warns Aschenbach, in advising him to leave the city at once. The unwholesome
odours of the canals in the sultry heat have become only one
indication of a city which festers with death, and which carbolic
and disinfectant try to conceal, only to draw attention to it the
more. The city's evil secret mirrors that in Aschenbach's own
heart; and it likewise cannot be hidden. But he too cannot bear
the thought of seeing the young boy leave any more than the city
can endure the thought of becoming out of pocket because the
tourists will leave, if news of the pestilence spreads. In each love
is possessive because of the self-gratification it brings. The city's
passion for its visitors is no less greedy and obsessive than
Aschenbach's for Tadzio; and each harbours its own form of
disease. 'Our adventurer felt his senses wooed by this voluptu-
ousness of sight and sound, tasted his secret knowledge that the

city sickened and hid its sickness for love of gain and bent an ever
more unbridled leer on the gondola that glided on before him.'[13]

The commercial greed of Venice (as in Shakespeare's play it
feeds on the trade and profit of all nations) reflects a degeneracy
similar to Aschenbach's – and on which its past also ironically
comments: the place in which painting and architecture triumphed over the mephitic waters of the lagoon, as Tadzio finally
will seem to do as well. As in the figure of St Sebastian who is
identified with Aschenbach's previous art (ironically, too!), art is
something won out of, and over: its spirituality is not a *donnée*,
but a reward for having a triumphed over the lure of corruption.
And this in its qualified way Venice stands for too. The spiritual
fact of the city in the lagoon is irresistible, and enduring over
against its inner stagnation.

What then of the narrator, who here becomes the invisible
observer? The style adopted by Mann in this novella achieves an
almost over-weaning omniscience. It is not merely that he can see
into Aschenbach's most private feelings and explore those recesses of behaviour for which no one else would be able to
understand the motive. Aschenbach in his moulding hands becomes a mythological being, inspired by daemonic power, in the
service of creativity. As a man he remains self-indulgent, egotis-
tic, more than a little preposterous, at times pathetic, even
repellent. His relationship with the world is based on an endless self-regard, which the narrator eyes ironically, but never
entirely deflates. He is after all an acknowledged master, the
news of whose death will be received by the world with shock
and respect.

There is something in Mann's summoning up of Aschenbach of
what the Spanish call *duende*, a dark wrestling with death, of
blood rebelling against the character imposed by time and convention on the acclaimed writer. The control and discipline of his
acquired classicism is subverted by the claims of paganism, and
of strange gods whose very existence has been overlaid by the
immobility of his life in Munich. His travelling in space, as well
as being a journey to the East, to the place where the tiger
crouches among bamboo thickets, involves a journey backwards
in time, to areas of primitive possession, of intoxication and
desire. 'Now daily the naked god with cheeks aflame drove his
fire-breathing steeds through heaven's spaces; and with him

streamed the strong east wind that fluttered his yellow locks ....'[14] The mysterious power which emanates from ancient culture becomes a call to the blood and to creative action. Tadzio may represent an image of perfect form, act as a ministering angel to the wearied spirit, but his presence would have no significance without his association with the abyss: the abyss which is struggle against death, the void, nothingness, in whose blackness other powers lurk. It is these unseen powers which Tadzio releases, and which carry Aschenbach to the edge of things: the edge of his own personal morality from which he quite literally looks down on the abyss, and the edge of his own creative nothingness, of which Venice also reminds him.

'He saw it once more, that landing-place that takes the breath away, that amazing group of incredible structures the Republic set up to meet the awe-struck eye of the approaching sea-farer: the airy splendour of the palace and Bridge of Sighs, the columns of lion and saint on the shore, the glory of the projecting flank of fairy temple, the vista of gateway and clock.'[15]

As these images pour through the empty arch of Aschenbach's mind they might be expected to inspire; in fact they carry the wind of death, the wind which blows from the dead in search of new places. The pestilence in Venice is what Aschenbach must encounter to find new power, not the beauty of Venice, nor the Venetian past. These belong to the dead, while the plague embodies the challenge of death to the living.

This strange encounter is what gives Aschenbach new power. Out of the conflict with the pestilence comes the increasing strength of Tadzio's image and his power to embody spiritual beauty. But as such it would be empty if it were not for the dark wind of which it was born.

Aschenbach cannot be separated from Mann's struggle with the creative imagination. *Death in Venice* is a mythological dramatisation of that struggle, done with all the ironic detachment of which Mann was a master. In it, the passion born of Eros in both his creative and destructive aspects is seen to be indispensable. *Death in Venice* provides a commentary on much in earlier novellas, where passion is seen as an effect of relationships and seldom so clearly as an instrument of creativity, which it has also been. 'Passion is like crime: it does not thrive on the established order and the common round; it welcomes every blow dealt *against* the bourgeois structure, every weakening of the social fabric.'[16] In this respect it reveals too the anarchic hand of the artist.

André Gide: *Strait is the Gate*

Except a corn of wheat fall into the ground and die, it abideth
alone: but if it die, it bringeth forth much fruit.   John 12:24

The history of passionate love in all great literature from the
thirteenth century down to our own day ... the account of the more
and more desperate attempts of Eros to take the place of mystical
transcendence by means of emotional intensity.
                    De Rougemont, *Love in the Western World*

Gide saw himself as a man of contradictions. His novella, *Strait
is the Gate*, is the product of a protestant imagination in a
Catholic culture. He had a dread of spiritual inertia, and a fear
of liberty. 'The great problem for the modern spirit,' he once
wrote, is not how to acquire freedom, but how to endure it.'[1] The
contradictoriness of the novella – Alissa's refusal of that spontaneous passion with which many of the previous works have been
concerned – provides a way of summarising some of the ideas in
this book; and at the same time it looks forward to a future where
the myth has almost disappeared because it has lost its context.
    The conflict between virtue and desire recalls *The Princess of
Clèves*. Gide and Madame de Lafayette share too a lyrical and
analytic style which enables them to reason about feeling. But
Gide's classicism is 'experimental', probing the inherited inhibi-
tions of class, family and religion, questioning the restraint
which prevents the individal from letting go, and recognising in
the faults of parents' lives the origins of tragic weakness in the
next generation. Desire and passion lack spontaneous expression, because of the weight of the past, which cannot be shaken
off, or is borne for the sake of a future reward which fails to
materialise. Gide takes up the problem of the twentieth century,
of what to do with the freedom it offers, whether psychological,
sexual or economic, and how to find in that freedom an identity

which is fulfilled. Prophetically that problem is embodied in the figure of a woman.

Strait is the Gate might be described as a novella in which passion is frustrated through various forms of inhibition. Like other works in this book, it deals with first love. When Jerome and Alissa meet, she is sixteen and he fourteen; they reflect Gide's own meeting with his future wife, when he was thirteen; and much in the subsequent narrative originates in auto-biographical experience. As in the novella, where Jerome remembers what took all his strength to live, memory slowly shaped and matured this work for Gide. In spite of its brevity, the actual writing took him more than three years, and it re-flected experiences which had occurred twenty years previously. It was, like other novellas, a work which could only be written when the desire had become a memory, and desire could be recaptured in the freedom which memory allows. But there also existed in Gide, as he confessed, a 'mystical tendency' which perhaps drew him to the myth of which the novella is an expres-sion, and with which it wrestles strenuously. As a homosexual who also remained devoted to his wife until her death in 1938, the deferment of passion to a world beyond death might have had at least an imaginative appeal. If so, he had the courage to reject it. Like Mann's *Death in Venice* it nonetheless is shot through with the pain of a love which is suppressed.

Gide's narrative is divided between Jerome's recollected ac-count of his relationship with Alissa, and her Journal which Jerome reads after her death. Gide himself thought the Journal to be among his most successful pieces of writing. It reveals the anguish of a soul determined to love God only, but drawn back irretrievably to the only love she can feel: her love for Jerome. As a rival for love of God, she almost hates him, seeing him as intervening between her and God. Gide's awareness of the role of the rival in structuring desire; and of the hatred he or she attracts as the proximity increases, recalls the examples of ear-lier novellas; but it also looks forward to the treatment of the same theme in more modern fiction such as Graham Greene's *The End of the Affair*.[2]

Tempted before her death to destroy her journal, Alissa real-ises that she has written it for Jerome. She has discovered the language in that 'powerful impetus of the mind' which brings passion to birth; and its need to declare itself reveals as much self-love as love for another. Alissa is in love with the idea of virtue. 'My God, allow him at times to catch in these lines the awkward accent of a heart, obsessed with the desire to urge him towards those heights of virtue which I despaired of reaching.'¹ She has turned to God to save her from the sexuality she cannot confront because for her it will always be tainted by her mother's infidelity. Her passion for Jerome expresses itself as a desire for a goal they might both reach together and independently, beyond sexuality and marriage, as a new kind of superhuman virtue. She conceives of happiness too, not as something to be found and grasped, but as something to be indefinitely deferred. 'And I ask myself now if it is really happiness that I desire, or rather the progress towards happiness. Oh, Lord! protect me from a happiness which I might be able to reach too quickly. Teach me to postpone my happiness, to move it as far away from me as You are.'⁴ As we have seen before, desire is intensified by the presence of an obstacle; and can take the form of wanting the beloved to be unfaithful so that one can court her again. In Alissa, desire and the happiness which might be achieved in its fulfilment is intensified by making the obstacle God, and therefore irremovable unless God himself disappears.

One of the characteristics of Gide's novella lies in a reticence, what he saw as a 'strength in reserve' about its central events. This may also be seen as a failure on Jerome's and Alissa's part to perceive the significance of what is happening to them at the time: in common with others they cannot possess full awareness of the myth they are living. Jerome's narration begins: 'Some people might have made a book out of it; but the story I am going to tell used up all my strength in living and my courage is exhausted. So I shall set down what I recall quite simply ....'⁵ Against the power of myth neither reason nor intelligence can provide an adequate defence. Memory alone perceives the shape in what has happened. What is often described in a cliché as the advantage of hindsight means in fact the bringing to light of what could not at the time be perceived. Human history would have been different if this were not the case. In Jerome's reconstruction the existence of the myth is laid bare through the simple device of a repetition.

One afternoon, Jerome decides to return unexpectedly to see

Alissa at home. Her mother, Lucile, suffers from hysterical
screaming attacks, and the maid warns him not to go up as she
is in the grip of one at the time. He brushes past her. On the first
floor the door of Lucile's room is open, and he sees her stretched
out on a sofa with the curtains drawn. The room is illuminated
by candelabra, and her two other children, Robert and Juliette,
are at her feet. Behind her is a strange young man in a lieutenant's uniform. When he comes to recall this scene, Jerome
comments that the presence of the two children seems to him
monstrous. The lieutenant is playing a game with Lucile, and
saying that if he had a pet lamb he would call her 'Bucolin' (the
family surname). 'My aunt herself burst out laughing. I saw her
hold out a cigarette for the young man to light. She took a few
puffs. The cigarette fell to the floor. He rushed forward to pick it
up, pretended he had caught his feet in a scarf, tripped and fell
on his knees before my aunt.'⁶ During this ridiculous performance Jerome slips upstairs to Alissa's room, where he finds her
on her knees by her bed, weeping. Jerome recognises that his
whole life is decided in that moment, when he determines to
'shelter this child, from fear, from evil, from life'.⁷ What he cannot
know is that her life is being decided in those moments too, and
set on a path where he will not have the power to intervene.
Shortly afterwards Lucile runs away from her husband.

In Alissa's Journal this scene is replayed with variations,
many years later. One evening, when Jerome is staying with the
family at Fongueusemare, Alissa is left alone. Her father comes
in and finds her lying on the sofa – a thing she hardly ever does.
She is aware of a feeling of shyness; he asks her to come and sit
beside him, and begins to talk about her mother, which he has
never done since their separation. She asks why he is telling her
about their early happiness; he replies that seeing her lying on
the sofa, 'I thought for a moment I saw your mother again.'⁸
Alissa then reveals to her Journal that she has asked her father
so insistently because of an incident which had occurred with
Jerome the same evening. He was standing, reading over her
shoulder. 'I could not see him, but I felt his breath and, as it were,
the warmth and pulsation of his body. I pretended to go on
reading, but I did not take it in any more. I was not even able to
make out the the lines. I became so disturbed that I had to get
out of my chair in haste, while I was still able to do so. I managed

to leave the room for a few minutes; and fortunately he noticed nothing ... But a little later, when I was alone in the drawing-room and was lying down on the sofa, where I reminded Papa of my mother, I was at that very moment thinking of her.'[9]

The sofa on which Jerome has seen Lucile is the same as that on which Alissa will remind her father of his wife, at the very moment when she is thinking of her. Both moments are associated with something monstrous and evil. Jerome will derive from his perception of Lucile his role as Alissa's protector; she will become a fugitive from the sexuality she now takes to be evil. Her awareness of his physical presence – and the pulsation of his body – awakens in her feelings so strong that she has to run from them. The reticent poetry of Gide's writing is nowhere better characterised than in the use which he makes of the sofa in these two episodes, so that it becomes a symbol of seduction and flight. For both participants, the significance of the scene is however only partially realised. Evil, for Gide, is something by which we are touched almost without realising that it has happened, and of which the significance seems to be transient until long after-wards. Through this simple repetition, and the image of the sofa, with all its associations, Gide narrates the power of obsessions, only half realised, which have to be lived through and overcome. In memory Jerome will attempt to do just this.

His narrative begins, as we have seen, with a defence of its selectivity; he intends to recollect – as best he can, and without invention – a story which took all his strength in living. The familiar claim to setting things down as they happened, without invention, is made again; but the intention is now more consid-ered: a weighing-up of their existential cost. Memory has become the means of exploring the self, of revisiting its landscapes, of mapping its contours, to discover what actually happened, of which the cost was so high. As we shall see by the end, the process always involves evasion, the slipping through of something es-sential, because memory works through a process of selection, beyond the control of even a rigorous narrator. In this, perhaps, exists the anguish of Gide's art, and its most deeply considered achievement.

Jerome's story concerns his triangular relationship with his two cousins, Alissa and Juliette, which begins in the year of his father's death, when he is twelve years old – a time when, as he says, he was predisposed to new emotions, and goes to stay with his uncle at Fongueusemare, near Le Havre.

Although in time Alissa admits her love for Jerome, she refuses to become engaged to him. She claims that she does not need so much happiness: her first move in a game of deferment which enables her to put divine before human love. Only after death can that which has been parted in life be brought together. Alissa feels and thinks in the language of a passion which seeks to find fulfilment outside the terms of human existence. But it is inside them that she has to continue to manoeuvre for her ends. When challenged by Jerome's aunt, she confirms her love but says that she does not wish to be married before her sister, Juliette. Juliette, a little later, will break the news to Jerome:

> 'And do you know whom she wants me to marry?'
> I did not answer.
> 'You!' she went on with a cry.
> 'But that's madness!'
> 'Yes! isn't it!' There was both despair and triumph in her voice. She straightened herself up, or rather threw herself backwards.
> 'Now I know what I have to do,' she added faintly, as she opened the door of the garden which she closed violently behind her.[10]

The full irony of this reaction will only become apparent ten years later, after Alissa's death, when Jerome goes to visit Juliette and her family in the south of France. Jerome admits that if he had married another woman he could only have pretended to love her.

' "Ah!" said she, as though with indifference; then turning her face away from me, she bent it towards the ground, as if she were looking for something she had lost. "Then you think one can keep a love without hope in one's heart for so long as that?" '[11]

When she gets up, she takes a step, and falls back again into a nearby chair, as though lacking all strength. 'She put her hands up to her face and it seemed to me she was weeping.'[12]

The presence of the rival, and the obstacle Juliette has presented to the fulfilment of his desire, has confirmed Jerome in his love for Alissa; while she in her life has felt mainly resentment of her sister for finding happiness elewhere than in her sacrifice. The so-called 'sacrifice' has of course been no more than an act of self-love, which permits that constant deferment of human love for the sake of a desire which she does not wish to fulfil.

Alissa's case, though, is not just a refusal of sexuality, a dislike of appropriation by the weak man which Jerome proves himself to be (Gide himself disliked him for his flabbiness). Her desire becomes an increasingly violent oscillation between her assertion of a devoutness she wants Jerome to share, and her attraction towards him which she cannot overcome or resolve. Having persuaded Jerome not to attempt to see her, she begins to admit in her renewed letters the violence with which she wants him – but only in his absence. 'Believe me, if you were with me I could not think of you more. I would not wish to hurt you, but I have come to the point of no longer desiring your presence – now. Shall I admit it? If I knew you were coming this evening I should flee.'[13] This necessity of flight indicates the impossibility of fulfilling a desire except through a myth which ends in death. Alissa wants nothing so much as an end to desire. On the infrequent occasions when she allows him to visit her, their solitude is accentuated by an ability to communicate with each other, an embarrassment even in the meeting of hands. For Alissa, at least it has proved true, that their correspondence has been a mirage: they have been writing only to themselves.

As with the sofa, Gide's writing works through images of which the significance accumulates as the narrative progresses, and each of which is inscribed with desire, and its denial. The amethyst cross, belonging to Jerome's mother, is given by him to Alissa on his mother's death. She uses it as a secret sign between them during one of his final visits to her. When she comes down to dinner without wearing it, Jerome knows that he must leave without saying good-bye. She does so after telling him that holiness not happiness matters most. The cross acts as a talisman defending her idea of virtue, but also unconsciously as a bond between Alissa and Jerome's mother (whom she is said to resemble) suggesting a taboo on sexuality and bolstering her rejection of it, associated with her sense of evil, derived from her own mother's infidelity and desertion.

So it is with *la porte étroite*, the strait gate of the Gospel according to Saint Luke, and the narrow door of Alissa's garden. The Gospel text is the subject of the sermon which Jerome hears preached in the company of Alissa, just after he has committed himself to protect her from evil. It precipitates a dream-like vision of their future as two people who will find the strait gate. He sees the gate too as being the door of Alissa's room through which he has recently entered. 'I had the presentiment of another joy, pure, seraphic, mystic for which my soul already thirsted. I imagined this joy like the song of a violin, at once strident and tender, like a sharp-pointed flame in which Alissa's heart and mine were consumed.'[14] The sexuality of his imagining is apparent enough, but beyond this there is also the mystical transcendence which exists beyond human reality and includes an immolation of it.

The lower garden of the house at Fongueusemare is approached by a 'little secret gate'; through this Jerome will pass at his last and unexpected meeting with Alissa. Unexpected at least to him. Three years after their previous meeting, Alissa comes to the garden, on three consecutive nights, knowing that she will see him: 'Yes, I knew I was going to see you again once more. For the last three days I have come here every evening, and have called you as I did tonight ....'[15] He tells her that he can love no one but her; and for the first time kisses her with passion. For her that risks spoiling their love. God intends them for some better thing which is about to begin. With those words the narrow door is shut and bolted upon him, confirming in him that despair which arises from the final rejection of sexuality. In St Luke's Gospel, the narrow gate stands for the rigorous path to salvation; here it becomes like a 'press and vice' which denies intimacy for the sake of some other and special vision. The myth of death as the goal of desire has become inseparable here from the death-wish which exists within the Puritan refusal of pleasure.

Alissa's Journal, which Jerome reads after her death, celebrates the possibility of Joy, but always a joy beyond human suffering. The deepening of this expresses itself in physical illness. Denial of the world can only be resolved by leaving the world; her journal which has been described as the 'diary of a mind annihilating its own desire'[16] leads to the inevitable end, but not before she has seen her life for what she has made of it. Alissa alone becomes capable of reading the myth she has lived, even as it is completed. 'It was like the sudden and disenchanting *illumination* of my life. It seemed to me that I saw for the first time the walls of my room atrociously bare. I was overcome by fear. Even now I am writing to reassure myself, to calm myself. O Lord! let me reach the end without blasphemy! ... I should like to die now, quickly, before realising again that I am alone.'[17] Emotional intensity can no longer give way to a mystical transcendence because that has proved to be empty, enclosing her in the silence of those infinite spaces of Pascal, whom she likes to quote: 'Whatever is not God cannot fill up my longing.'[18] And so her longing is left without satisfaction.

But as has often been noted, aesthetic emotion is not the same as actual emotion. Jerome's revivification of that experience which took all his strength to live through does not end with her death. 'I saw Juliette again last year. More than ten years had gone by since her last letter, in which she told me of Alissa's death.'[19] As often in the novella, the eclipse of time does not interfere with the continuity of the narrative. Jerome, however, does not possess Alissa's power to read his own story. The account of Juliette's continuing love for him is given without any indication on his part that he has read her words or her responses correctly; or it may be that he is incapable of responding to them, that both of them are doomed to keep a love without hope in their hearts for as long as they live.

The magician behind the story has the final words; or, at least, they belong as much to him as to a final observation by Jerome: 'A servant came in, carrying the lamp.'[20] In this gesture towards completion, a stillness as at the end of a play, the aesthetic act is completed. In that completion – as with the light cast by the lamp – there is a sense of shadows which have been temporarily driven back, revealing in the illuminated space, an action complete in itself, but still going on in our minds. In dismissing the myth, Gide looked forward to a time which Lawrence foresaw when narratives of passion would lack altogether that 'mystical tendency' which had characterised these novellas in the past; and which had given to them that intensity they also questioned with the lucidity which memory allows.

D.H. Lawrence: *The Fox*

And the further and further she had gone, the more fearful had become the realisation of emptiness. An agony. An insanity at last.
D.H. Lawrence, *The Fox*

Because he cannot face his nothingness he throws himself on another who seems to be spared by the curse.
René Girard, *Deceit, Desire and the Novel*

D.H. Lawrence wrote *The Fox* in 1923, but the story is set in 1918, when 'there was not much food to buy', and the men who have not returned from the war have left behind a generation of women, forced to earn their own living and with little prospect of finding a husband. The two women at the centre of this novella, known by their surnames as Banford and March, are 'neither of them young; that is, they were near thirty. But they certainly were not old'. On the death of Banford's grandfather, the two 'girls' have been left to work a farm alone. In spite of their hard work, Bailey Farm does not prosper: 'they seemed to be losing ground, somehow, losing hope as the months went by.'[1]

Seventy years have passed since Mrs Gaskell wrote about Hope Farm. Rural life has changed fundamentally. Even the name of Lawrence's farm suggests the threshold of bankruptcy, where uncertainty is implicit, and old ways are threatened. The absence of family life, of natural and fulfilling relationships, however strained, is as marked as the void left by the absence of any religious or spiritual tradition, which mitigates and gives meaning to the harshness of toil. The rotation of the seasons, which provides a pattern for human life and a way of ordering it, broken only by the call of worship, has lost its power to solace and give pleasure. Nature is hostile, forbidding and indifferent. In Hardy's novels, this acts as a backdrop for man's struggle against a harsh fate in a drama of pain. In Lawrence's novella, it is merely another aspect of an estrangement and strain between people and things which reflects the aftermath of war and Lawrence's awareness of how radically Europe has been changed by the war. The 'mystical tendency', of a transcendence of desire in death has now become replaced by a psychological probing of the present in which memory has no part, and desire is sightless, uncertain of itself, but no less obsessive. The goal of an attempted union has been replaced by an acceptance of isolation from which release is sought and not found: not least because the bonds between man and nature have been loosened as well as those between men and women. Even as an aesthetic emotion, harmony has lost its force to compel and bind.

'The months passed, the dark evenings came, heavy, dark, November, when March went about in high boots, ankle deep in mud, when the night began to fall at four o'clock, and the day never properly dawned. Both girls dreaded these times. They dreaded the almost continuous darkness that enveloped their desolate little farm near the wood. Banford was physically afraid. She was afraid of tramps, afraid lest someone should come prowling around. March was not so much afraid as uncomfortable, and disturbed. She felt discomfort and gloom in all her physique.'[2] This sense of disturbance will manifest itself concretely in the figure of the fox, and later in his human counterpart, the soldier who has returned from the war. Unlike the men in *Cousin Phillis*, Paul and Mr Holdsworth, this 'youth' has no prospects or home. He ran away from his grandfather who once owned Bailey Farm, went to Canada, joined the army, and so returned to Europe. Now, with the war over, he has returned in search of his roots, only to find strangers in what had once been his home. In Mrs Gaskell's time, the building of railways around the world (Mr Holdsworth, it will be remembered, goes to Canada) offered a new skilled occupation for young men, as well as standing for a technological progress of which the effects seemed likely to be positive. No such signs, either for the individual or society at large, are visible in the world of 1918. In the brief glimpse of life away from the farm, when the youth has to seek leave of absence from his unit in order to solve the problem of his broken engagement, army life also seems to lack any redeeming sense of purpose. 'In that great camp of wooden huts and tents he had no idea where his captain was ....'[3] Individuals like institutions are dispirited, and uncertain where to turn. In the end he will leave once more for Canada, with March ... but whether to anything better remains uncertain and unclear.

Mrs Gaskell's narrative reaches back into the past: to the skills of Paul's father as an inventor, to the tradition of nonconformist chapel-going and preaching, as well as into the future, symbolised in the ever-extending railway lines. Lawrence's narrative, on the other hand, is self-enclosed. The legacy of the past offers toil without hope. The farm exists in a kind of limbo, created by the war, and the straining away from it in search of happiness will lead March into a 'horrible abyss of nothingness'.[4] It is as though in the aftermath of the war life has drained away from the farm, leaving it sterile and unpeopled, except for the fox. A way of life, in which a natural reciprocity between man and nature has been reduced to the conflict between hunter and hunted, reflecting the upheaval and shrinkage of vision which the Great War has brought about.

'She lowered her eyes, and suddenly saw the fox. He was looking up at her. Her chin was pressed down, and his eyes were looking up. They met her eyes. And he knew her. She was spellbound – she knew he knew her. So he looked into her eyes, and her soul failed her. He knew her, he was not daunted.'[5]

This 'strange encounter' recalls that other encounter in Wilfred Owen's poem, and also results in an inability to kill. 'She put her gun to her shoulder, but even then pursed her mouth, knowing it was nonsense to pretend to fire .... She was possessed by him.'[6] The locking together of eyes involves a mutual hypnosis, a joining together of wills, a battle for mastery, a struggle for power. Even before the young man returns from the war, the battle has been joined: a struggle which he takes over in becoming the fox.

Lawrence's technique is simultaneously one of absence and presence. He is present in the battle of wills, but in this novella we have no narrator, or listener. His method is investigative: from the first encounter with the fox, eyes speak and are silent, communicate and hold back. The dialogue of souls is constantly implied in looks. (The word 'eyes' recurs many times, often several times in a single paragraph.) It is as though in this world where the past has been wiped out, and the future has not yet come into being, the present alone can be asked to yield its meaning. As the two women and the young man watch each other, so the narrator watches them with his eye of steel, which comments only in metaphors: 'He seemed as remote from her as if his red face were a red chimney-pot on a cottage across the fields, and she looked at him just as objectively, as remotely.'[7] The homeliness of the metaphor ironically confirms the distance which separates them.

Almost immediately after March's encounter with the fox, Henry Grenfel appears at the farmhouse door. Like the stranger or revenant in Ibsen's plays, he appears to disturb the even flow of life, for all its problems, between the two women. Their exist- ence is settled, and apparently content, if sterile. By March he is greeted, appropriately, with a gun, because his appearance at night seems like a threat, and because almost at once, she recognises whom she has encountered again: 'To March he was the fox. Whether it was the thrusting forward of his head, or the glisten of fine whitish hairs on the ruddy cheek-bones, or the bright keen eyes, that can never be said: but the boy was to her the fox, and she could not see him otherwise.'[8] As with the other fox, the hunted also hunts: 'The youth watched her as she bent over the table, looked at her slim, well-shapen legs, at the belted coat dropping around her thighs, at the knot of dark hair, and his curiosity, vivid and widely alert, was again arrested by her.'[9]

At the same time his arrival fills a vacancy. He is right to observe, 'there wants a man about the place'.[10] And ironically again, it is Banford who tells the young man of twenty to stop. He has succeeded in entering their privacy, and as March re- marks, 'the village doesn't matter to me, anyhow.'[11] Once the door has been opened to him, he begins to act as a catalyst upon their lives in ways which none of them can foresee. His presence in March's subconscious is reflected in her dreams, where she hears singing in the night – the fox singing – and follows him only to be bitten. 'She stretched out her hand, but suddenly he bit her wrist, and at the same instant, as he drew back, the fox, turning round to bound away, whisked his brush across her face, and it seemed his brush was on fire, for it seared and burned her mouth with a great pain. She awoke with the pain of it, and lay trembling as if she were really seared.'[12] The sexuality to which she has never been exposed arouses in her that sense of pain which the woman's fear of penetration can induce.

For Banford, on the other hand, who is afraid of Nature, the presence of the young man offers the possibility of a new social and domestic gratification. She was as pleased and thoughtful as if she had her own younger brother home from France. He draws out her natural warmth and kindliness, and enjoys her sisterly attention, providing the opportunity for her to indulge a liking for hospitality, thwarted again by the war. To March he is invested with all the obsessive power and interest of a dream-image; to Banford, he acts as a liberator of her natural and undemanding affection. In these circumstances she under-estimates her enemy's cunning.

The idea comes into his mind: 'Why not marry March?'[13] And with that the balance of the relationship between the three of them shifts. He sees himself as a hunter: 'even before you come in sight of your quarry, there is a strange battle, like mesmerism. Your own soul, as a hunter, has gone out to fasten on the soul of the deer, even before you see any deer.'[14] Lawrence characterises the struggle between man and woman as a profound battle of the wills 'which takes place in the invisible'.[15] Like Zeus concealed in the cloud before the 'rape' of Io, the young man hunts his fright-ened prey, in a manner which Lawrence represents as mythopoeic. 'The bullet's flight home is a sheer projection of your own fate into the fate of the deer. It happens like a supreme wish, a supreme act of volition ....'[16] It occurs within a kind of invisibil-ity, making him the more dangerous to his prey, and to Banford who does not know of the struggle going on, or the power which now possesses him. Lawrence writes of sexuality here in its psychic manifestation, as something which takes possession of, and modifies consciousness, without any outward change. 'So he remained in appearance just the nice, odd stranger-youth, stay-ing for a fortnight on the place.'[17] The concealed hunter becomes the more deadly when he strikes, leaving March as though killed. The fox she wanted to kill has become the one who has mastered her. The interrogatory nature of the relationship between them is explored through looks as keen and sharp as they are ulti-mately unrevealing, except as a struggle of wills.

When Henry announces to Banford that he and March are going to get married, he wounds her as a huntsman too: 'Banford looked at her like a bird that has been shot: a poor little sick bird. She gazed at her with all her wounded soul in her face, at the deep-flushed March.' But the response is a resounding 'Never'.[18] Her desire to keep possession of March is fought as fiercely by her as by him. She would die if they tried to continue living together after the marriage; his physical presence revolts her; he is out for what he can get; and he wants to be master of them both, as he is master of March already. She sees now their mistake in letting him stop, in showing him kindness of which he has taken advantage.

Lawrence sees the enclosure of their relationship in the farm with its murderous embrace as being like a metaphor for England after the war. 'And suddenly it seemed to him England was little and tight, he felt the landscape was constricted even in the dark, and that there were too many dogs in the night, making a noise like a fence of sound, like the network of English hedges netting the view.'[19] In such an environment the fox doesn't stand a chance. 'It seemed to him it would be the last of the foxes in this loudly-barking, thick-voiced England, tight with innumerable little houses.'[20] England stands for repression and suffocating restriction, in which the wild represented by the fox has no place. In killing the fox, as Henry does, he is only doing England's work; March dreaming of Banford's death will symbolically do the same in covering Banford's body with the fox's skin. The nailing of the fox's skin to a board in reality appears as a kind of crucifixion, a sacrifice of their inner and spiritual life to something meaner and impoverished.

The conflict thus set up is not easily concluded. The young man's rage at being thwarted by Banford intensifies, as does her resentment at his presence. The burgeoning physicality of his desire for March is fired by his sense of a 'secret bond, a secret thread'[21] between them with which Banford attempts to interfere, while March is tormented by her knowledge of Banford's unhappiness. Under the influence of his passion (his desire to master her) March agrees to marry him, only to retract once he has left her and returned to the army on Salisbury Plain, from which he has not yet been demobbed. Though the war is 'really over' it still holds them in a limbo, preventing for a while their setting out for another life in Canada.

The letter with which March rejects his proposal expresses both her sense of his strangeness and of Jill's proximity to her. 'I love Jill and she makes me feel safe and sane, with her loving

anger against me for being such a fool.'[22] Being balked of his prey
– his doom, his destiny and his reward – intensifies Henry's rage
against Banford, who becomes the thorn he must remove from
his life: a thorn which rankles to insanity.

When he goes to ask for a special twenty-four-hour pass to
return to the farm, the Captain senses at once that he has
problems with a woman and warns him against causing trouble.
Briefly, at this moment, Lawrence's narrative steps outside the
parameters of conflicting wills, and sees them objectively as
expressions of a common problem, so simplified as to render the
analysis a meaningless cliché.

Sixty miles of wet and muddy cycling separate him from the
farm, and he arrives to find March attempting to fell a dead tree.
Once again the shadow of the war is to be felt in the absence of
men, and in the prohibition against cutting timber. Metaphori-
cally, it seems symbolic of what the war has done to Europe.

March is determined to succeed because in these days of scarce
fuel, the tree would make such splendid firing. Even her chop-
ping at the trunk has had to be done close to the ground so that
no one will notice. But the tree has not fallen. Banford's father
and his wife have (somewhat surprisingly) appeared to witness
the felling; and Henry now joins them, immediately asserting his
dominion over March who with her rabbit look succumbs to her
fox. Henry at once perceives that if he fells the tree in a certain
way, then the branch will strike Banford; and he becomes again
like the huntsman who is watching a flying bird. 'In his heart he
had decided her death. A terrible still force seemed in him, and a
power that was just his.' But he warns her against not moving.
And she responds by mocking his skill. ' "Let us see some crack
Canadian tree-felling," she retorted.'[23] No one, except the hunter
who watches with his intense bright eyes, knows what happens
until they see she is dead. And he knows it for its inner significance: 'the inner necessity of his life was fulfilling itself, it was he
who was to live.'[24] He, like March, knows he was won, and he is
glad. He has won over Banford, but he has also won March. 'His
life must have her. And now he had won her. It was what his life
must have.'[25] A death has cleared the way to the fulfilment of his
obsession.

So he comes to possess her; but although she *wanted* him to
possess her, he still did not quite succeed. 'Something was miss-

ing.' In her 'dark, vacant eyes' – even when they have left the farm for Cornwall – there remains a wound, as though she could not 'accept the submergence which his new love put upon her'. As a woman she could only exist under the surface, like the sea-weeds she watches. 'Beneath the water they might be stronger, more indestructible than resistant oak trees are on land. But it was always under-water, always under-water. And she, being a woman, must be like that.'[26] But in the past she had been the opposite of that, taking responsibility for Jill's well-being, and in her own small sphere, for the 'well-being of the world'. In this she has failed, and with the knowledge of failure comes also the awareness of nothingness, of a striving for what could never be achieved. The search for happiness always ends 'in the ghastly sense of the bottomless nothingness into which you will inevitably fall if you strain any further'.[27] And happiness – the responsibility for another's or others' happiness is the one goal which a woman can conceive; and which will inevitably leave her with the realization of emptiness. As for the 'boy', he wanted her to give herself to him without defences; and 'she wanted to be alone; with him at her side'.[28] He wanted to take away her 'consciousness' and make her just his woman. 'She would be an independent woman to the last ... but she was so tired, so tired ....'[29]

He believed that when they left England, when they sailed across the sea that they now only watched from Cornwall, she would close her eyes at last and 'give in to him'. What irks him still is the feeling that he has not got his own life, and he cannot have his own life until she yields to him and sleeps with him. 'She would not be a man any more, an independent woman with a man's responsibility. Nay, even the responsibility for her own soul she would have to commit to him.'[30] He tells her she will feel better once they get over the sea to Canada. And she tells him she may. She can't tell what it will be like over there.

Lawrence's novella differs from all those previously considered in that it enters the psychic worlds of a man and a woman, perceiving in each a different kind of yearning which cannot be satisfied: a difference which originates in gender, and which incorporates inherited attitudes as well as individual aspirations. The woman looks towards a goal – the only goal she can conceive as possible for her – which dooms her to lack of fulfilment; the man yearns only for her immersion in him. Both, though not without a certain kind of goodness, involve a distortion and restriction of their humanity, force them to live quite literally on an island which restricts and suppresses, perpetuates conflict through the setting of impossible goals. The passion which she arouses in the soldier home from the war is seen once again to involve an estrangement from the rest of the world, even to involve the desire to bring about 'its' death, so that the obstruction to the totality of their relationship can be removed. But the conflict is played out only in the theatre of their own wills: desire is never transcended; and the attempt to fulfil it leads deeper into a feeling of void. Here, there exists none of the ritual compensation which Werther creates from his self-dramatisation.

Remorse and guilt – even a sense of loss – play little part in their response to Banford's death. The narrative shows little interest in external event or consequences. No mention is made of a coroner's inquest, of his demobilisation, or of anything other than their inner state, except those few telling details which mirror it. 'They went to Cornwall, to his own village, on the sea.'[31] What matters to him is to go to his village, and look out over the sea to the land where their new life can begin.

Throughout this novella what happens without matters less than what happens within. Eyes as mirrors of the soul speak volumes but tell less than they might be expected to. Like the camera in a film of the *nouvelle vague*, the narrator keeps on returning to their faces to scrutinize and question; but he, like the camera, can only see so much. What the eyes imply can only be taken up in the mythopoeic language of will, mastery, possession and power. And at this level the novella ceases to be about particular individuals (the use of surnames through much of the tale suggests a certain impersonality); it uses names as a focus for drives, and impulses of a more general human kind: drives which themselves lack any very sharp definition, and where the words used to name them – such as 'will' and 'mastery' – invoke complex problems of psychology, semantics and philosophy. If these problems were dwelt upon, the tale would be ruined. Lawrence avoids them through a more musical solution, through the reiteration of the concrete, the 'eyes' and 'looks' which the reader must imagine as best he or she can, through the pulsations of this reiterative prose, which responds to passion and rejection, advance and withdrawal, mastery and submergence, like the waves of the sea, invoked at the end. The movement of the narrative to Cornwall at its conclusion seems as much a musical solution as a geographical one, because it is there on that remote promontory that their isolation with one another, and their unresolved conflict is reflected in the intransigence and tenacity of cliffs and sea, where what happens beneath the surface matters more than what can be seen. In the invisible depths, as in Ibsen's late plays, the currents which result in fixity of emotion, or its renewal are at play. About the outcome Lawrence's narrative remains tentative and uncertain, as also about the cost of victory for either or both. And this is no doubt because the whole environment in which such conflicts come to be played out has crumbled into the sea, leaving individuals estranged from each other, and from it, in a kind of no man's land. Passions have lost any clear social context; and the context itself has lost its clarity of contour. They are 'social solitaries', searching for a wholeness which neither exists in them, nor in the world in which they live. For the past to be transcended through memory, the past must exist; and for them the past too has been blasted.

The narrative mentions that Henry must cycle from Salisbury Plain to Blewbury to return to Bailey Farm. But the geography of the village, and of the surrounding Berkshire Downs, has no significance in the narrative; they are only names on a map; just as the characters' names identify them only to reveal the 'void' which lies beneath such forms of identification: a void, like that of the sea, full of invisible currents. March's sense of her own nothingness emerges from ideas of her self which do not coincide.

The void within cannot be separated from the destruction of the world without. The elaborate social conventions of *Death in Venice*, of a leisured *haute bourgeoisie* immersed in pleasure and indulgence, have been quite simply obliterated, leaving a landscape as bleak as it is austere. The nature, the quality of human feelings as they emerge from the sea of the unconscious is determined by the social environment upon which and in which they play. And here there is a creeping nothingness within and around Bailey Farm. A future containing any promise lies outside

Europe, in another world which has yet to be encountered and made; and where the fading European myths will be left far behind.

12

Myth and the Novella

Perhaps it is not-being that is the true state, and all our dream of
life is without existence; but, if so, we feel that it must be these
phrases of music, these conceptions which exist in relation to our
dream, are nothing either. We shall perish, but we have for our
hostages these divine captives who shall follow and share our fate.
And death in their company is something less bitter, less inglori-
ous, perhaps even less certain.   Proust, *Swann's Way, Part Two*

The assurance of Aschenbach, whose whole being is geared to
fame, is underpinned by the idea of German greatness, and its
rootedness in the European spirit, which Goethe personifies. His
certainty embodies the survival of a tradition which the Great
War was to shake to its foundations, and the Second World War
to destroy. Convictions about the self based upon the Christian
belief in the individual soul and the assumption of European
cultural superiority began to founder more widely as well. 'We
shan't', wrote W.H. Auden, 'not since Stalin and Hitler, trust
ourselves ever again: we know that, subjectively, all is possible.'[1]
Nor would it be possible to feel that sense of individual worth by
which an Aschenbach is inspired. Some may judge that a good
thing; others a threat to human creativity, to the attempt upon
great endeavour. Belief in the self makes possible the myth of the
self of which all forms of creativity are a projection. In this book
I have been concerned with certain forms of projection, in a
particular form of fiction, and with the changing nature of that
projection in different national and cultural contexts.
   Underlying this was the view that the novella of passion
projected a particular type of myth which despite its variations
had many similarities. These tales embody the projection of a
desire, however formed, which seeks a fulfilment that can only
be achieved through the overcoming of desire. This is not the
result of holding a mirror up to nature, of truth to life; but of

truth to myth, of finding a narrative appropriate for, and expres-
sive of, those cycles which exist between the conscious and
unconscious mind, which have to be lived through and which
result in our obsessions. Of these the season myth is the most
ancient and prominent. *Werther*, the story of an obsession, is
given its structure by this myth, opening in May, and ending with
Werther's death on Christmas Day, which brings to winter the
promise of resurrection and life.

De Rougemont has argued that the myth of passion originates
in the Catholic culture of the middle ages, giving form to a belief
in love beyond death, and a union which can only be achieved
when the human world has been transcended. The manifestation
of this myth in these short fictions is not overtly religious, except
perhaps in the conclusion of *The Princess of Clèves*, and Gide's
Strait is the Gate. But in the foreshortening of the myth, as of the
narrative in general, there is a recurrent insistence upon the
nature of passion as attempting an appropriation, a possession,
which cannot be achieved, and which seeks relentlessly to find a
form of satisfaction doomed to failure. The conditions which
cause this failure are social in part, the result of pressures to
conform and to live within existing social conventions and stereo-
types; the intrinsic cause is however more important: it lies in the
'death-devoted' nature of the desire itself, in its innate powerlessness to find satisfaction or fulfilment in the world such as it is.
But this implies the existence, or the possible existence, of some
other world, where the obstacles to the fulfilment of desire no
longer exist, not necessarily as a matter of metaphysical belief,
but as a psychological goal where the contingency of the present
can be overcome in a timeless moment or moments. And this
itself is a defence against a sense of rootlessness and meaning-
lessness which permeates the later twentieth century.

Gide's *Strait is the Gate* (1909) exemplifies the declining power
of the myth of passion. It concerns the rejection of desire for the
sake of some other and higher love, only to reach the view of the
non-existence of any such thing, and the rejection of the myth
which derives from it. This involves a rejection of something
intrinsic in the European spirit, bringing about a transformation
of an important element in its structure. The myth was itself a
defence against, a protection from those 'cliffs of fall, no man
fathomed' beyond which lie the extremes of psychopathology

with which so many modern narratives, true and fictional, are concerned. Desires, like obsessions, could be transcended. There is no way in which myths which partly belong to the unconscious can be recovered once discarded; but the awareness of the particular void left by their death offers a warning.

As the discussion at the beginning and end of *Adolphe* suggests, this is not just a matter of 'character', or rejecting the 'accepted order of things', or in more fictional terms of the overcoming of an obsession (though it involves all of them); it is a question of the way in which desires are shaped by structures of which we are unaware, by myths which exist within us, whether the result of genetic or emotional inheritance, or what Samuel Butler once called 'unconscious memory'. By this he meant those mental or physical processes which we instinctively repeat because they have been gone through by many generations before us: a facilitated pathway which we use without conscious thought or awareness, and of which literature is one expression, involving, as has been frequently shown, the use of archetypes.

In Christianity, and in the literature shaped by the vocabulary of Christianity, the struggle between good and evil expresses one such pattern; and this in turn represents an articulation of the myth of the fall. What this book has been concerned with is the way in which imaginative fictions depict such myths without necessarily making a conscious reference to them.

The myth of passion is at root a myth of wholeness, older than Christianity, though modified by it. The seasons, in their cyclic pattern reflect the processional and recurrent nature of human life, in which, in each generation, the same forces are at work. Nothing is separable from them; and within them Eros acts as a 'mighty lord'. In the myth of Cupid and Psyche, Psyche is forbidden to look on the lover who visits her every night; when she tries to discover who he is by lighting his face, as he sleeps, with her candle, Cupid vanishes into the night. In Claude's famous painting of 'The Enchanted Castle', the artist captures the mysterious nature of the place, and its ever-present but invisible master. The castle, immense in size and with innumerable rooms, is a place of splendour but also of unknown dangers, which the traveller enters at his or her peril. It is part of Nature, and its hidden mysteries are always latent in the human traveller. This sense of Eros as being present in the natural world was grounded in a sense of wholeness, of which the union between men and women was one example.

In all these novellas, human involvement with Nature is present as a force. Frequently the country is associated with feelings which are natural, and the city with passions which are destructive and unnatural. The unnaturalness intensifies the more this sense of involvement with nature is lost; man as an urban animal is often and deeply bewildered.

As the twentieth century proceeds, this sense of Eros as a mysterious and natural force, often more brutal and destructive in its effects within the city, becomes gradually displaced by man's changing relationship with Nature. His transformation from being a rural being who sometimes lived in the town to being an urban being who sometimes visited the country dispossessed the gods of Nature of their old sway.

As science too began to proclaim that one day all the secrets of Nature would be revealed, Nature moved from its place in the private domain, where its forces had given names to the internal impulses of a psycho-drama, into the public arena of dispute and interpretation. In this change, a loss began to occur in the European psyche which had evolved out of, but never apart from, man's participation in Nature. Since the time of pre-history, and his first cave-drawings, European man had been haunted by the images of animals which he hunted and which were part of those natural forces he could not control. This demotion meant that Eros, as the urgent and aphrodisiac force of that natural world, began to fade in the human perception of things, and at the same time to lose that invisibility on which his power and mystery depended. Sex as a physical activity, through which needs are expressed and pleasures obtained, was taking his place, as Psyche herself was being reduced to an agitation of neurones.

With the disappearance of Eros and the emptying of the Western world of all forms of the numinous, even the death of God himself, the myth of passion began to lose its power or to be directed ever more intensely inwards, where it could only feed on its own impacted distress, weeping and anarchic, in the knowledge that wholeness was not to be found.

The passion, or suffering, ceased to be part of some natural, if disordered process, and became a further instance of human solitariness: no other world existed in which harmony could be hoped for, and no power of grace operated in this to assuage the suffering caused. The mind was enclosed with emotions it could not control or overcome.

The gradual unlocking of the secrets of Nature, and the weakening of a sense of mystery in her operations (which culminated in the arrival of the first men on the moon) brought about the disappearance of those deities who since pagan times had operated in her, and continued to exercise their powers throughout the Christian era. The conversion to Christianity of the centaur did not cause his disappearance. Milton was right when he wrote in the Nativity Ode:

> The flocking shadows pale,
> Troop to th' infernal jail,
>   Each fetter'd ghost slips to his several grave,
> And the yellow-skirted fays,
> Fly after the night-steeds, leaving their moon-loved maze.[2]

Milton was wrong, however, in thinking them defeated. Dispersed and driven underground they were, but their power to amaze, bewilder and blind remained undiminished.

In Lawrence's *The Fox*, we can see this period in the European spirit beginning to draw to its end – a period in which man and Nature had a reciprocal relation and myths which expressed that relation. Christianity grew out of a sense of wholeness, and gave it a new meaning, to which the cathedrals of Europe bear witness in splendour and glory. They are the expression of the European spirit raised to the highest power; and anyone who loves Europe loves them. On the doorway of the church at Aulnay, the donkey playing the harp symbolizes this integration of time and eternal, of man's inseparability from pagan mysteries, and Christianity's rewriting of them in a new myth which overlaid the old. The melancholy slow withdrawing roar of the sea of faith in the nineteenth century saw also the demise of that pagan world, so richly and mysteriously peopled, which had shaped the European spirit, and had remained for so long a central part of its make-up.

In different countries of Europe, and at different times, the myth of passion has presented itself in various guises, shaped by culture, society and language at a particular time. In France, the high culture of Paris in the seventeenth century structured the way in which Madame de Lafayette conceived of desire, and the dangers which resulted from giving way to passion in a society of intrigue. The higher and more detached vision which the Princess of Clèves achieves enables her to see the entanglements of the world for what they are, and to smother the remains of her passion. This withdrawal from society is in mythical (and literary) terms a metaphor for overcoming her obsession.

The appropriateness of the novella form for a narrative of sharp focus and foreshortened effects is self-evident. The recurrence, within the form, of these narratives of passion points to the similarity with the lyric mode in poetry, where intensity of feeling is achieved through economy of expression and compression of language. At the outset, I referred to certain forms of projection in these novellas, and have tried to suggest that within very individual contexts (themselves of great interest) these projections embody an abbreviated form of mythical experience. The argument might be summarised like this. In each case, some form (though they may be very different) of autobiographical experience underlies the narrative; as in all creative acts it is transformed but not altogether lost. In fact, because of the brevity and intensity of the narrative, it often lies rather closer to the surface, is more germane to the subject than in more discursive fictions. This autobiographical experience involves an obsession, which when it has been burned out is revisited by memory – sometimes after a long interval – and the desire which prompted it is re-examined in order to question its nature. This is not an intellectual exercise, but a revisiting of a landscape where particular and decisive events occurred: events which determined the future course of a life. The resurrection of desire cannot be separated from the need to question its nature, to elucidate the intensity of its feeling and examine its moral properties. But no more than in the original experience can the whole nature of the desire be examined; and this is because it involves a myth which can no more be perceived in its recreation than in the original experience. The existence of the myth is what turns it into an obsession. In this case the myth involved concerns a desire so intense that it cannot be fulfilled in the human world, and which owes its origin to the long history of a belief in the existence of another world where such dissatisfactions and frustrations would be overcome, or would no longer exist.

Here, as in all these fictions, the erotic basis of creativity, the desire which is the absence of words, and which ends in the completion of the work, is inseparable from the destructiveness revealed in the narrative. The creative passion is always destructive; but the destructiveness liberates the creativity. The labyrinth of desire, a place of darkness, leads to an unseen centre, where death waits; the thread which enables the survivor to return to the light is that of memory.

In the work of Mrs Gaskell, the extremity of the continental examples is less apparent. The continuity of rural life, the lack of emotional sophistication and the foundation of firm beliefs gives the myth a different tone, and offers a more subdued, if no less resonant account of its perils. This world offers the chance of a new beginning, with the past overcome. But this is a question of degree, not of substance, and reflects the modification of the myth in a Protestant as oppposed to a Catholic culture. Punishment, sacrifice and violence are imagined more moderately; social disapprobation and personal unhappiness are the fruits of transgression, and must be borne up against with stoicism and resolve to start afresh. Death has none or little of the mythic status which it acquires in the case of Manon, Werther, Ellenore or Aschenbach; and the problems which passion creates are not in the end insoluble. Desire simply comes to an end, or is truncated; and the myth itself is left unfinished. The overcoming of the obsession is symbolised in the passing of a fever; mind and body are suddenly purged, as in a still morning after storm. There is no sense of absoluteness, or finality; and also no assurance it will not happen again. Mrs Gaskell does not write here of an emotion which consumes for ever, which destroys (though it comes very close to doing so); and there exists in her imagining a a resilience, a moderation, and cautious courage, which the grander, more terrible passions do not permit.

In the classical world, gods bewildered men to further their own ends; men who were blind followed their impulses. The tragedy of the blind leading the blind was apparent in antiquity as in the Christian era; but in that later time the myth had been transformed by the addition of one leader who could lure men to their destruction, and another who could save them through grace. The legacy of the fifteen hundred years of Christianity absorbed into the Western imagination the vision of a world where an absolute union could occur: a place where division, conflict and estrangement came to an end. The myth of harmony which this presented involved an insoluble paradox; human desire could not be fulfilled in this world; but the absence of such fulfilment condemned human beings to endless suffering. Freedom from desire could only occur in death. The greater the intensity of the desire the more the passion or suffering would be heightened without prospect of resolution.

With increasing secularism, and no promise of future rewards and punishments, memory becomes the sole arbiter. Memory as a recreative force does not sit in judgement on desire (though it may beget remorse which judges the effect of actions on others); and in recalling desire it becomes subject to the demands and distortions of the ego, which wishes to represent desire in the best possible light as life-affirming, as a form of renewal, or as a resistance to dying.

In these novellas of passion there remains the substance of a myth created by the belief in the possibility of an absolute union beyond death, which creates the obsession. Only in art can the obsession be overcome, after desire itself has died, and memory revisits it with the lucidity which the creative imagination inspires, when memory and desire stir dull roots with spring rain.

Notes

Introduction: Memory, Desire and Passion

1. The novella as a form is discussed in detail in Chapter 1.

2. Roy Porter, Review of Adam Philips's *Flirtation*, *Sunday Times*, September 1994, 7.3.

3. Dennis de Rougemont, *Love in the Western World*, translated by Montgomery Belgion, New York, 1983, pp. 145-6.

4. ibid., p. 21.

5. René Girard, *Deceit, Desire and the Novel*, translated by Y. Freccero, Baltimore, 1966, p. 297.

6. ibid., p. 300.

7. Rougemont, p. 173.

8. In Werther's intensely solipsistic state, the replies only interest him as fuel to his obsession.

9. J.W. von Goethe, *The Sorrows of Young Werther*, translated by Victor Lange, New York, 1949, p. 23. This is a useful translation, though 'sufferings' is preferable to 'sorrows'.

10. Marcel Proust, *Remembrance of Things Past*, translated by C.K. Scott Moncrieff, London, 1952, vol. 3, p. 56.

11. *Werther*, p. 124.

12. ibid., p. 3.

13. Rougemont, p. 167.

14. *Werther*, p. 95.

15. ibid., p. 128.

16. Girard, p. 21.

17. ibid., p. 48 (Girard is quoting de Rougemont).

18. *Remembrance*, vol. 3, p. 219.

19. M. de Cervantes, *The Adventures of Don Quixote,* translated by J.M. Cohen, Harmondsworth, 1950, p. 936.

20. *Werther*, p. 1.

21. ibid., p. 20.

22. ibid., p. 77.

23. Quoted in Stendhal, *Love*, translated by Gilbert and Suzanne Sale, Harmondsworth, 1975, p. 209

24. *Remembrance*, vol. 2, p. 69.

25. *Werther*, p. 50.

26. *Love*, p. 211.

27. M. Lermontov, *A Hero of Our Time*, translated by Paul Foote, Harmondsworth, 1956, p. 157.

28. ibid., p. 91.

29. ibid., p. 109.

30. ibid., p. 98.

31. ibid., p. 145.

32. ibid., p. 157.

33. ibid.

34. ibid., p. 127.

35. ibid., p. 126.

36. *Remembrance*, vol. 2, p. 92.

37. Rougemont, p. 207.

38. Quoted by Girard, p. 59.

39. Girard, p. 296.

40. Quoted in R. Jean, *Lectures du Désir*, Paris, 1977, p. 8 (my translation).

41. I am indebted again to Girard in this passage. See p. 299 and following.

1. Form and the Novella

1. I have not included Mérimée's *Carmen* in this book for a number of reasons. Although it superficially resembles other works in this book in theme, and is certainly a novella, it has relatively little interest in the state of mind of the lovers, except as Carmen personifies the *rom* or gypsy. Its power derives from its Andalucian setting (in this sense an exotic traveller's tale); and from the desire for revenge which Carmen's flaunting of her infidelity arouses in Don Jose when his love is spurned. But the novella shows little interest in the internal development of the feelings which lead to this melodramatic climax. *Carmen* is about a 'crime passionel', but it does not analyse passion.

2. A.D. Harvey has interestingly argued in 'Why the "Novelle"?', *New German Studies*, vol. 16, 1990-91, pp. 159-72 that the Germans needed the concept of the 'novelle' because, in contrast to France, England and Russia, they had produced so few outstanding novels. 'They simply invented a new category of success.'

3. M. Swales, *The German Novelle*, Princeton, 1977, p. 33

4. L. Wittgenstein, *Tractatus Logico-Philosophicus*, London, 1961, p. 56.

5. Swales, p. 33.

6. The German *novelle* has been, and continues to be, the subject of intense critical and theoretical debate. The significance of the form in German literature, particularly of the nineteenth century, is beyond question. The vagueness of the term in other languages and literatures, including English, is equally indisputable. My intention in this book is not to become involved in a conceptual debate about what the novella is, but to show how works of fiction which fall appropriately within the scope of this term (i.e. works which are clearly not short stories, or novels of a discursive kind) have been used for telling a particular kind of narrative in particular ways.

7. L. Leibowitz, *Narrative Purpose in the Novella*, The Hague, 1974, p. 51.

8. ibid., p. 13.

9. Leo Tolstoy, *Anna Karenin*, translated by Rosemary Edmonds, Harmondsworth, 1954, p. 534.

10. ibid., p. 62.

11. ibid., p. 827.

12. ibid., p. 826.

13. ibid., p. 830.

14. ibid., p. 835.

15. ibid., p. 852.
16. ibid., p. 853.
17. ibid., p. 814.
18. ibid., p. 853.

2. Madame de Lafayette. *The Princess of Cleves*

1. Madame de Thianges, a friend of Madame de Lafayette, knew that she wished to be received at court again. She therefore gave to the King's son on New Year's Day, 1675, a model of a room, called *Chambre du Sublime*, in which the figures of Madame de Lafayette and her friends were represented. This beautiful toy became the subject of conversation at court, and led the King to invite Madame de Lafayette to court entertainments.

2. Quoted by Leonard Tancock in his Introduction to the Penguin Classics translation of *The Princess of Clèves*, Harmondsworth, 1978, p. 9.

3. I am indebted here to J.W. Scott: *Madame de Lafayette: La Princesse de Clèves*, London 1983.

4. The page references given below are to Garnier-Flammarion edition, Paris, 1966.

5. pp. 44-5.
6. p. 50.
7. p. 37.
8. p. 67.
9. p. 68.
10. p. 171.
11. p. 180.
12. ibid.
13. p. 174.
14. ibid.
15. pp. 125-6.
16. p. 168.
17. p. 122.
18. p. 60.
19. pp. 166-7.

3. Abbé Prévost: *Manon Lescaut*

1. A.-F. Prévost, *Manon Lescaut*, translated by Helen Waddell, with a preface by Christopher Smith and an introduction by George Saintsbury, London, 1987, p. xlvi.

2. See quotation from Prévost, *Le Pour et le Contre*, in '*Préface*' to *Manon Lescaut* by J.-L. Bory, Paris, 1972, p. 31.

3. See Saintsbury, op. cit, p. l.

4. As in *The Princess of Clèves*, coincidence recurs in Prévost's narrative. What appears as a structural device within the story also reflects the powerful element of chance in the occurrence of even the profoundest emotions.

5. Abbé Prévost, *Manon Lescaut*, Paris, 1972, p. 74.

6. Richard A. Smernoff, *L'Abbé Prévost*, Boston, 1985, p. 50.

7. *Manon*, p. 213.

8. ibid., p. 42.

9. ibid., p. 169.

10. ibid., p. 98.

11. See Introduction, n. 38.

12. *Manon*, p. 201.

13. Saintsbury, op. cit., p. xli.

14. *Manon*, p. 53.

15. ibid., p. 92.

16. ibid., p. 95.

17. Stendhal in *Love* writes extensively about the idea of crystallisation in Book One, Chapters 6 to 12.

18. *Manon*, p. 213.

4. Benjamin Constant: *Adolphe*

1. Benjamin Constant, *Adolphe*, Paris, 1957, p. 33.

2. The presence of these letters perhaps also suggests the unsatisfactoriness or incompleteness of the narrative to Adolphe.

3. *Adolphe*, p. 119.

4. ibid., p. 122.

5. ibid., p. 27.

6. ibid., p. 29.

7. As in Prévost's case, the least laborious work proved the most lasting.

8. See H. Nicholson, *Benjamin Constant*, London, 1949, p. 24.

9. *Adolphe*, pp. 37-8.

10. ibid., pp. 116-17

11. See D. Dennis: *Benjamin Constant: Adolphe*, Cambridge, 1987, p. 11.

12. *Adolphe*, p. 96.

13. ibid., p. 40.

14. ibid., p. 42.

15. ibid.

16. The theme of parental influence, both Freudian and explicit, is one to which I shall return later in this chapter, and subsequently. We have already seen it at work in the influence of Madame de Chartres on her daughter, and of M. Des Grieux on his son. Both the presence and absence of parental influence may be instrumental in the arousing of passion, and continues to exert a powerful pressure in some direction on its subsequent evolution.

17. *Adolphe*, p. 85.

18. I.W. Alexander, *Adolphe*, London, 1973, pp. 32-3.

19. *Adolphe*, p. 105.

20. ibid., p. 111.

21. ibid., p. 119.

22. ibid., p. 89.

23. See B. Constant, *De la religion*, vol. 1, 1826, p. 170.

24. *Adolphe*, p. 59.

5. Ivan Turgenev: *First Love*

1. D. Magarshack, *Turgenev*, London, 1954, p. 66.

2. I. Turgenev, *First Love*, translated by Isaiah Berlin, Harmondsworth, 1978, p. 106.

3. Proust, *Remembrance*, vol. 3, p. 215.

4. Magarshack, p. 80.

5. ibid., p. 78.

6. *First Love*, p. 50.

7. ibid., p. 103.

8. ibid., p. 24.

9. ibid., p. 25.

10. ibid., p. 61.

11. ibid., p. 28.

12. ibid., p. 23

13. ibid., p. 42.

14. ibid., p. 54.

15. ibid., pp. 38-9.

16. ibid., p. 97.

17. ibid., p. 49.

18. ibid., p. 52.

19. See Magarshack, p. 77. 'I bought it [love] at the cost of my life because I am dying a slave.'

20. *First Love*, p. 67.

21. ibid., p. 72.

22. ibid., p. 76.

23. ibid., p. 88.

24. ibid., p. 91.

25. ibid., p. 96.

26. ibid., p. 97.

27. ibid., p. 100.

28. I am indebted to Dr V. Goldsworthy who has checked the Russian text, where Turgenev writes literally: 'Then the words were heard: "Vous devez ..."' etc.

29. *First Love*, p. 102.

30. V.S. Prichett, Introduction to Berlin's translation, p. 17.

6. Mrs Gaskell: *Cousin Phillis*

1. Stendhal, *Love*, p. 142.

2. ibid., p. 156 (quoted anecdotally).

3. ibid., p. 152.

4. ibid.

5. The question of whether Dostoevsky succeeds in justifying the end of *Crime and Punishment* is often debated. The existence of the aesthetic problem points to a specifically Russian outlook, and a Russian myth of redemptive love. It is impossible to imagine a writer from Western Europe ending the novel in quite this way.

6. *Love*, p. 142.

7. E. Gaskell, *Cousin Phillis* (Everyman), London, 1970, p. 44.

8. ibid., p. 2.

9. ibid., p. 3.

10. ibid., p. 7.

11. ibid., p. 23.

12. ibid., p. 28.

13. ibid., p. 35.

14. ibid., p. 43.

15. ibid.

16. ibid., pp. 49-50.

17. ibid., p. 50.

18. In *The Princess of Clèves*, Madame de Lafayette uses the device of the stolen portrait to reveal the love of Nemours. In both cases the revelation

happens by chance.
19. *Cousin Phillis*, p. 77.
20. ibid., pp. 81-2.
21. ibid., p. 89.
22. ibid.
23. ibid., p. 64.
24. ibid., p. 7.
25. ibid., p. 80.
26. ibid., p. 25.
27. See the discussion of *The Fox* in Chapter 11 in relation to this point.
28. *Cousin Phillis*, p. 6.
29. ibid., p. 10.
30. ibid., p. 69.

7. Alexandre Dumas *fils*: *The Lady of the Camellias*

1. F.A. Taylor, *The Theatre of Aexandre Dumas, fils*, Oxford, 1937, p. 10.
2. This might be seen as illustrating a raging consumption (and consumerism) in society which still continues to accelerate.
3. It has been suggested that this relates to her menstrual cycle, and is a signal to potential lovers of the time when she has her period.
4. An interesting comparison with *The Princess of Clèves* exists here. The portrait which Nemours steals of the Princess has a supreme importance for him; but objects are not of general significance. In Dumas's work they suggest how close human life has come to be being regarded as a commodity.
5. Alexandre Dumas, *fils*, *La Dame aux Camélias*, Paris, 1975, pp. 68-9.
6. ibid., pp. 81-2.
7. ibid., p. 110.
8. R. Barthes, *Mythologies*, translated by A. Lavers, London, 1972, pp. 103-5.
9. *La Dame*, p. 106.
10. ibid., p. 113.
11. ibid., p. 120.
12. ibid., p. 130.
13. ibid., p. 186.
14. ibid., p. 206.
15. ibid., p. 214.
16. This same pressure is placed on Adolphe. It is one way in which society attempts to break down on the self-enclosure of lovers, at a time when male identity depends a great deal on the pursuit of ambition.
17. *La Dame*, p. 249.
18. ibid., p. 250.
19. ibid., p. 286.
20. ibid., p. 247.

8. Leo Tolstoy: *The Kreutzer Sonata*

1. Henri Troyat, *Tolstoy*, translated by Nancy Amphoux, Harmondsworth, 1980, p. 656.
2. ibid.
3. *The Kreutzer Sonata* was banned for some time by the censor. During this period it was circulated clandestinely in lithographed copies.
4. Troyat, p. 665

5. ibid., p. 672.

6. Leo Tolstoy, *War and Peace*, translated by Louise and Aylmer Maude, Oxford, 1991, p. 28.

7. ibid., p. 1239.

8. Leo Tolstoy, *The Kreutzer Sonata, and other tales*, translated by Aylmer Maude, 1960, p. 111.

9. ibid.

10. ibid., p. 210.

11. ibid., p. 121.

12. ibid., p. 123.

13. ibid., p. 212.

14. Tolstoy's last great novel, *Resurrection* (1899), concerned the life of a woman driven to prostitution. The regular inspection of prostitutes to check the spread of venereal disease was a theme to which he returned.

15. *Kreutzer Sonata*, p. 131.

16. ibid., p. 144.

17. ibid., p. 146.

18. Oscar Wilde, *The Ballad of Reading Gaol*, London, 1980, p. 15.

19. *Kreutzer Sonata*, p. 163.

20. ibid.

21. ibid., p. 161.

22. ibid., p. 168.

23. ibid., p. 169.

24. The breaking of an object as a way of breaking the power of an emotion, and as a substitute for violence against the person, is common enough; but it serves here as an effective narrative device for transcribing the force, and danger, of Trukachévski's feelings.

25. *Kreutzer Sonata*, p. 186.

26. ibid., p. 189.

27. ibid., p. 196.

28. ibid., p. 204.

29. ibid., p. 208.

30. ibid., p. 209.

31. Graham Greene, *The Quiet American*, Harmondsworth, 1962, p. 189.

32. *Scarlet and Black*, p. 462.

9. Thomas Mann: *Death in Venice*

1. Thomas Mann, *Death in Venice*, translated by H.T. Lowe-Porter, Harmondsworth, 1962, p. 7.

2. M. Reich-Ranicki, *Thomas Mann and His Family*, translated by Ralph Manheim, London, 1989, p. 32.

3. ibid.

4. *Death in Venice.*, p. 7.

5. ibid., p. 39.

6. ibid., p. 40.

7. ibid., p. 52.

8. ibid., p. 76.

9. ibid., p. 41.

10. ibid., pp. 47-8.

11. ibid., p. 78.

12. ibid., p. 83.

13. ibid., p. 63.
14. ibid., pp. 46-7.
15. ibid., p. 24.
16. ibid., pp. 60-1.

10. André Gide: *Strait is the Gate*

1. A.J. Guerard, *André Gide*, Harvard, 1969, p. 80.
2. *The End of the Affair* (1951) ends with Bendrix's prayer: 'O God, You've done enough, You've robbed me of enough, I'm too tired and old to learn to love, leave me alone for ever.' This rejection of a God, who has robbed him of love, has much in common with the preoccupations of Gide's novel.
3. A. Gide, *La porte étroite*, Paris, 1959, p. 177.
4. ibid., p. 162.
5. ibid., p. 13.
6. ibid., p. 26.
7. ibid., p. 28.
8. ibid., p. 165.
9. ibid.
10. ibid., p. 81.
11. ibid., p. 182.
12. ibid.
13. ibid., p. 103.
14. ibid., p. 30.
15. ibid., p. 147.
16. Guerard, op. cit., p. 127.
17. *La porte étroite*, p. 178.
18. ibid., p. 176.
19. ibid., p. 179.
20. ibid., p. 182.

11. D.H. Lawrence: *The Fox*

1. D.H. Lawrence, *The Fox*, Harmondsworth, 1960, p. 88.
2. ibid., p. 91.
3. ibid., p. 144.
4. ibid., p. 156.
5. ibid., p. 88.
6. ibid.
7. ibid., p. 118.
8. ibid., p. 93.
9. ibid., p. 95.
10. ibid., p. 97.
11. ibid.
12. ibid., p. 100.
13. ibid., p. 103.
14. ibid., p. 104.
15. ibid.
16. ibid., p. 105.
17. ibid.
18. ibid., p. 116.
19. ibid., p. 121.

20. ibid.
21. ibid., p. 131.
22. ibid., p. 143.
23. ibid., p. 151.
24. ibid., p. 152.
25. ibid., p. 153.
26. ibid., p. 154.
27. ibid., p. 156.
28. ibid., p. 157.
29. ibid.
30. ibid.
31. ibid., p. 153.

12. Myth and the Novella

1. W.H. Auden, 'The Cave of Making', *About the House*, London, 1966, p. 18.
2. J. Milton, 'On the morning of Christ's Nativity', *Complete Shorter Poems*, edited by John Carey, London, 1968, p. 112.

Further Reading

Introduction

Girard, R., *Deceit, Desire and the Novel: self and other in literary structure*, translated by Yvonne Freccero (Baltimore, 1966).
Bloom, A., *Love and Friendship* (New York, 1993).
Jean, R., *Lectures du Désir* (Paris, 1977).
Rougemont, Denis de, *Love in the Western World*, translated by Montgomery Belgion (New York, 1983).
Stendhal, *Love*, translated by G. and S. Sale, with an introduction by J. Stewart and B.C. Knight (Harmondsworth, 1975).

1. Form and the Novella

Bennett, E.K., *A History of the German Novelle*, revised and continued by H.N. Waidson (Cambridge, 1961).
Leibowitz, L., *Narrative Purpose in the Novella* (The Hague, 1974).
Paine, J.H.E., *Theory and Criticism of the Novella* (Bonn: Bouvier, 1979).
Paulin, Roger, *The Brief Compass: the nineteenth-century German novelle* (Oxford, Clarendon Press, 1985).
Springer, Mary Doyle, *Forms of the Modern Novella* (Chicago, 1975).
Swales, Martin, *The German Novelle* (Princeton, 1977).

2. Madame de Lafayette: *The Princess of Clèves*

Adam, A., 'Préface' to *La Princesse de Clèves* (Paris, 1966).
Danahy, Michael, *The Feminization of the Novel* (Florida 1991).
Henry, Patrick, ed., *An Inimitable Example: the case for the Princesse de Clèves* (Washington, DC, 1992).
Kamuf, Peggy, *Fictions of Feminine Desire* (Nebraska Press, 1982).
Mouligneau, Geneviève, *Madame de Lafayette, romancière?* (Bruxelles, 1980).
Niderst, Alain, *La Princesse de Clèves* (Paris, 1977)
Scott, J.W., *Madame de Lafayette, 'La Princesse de Clèves'* (London, 1983).
Tancock, L., 'Introduction' to *The Princesse de Clèves* (Harmondsworth, 1978).
Woshinsky, Barbara R., *'La Princesse de Clèves': the tension of elegance* (The Hague, 1973).

3. Abbé Prévost: *Manon Lescaut*

Francis, R.A., *Prévost, Manon Lescaut* (London, 1993).

Francis, R.A., 'The Abbé Prévost's first-person narrators' (Oxford: Voltaire Foundation at the Taylor Institution, 1993).

Jaccard, Jean Luc, *'Manon Lescaut': le personnage romancier* (Paris, 1975).

Segal, Naomi, *The Unintended Reader: Feminism and 'Manon Lescaut'* (Cambridge, 1986).

Smernoff, R.A., *L'Abbé Prévost* (Boston, 1985).

Syard, Jean, *L'Abbe Prevost: labyrinthes de la memoire* (Paris, 1986).

4. Benjamin Constant: *Adolphe*

Alexander, I.W., *Benjamin Constant: 'Adolphe'* (London, 1973).

Fontana, Biancamaria, *Benjamin Constant and the Post-revolutionary Mind*, (New Haven, 1991).

Gouhier, Henri, *Benjamin Constant devant la religion* (Paris, 1987).

Holmes, G., *The 'Adolphe Type' in French Fiction in the First Half of the Nineteenth Century* (Leeds, 1975).

Holmes, Stephen, *Benjamin Constant and the Making of Modern Liberalism* (New Haven, 1984).

Kloocke, Kurt, *Benjamin Constant: une biographie intellectuelle* (Geneva, 1984).

Murry, John Middleton, *The Conquest of Death* (London, 1951).

Nicolson, H., *Benjamin Constant* (London, 1949).

Poulet, George, *Benjamin Constant par lui-même* (Paris, 1968).

Unwin, Timothy A., *Constant, 'Adolphe'* (London, 1986).

Wood, Dennis, *Benjamin Constant: a biography* (London, 1993).

5. Ivan Turgenev: *First Love*

Costlow, Jane T., *Worlds within Worlds: the novels of Ivan Turgenev* (Princeton, 1990).

Lowe, David A., ed., *Critical Essays on Ivan Turgenev* (Boston, 1989).

Magarshack, D., *Turgenev* (London, 1954).

Pritchett, V.S., Introduction to *First Love* (Harmondsworth, 1978).

Pritchett, V.S., *The Gentle Barbarian: the life and work of Turgenev* (London, 1977).

Seeley, Frank Friedeberg, *Turgenev: a reading of his fiction* (Cambridge, 1991).

Troyat, Henri, *Turgenev*, translated by Nancy Amphoux (London, 1980).

Woodward, James B., *Metaphysical Conflict: a study of the major novels of Ivan Turgenev* (Munich, 1990).

6. Mrs Gaskell: *Cousin Phillis*

Brown, Pearl, 'The pastoral and anti-pastoral in Elizabeth Gaskell's 'Cousin Phillis', *Victorian Newsletter* 82 (1992), pp. 22- 7.

Craik, Wendy, 'Lore and learning in *Cousin Phillis*', *Gaskell Society Journal* 3 (1989), pp. 68-80.

Duthie, Enid L., *The Themes of Elizabeth Gaskell* (London, 1980).

Lucas, John, *The Literature of Change: studies in the nineteenth-century provincial novel* (Brighton, 1980).

Recchio, Thomas E., 'A Victorian version of the fall: Mrs Gaskell's *Cousin Phillis* and the domestication of myth', *Gaskell Society Journal* 5 (1991), pp. 37-50.

Spencer, Jane, *Elizabeth Gaskell* (Basingstoke, 1993).

Stoneman, Patsy, *Elizabeth Gaskell* (Brighton, 1987).

Uglow, Jennifer, *Elizabeth Gaskell: a habit of stories* (London, 1993).

7. Alexandre Dumas: *The Lady of the Camellias*

Issartel, Christiane, *Les dames aux camélias: de l'histoire à la légende* (Paris, 1981).

Schopp, Claude, *Alexandre Dumas: le génie de la vie* (Paris, 1985).

Taylor, F.A., *The Theatre of Alexander Dumas, fils* (Oxford, 1937).

8. Leo Tolstoy: *The Kreutzer Sonata*

Bayley, J., *Tolstoy and the Novel* (London, 1966).

McLean, Hugh, ed., *In the Shade of the Giant: essays on Tolstoy* (Berkeley, 1989).

Redfearn, David, *Tolstoy: principles for a new world order* (London, 1992).

Sharma, T.R., ed., *Essays on Leo Tolstoy* (Meerut, 1989).

Troyat, Henri, *Tolstoy*, translated by Nancy Amphoux (Harmondsworth, 1980)

9. Thomas Mann: *Death in Venice*

Berlin, Jeffrey B., ed., *Approaches to Teaching Mann's 'Death in Venice' and Other Short Fiction* (New York, 1992).

Colin, René-Pierre, *Les privileges du chaos: 'La mort à Vénise' et l'esprit décadent* (Tusson, 1991).

Ezergailis, Inta M., ed., *Critical Essays on Thomas Mann* (Boston, 1988).

Hollingdale, R. J. *Thomas Mann* (London, 1971).

Leser, Esther H., *Thomas Mann's Short Fiction: an intellectual biography* (London, 1989).

Marcel, Odile, *La maladie européenne: Thomas Mann et le XXe siècle* (Paris, 1993).

Miller, R.D., *Death in Venice: an essay on Thomas Mann's 'novelle'* (Harrogate, 1983).

Reed, T.J., *Thomas Mann: uses of tradition* (Oxford, 1974).

Reich-Ranicki, M., *Thomas Mann and His Family*, translated by Ralph Manheim (London, 1989).

Swales, Martin, *Thomas Mann: a study* (London, 1980).

Travers, Martin Patrick Anthony, *Thomas Mann* (Basingstoke, 1992).

10. André Gide: *Strait is the Gate*

Goulet, Alain, *Fiction et vie sociale dans l'oeuvre d'André Gide* (Paris, 1985).

Guerard, A.J., *André Gide* (Harvard, 1969).

Masson, Pierre, *André Gide: voyage et écriture* (Lyon, 1983).

Pollard, Patrick, *André Gide: homosexual moralist* (New Haven and London, 1991).

Thierry, Jean-Jacques, *André Gide* (Paris, 1986).
Walker, David H., *André Gide* (Basingstoke, 1990).

11. D.H. Lawrence: *The Fox*

Bell, Michael, *D.H. Lawrence: language and being* (Cambridge, 1992).
Heywood, Christopher, ed., *D.H. Lawrence: new studies* (Basingstoke, 1987).
Hyde, G.M., *D.H. Lawrence* (Basingstoke, 1990).
Moore, H.T., *The Priest of Love: a life of D. H. Lawrence* (London, 1974).
Myers, Jeffrey, *D.H. Lawrence: a biography* (London, 1990).
Preston, Peter, and Peter Hoare, eds., *D.H. Lawrence in the Modern World* (Cambridge, 1989).
Sagar, Keith, *D.H. Lawrence: life into art* (Harmondsworth, 1985).
Salgado, Gamini, and G.K. Das, eds., *The Spirit of D.H. Lawrence: centenary studies* (Basingstoke, 1988).
Sharma, T.R., ed., *Essays on D.H. Lawrence* (Meerut, 1987).
Trebisz, Malgorzata, *The Novella in England at the Turn of the XIX and XX Centuries: H. James, J. Conrad, D.H. Lawrence* (Wroclaw: Uniwersytetu Wroclawskiego, 1992).
Worthen, John, *D.H. Lawrence: a literary life* (London, 1989).

Index